digital enhancement for landscape photographers

digital enhancement for landscape photographers

arjan hoogendam and herb parkin

Guild of
Master Craftsman
Publications

First published 2003 by
Guild of Master Craftsman Publications Ltd,
166 High Street, Lewes,
East Sussex BN7 1XU

ISBN 1 86108 386 6
A catalogue record of this book is available from the British Library.

Publisher: Paul Richardson
Art Director: Ian Smith
Production Manager: Stuart Poole
Managing Editor: Gerrie Purcell
Commissioning Editor: April McCroskie

Editor: James Evans
Cover design: Francis & Partners
Additional cover design: Sam Reeves
Book design: Francis & Partners
Typeface: Trade Gothic

Colour origination: Articolor Italia srl, Italy
Printed and bound: Kyodo Printing Co. Pte Ltd, Singapore

Our thanks to the following, without whom this book would not have been possible:
our wives, Mieke and Alyke; our publishers GMC, especially April and James; and to all the others who gave us their time and support.

To Denis, who is still searching for the perfect landscape

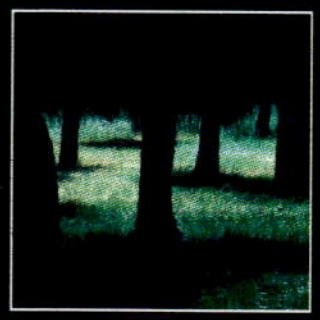
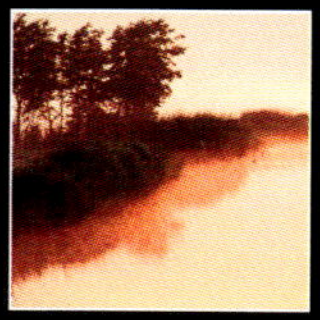
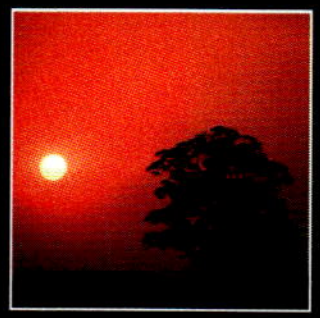
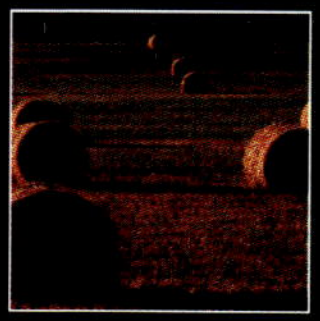
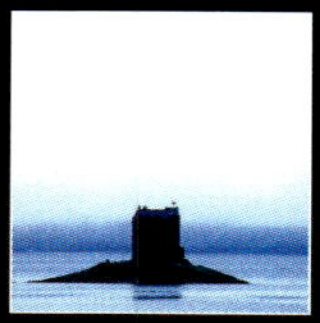
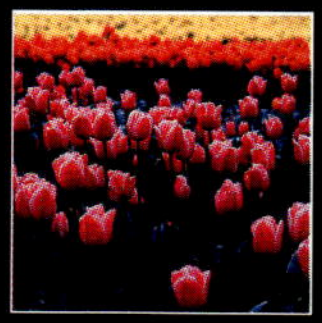

contents

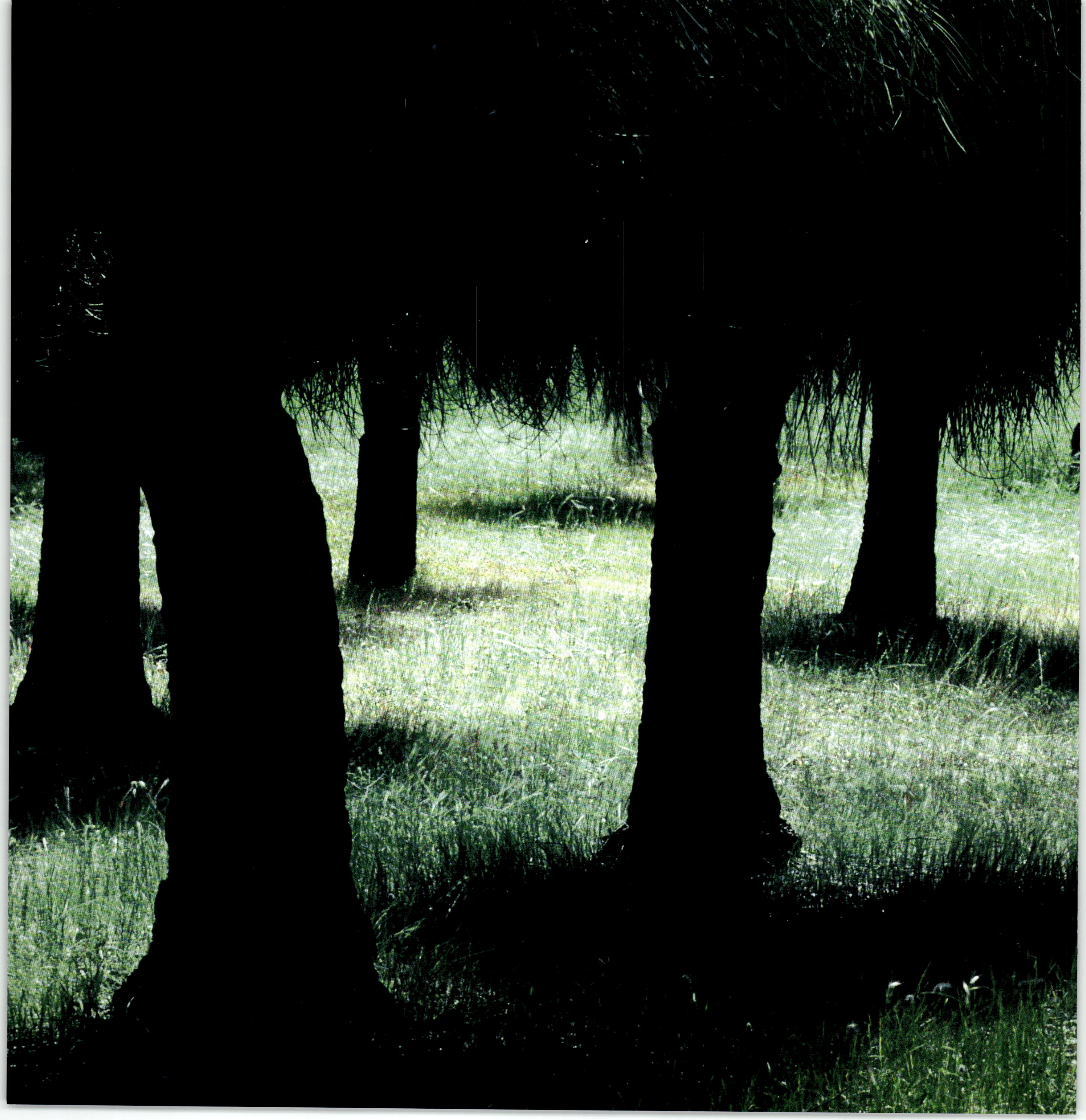

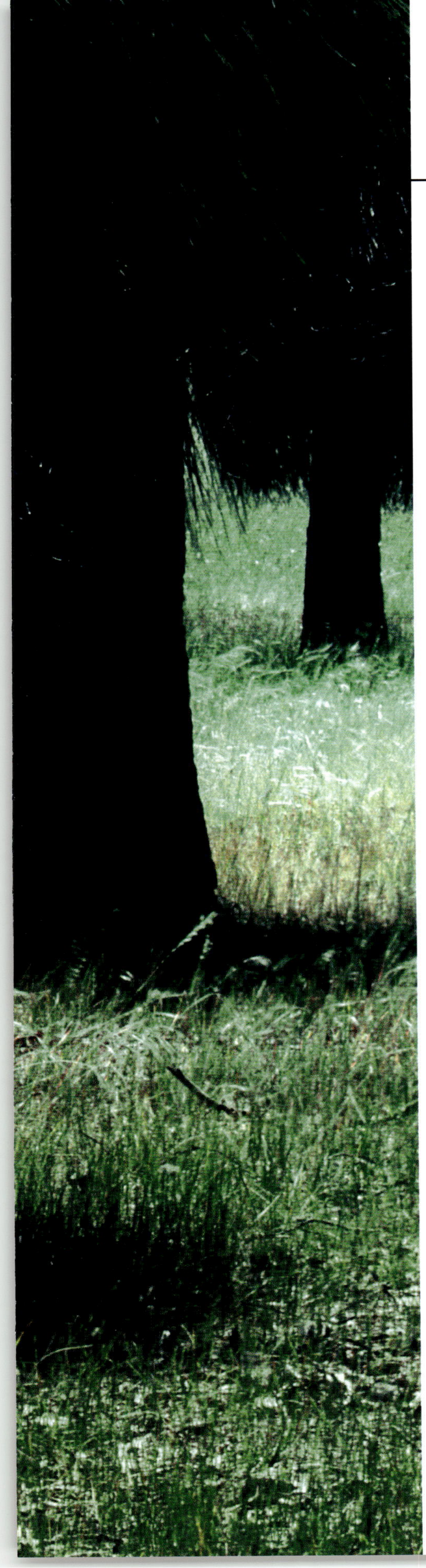

introduction

The rubbish bin has played a part in our landscape photography all too often in the past. Now, courtesy of the computer, we need never throw away another image. Even if you know little about the computer, and even less about digital photography, this book is designed for you.

The projects in this book present views of the landscape, portrayed through photographs, screen grabs, computer-enhanced images, and words. The techniques covered are not exhaustive, but were they to enter into too much detail the result would become little more than the photographic equivalent of painting by numbers. There would be little, if any, creative value in that. This is not to deny the importance of the views shown here; the information and inspiration are there to be found. However, photography – with or without the computer's help – is about individual creativity, exploration and expression. In spite of any supposed rules, there can never be a universal set of formulae for photography. It is as individual as thinking.

This book has many levels of application. One option is simply to enjoy the journey through its pages, picking up snippets of instruction and inspiration on landscape photography, and, perhaps, keeping the book on hand for that future time when theory develops into action at the computer. On another level, it might make you aware of where photography is going in light of advances in computer technology, and inspire you to apply the techniques we use here to your own photographs. A third level goes beyond this. It is taking what is seen, and seeing the unseen.

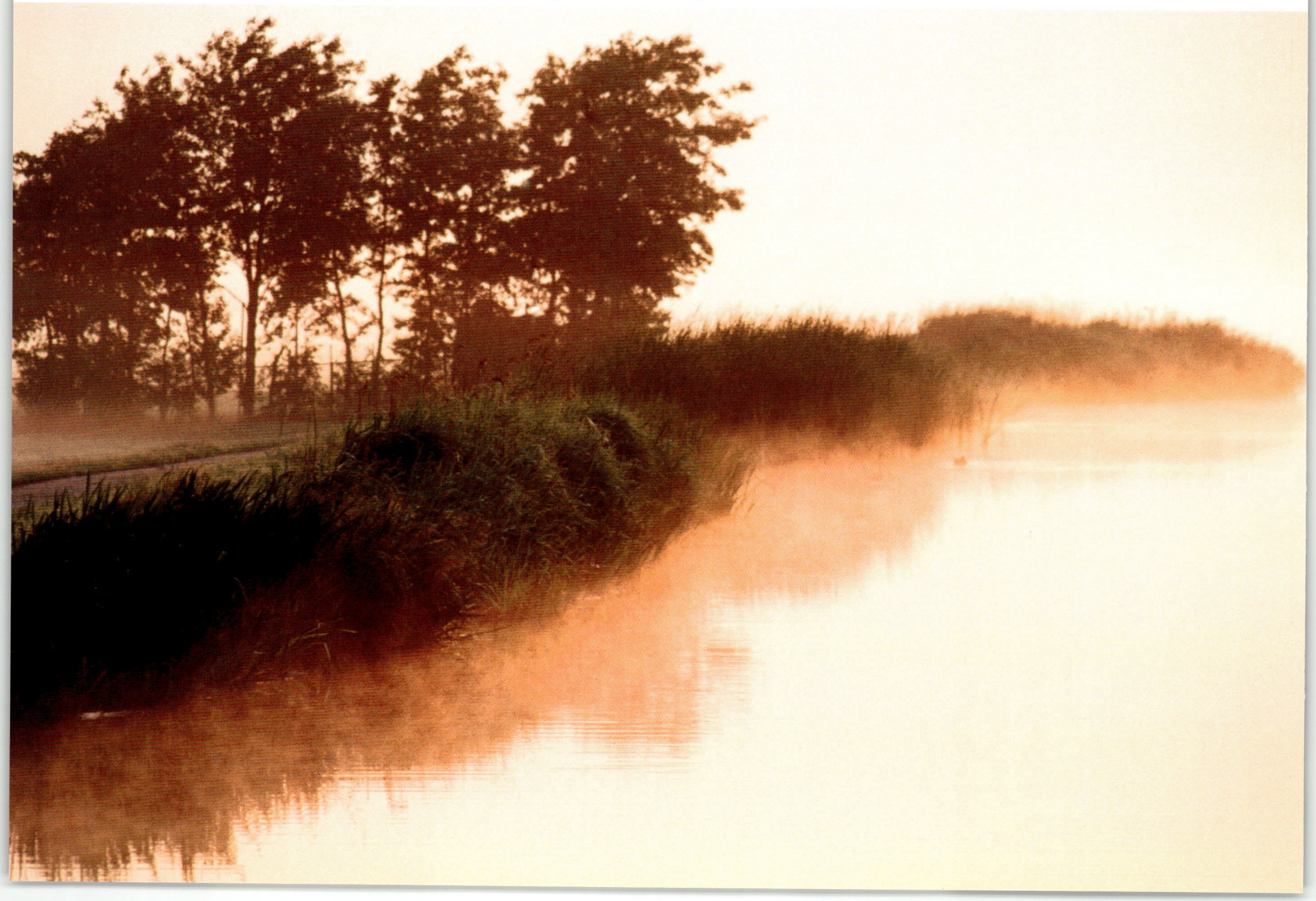

in search of the perfect landscape

A landscape photograph is not, generally, a group accomplishment. It is not a team effort, but something much more personal. When I make a photograph it is up to me whether I like it or not, and to decide how good it is. Perfection, to some readers, may be an ideal or an elusive quality. If I find that I am completely satisfied with a photograph I have taken and choose to see it as perfect, then this has nothing to do with being presumptuous. If I want to sell it to you as a 'perfect photograph' then that is another story. When in the business of selling photographs I have to be aware of a potential client's situation and needs. However, my aim when making a landscape photograph is to try to show what I am seeing and feeling when I release the shutter. If I am to produce my perfect photograph, I need to be aware of my own needs as a photographer. This book is about understanding those needs.

Like the computer-based enhancing techniques you will discover here, the basic techniques of photography are not hard to follow or complex to understand. So why do so many photographs disappoint? Perhaps it is because before we know 'how', we need to know 'why'. Many photography books abound on technique. They delve into detailed descriptions on the depth of field, they cover the elements of composition, suggest which equipment to use, and look at light. All too often, however, they fail to reveal the reasons *why* a particular technique, a certain lens or a specific light is desired in the first place.

Before we [Arjan and Herb] describe the relevant enhancing techniques in each project, I [Herb] address the thinking behind that photograph. Obviously this is personal, but as a consequence it is hoped that you will find it an inspiration for producing your own perfect landscape.

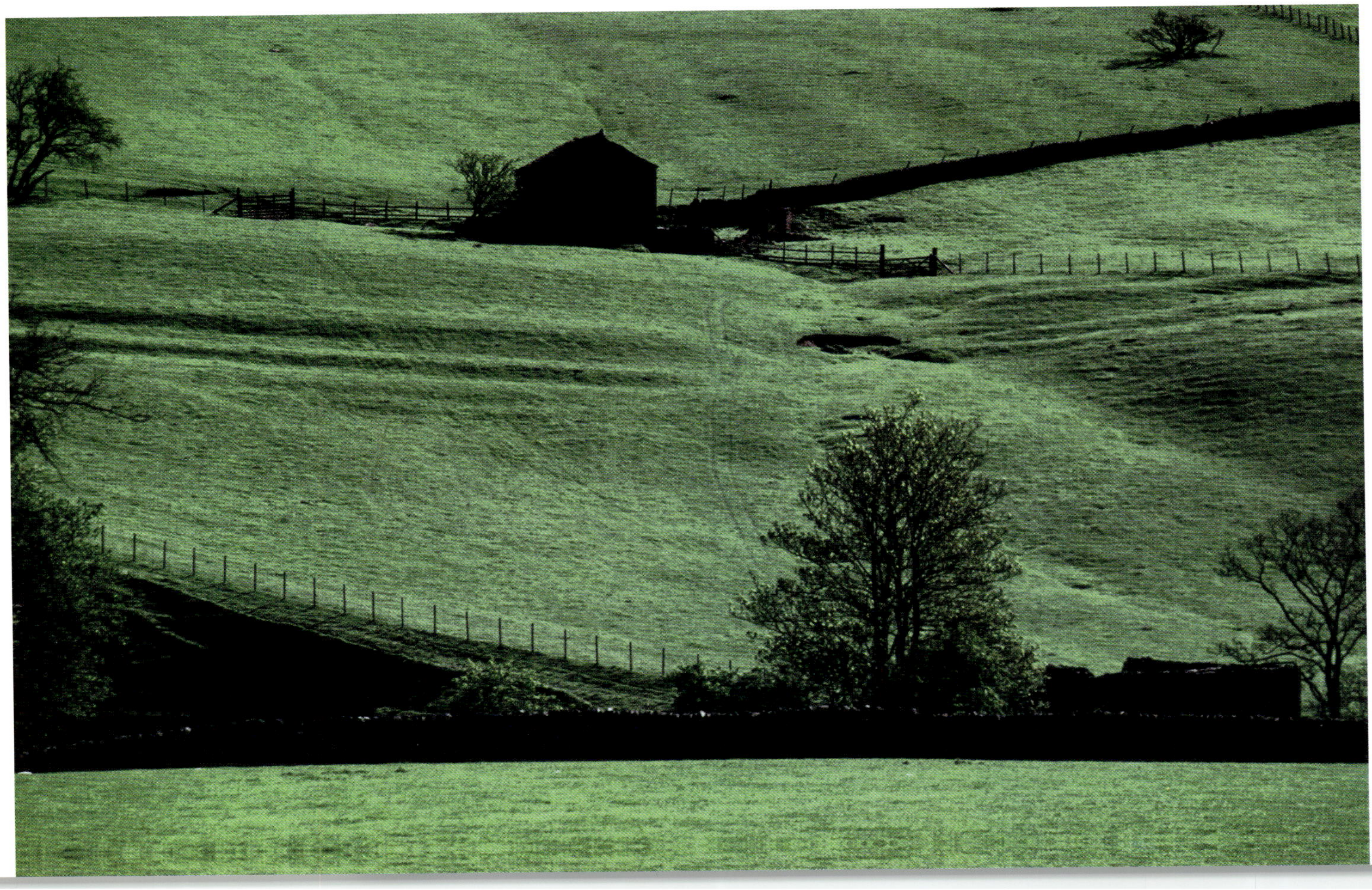

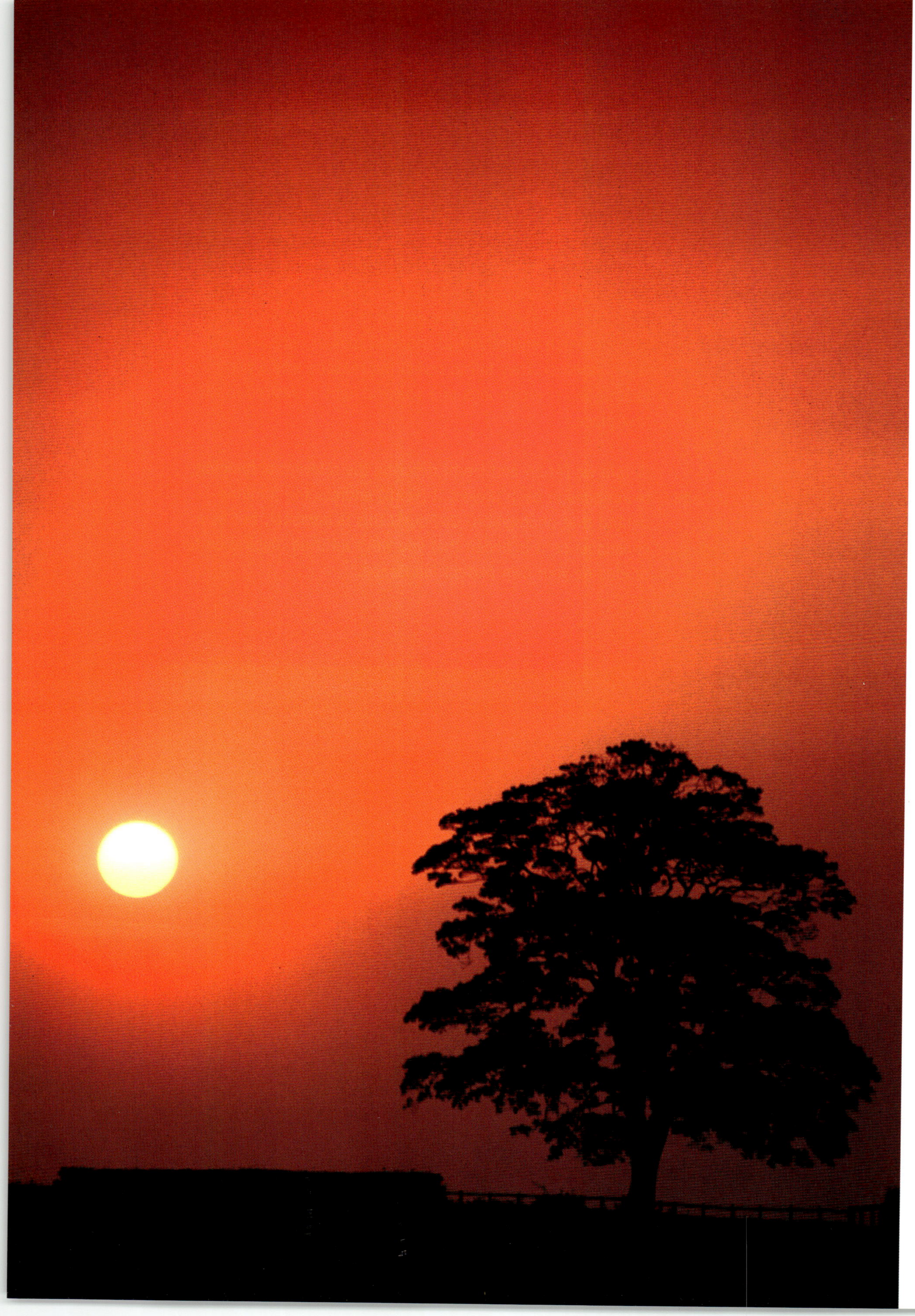

the computer as a tool

Landscape photography can be wonderfully rewarding. However, is there a photographer who has not wished to change something in a landscape photograph at some time or other? Of course, when things go wrong there are a number of possible solutions. The lab can fix some problems, but at a price. Alternatively, the darkroom offers many treatments, provided you have the time and expertise. When on location there is the option of extra equipment, which again is expensive, as well as unwieldy.

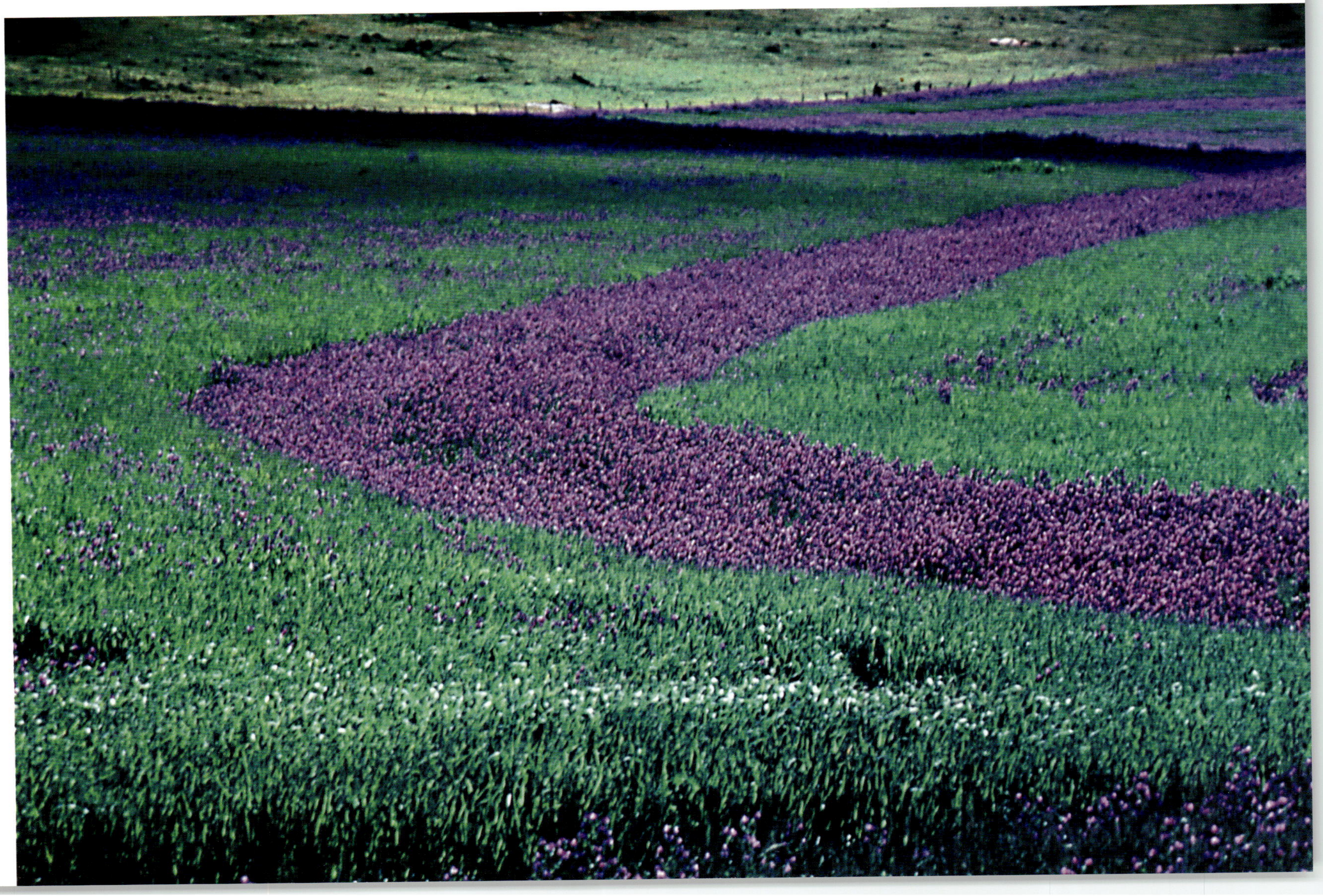

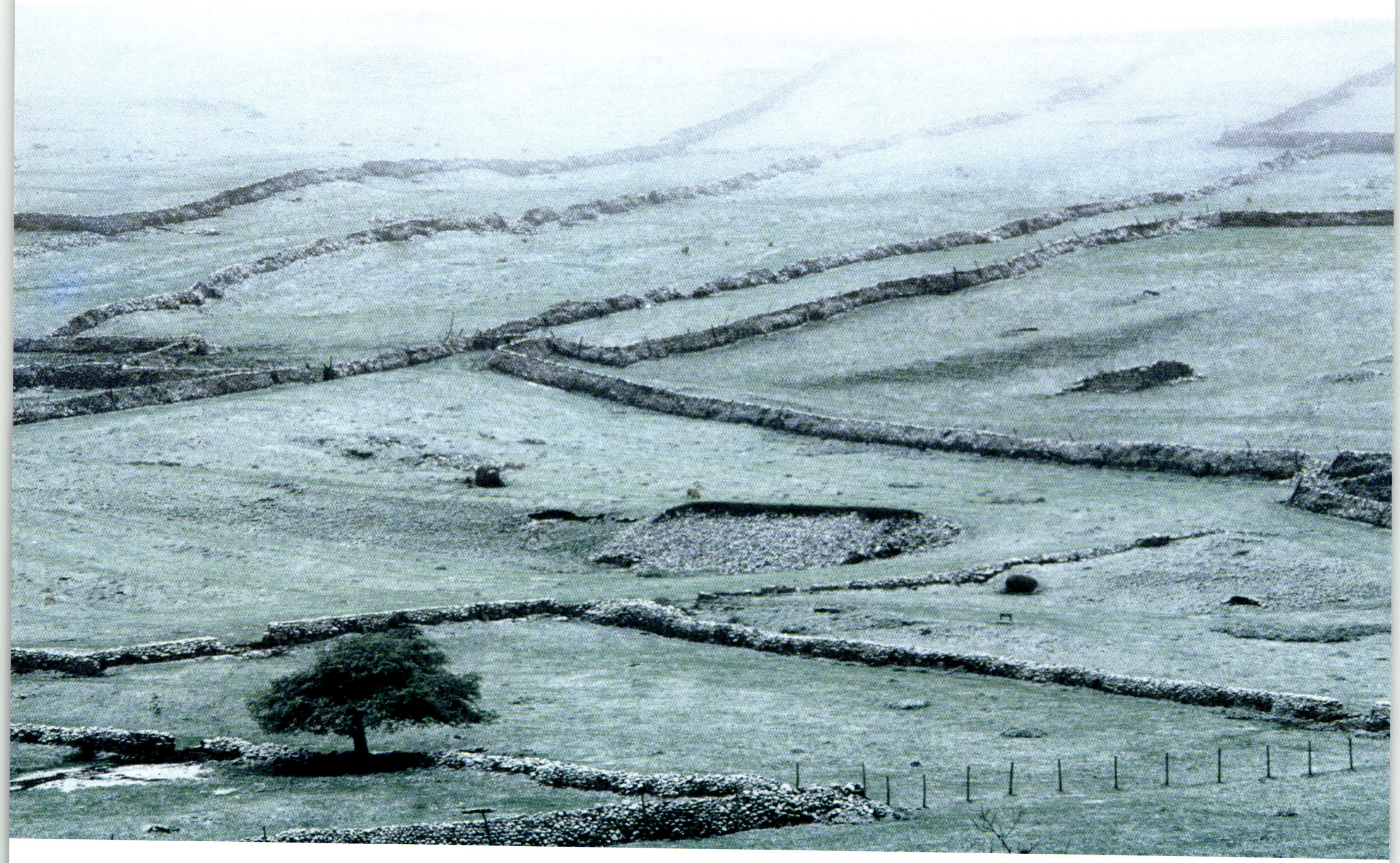

Landscape photography has come a long way since the days when a photographer would disappear under a black cloth to fiddle with a heavy and cumbersome camera in an attempt to make an exposure. Today, the computer means that previously undreamed of procedures can be effected at the touch of a button.

As a photographer, look upon the computer as a tool awaiting your instruction to help you perfect an image. Computers are a fact of modern life and are here to stay. We can avoid them in fear and ignorance, or we can accept them and try to use them to our advantage.

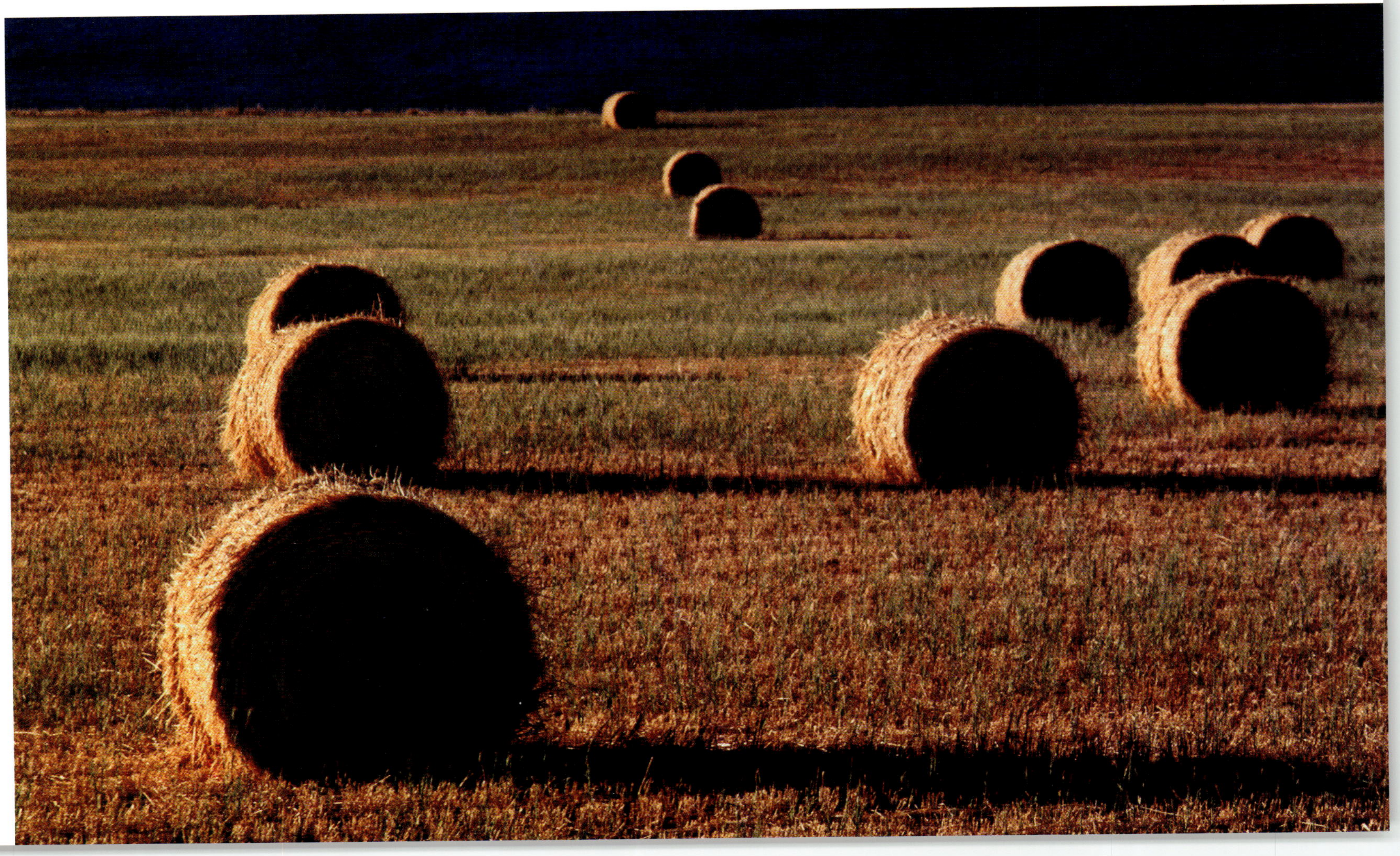

There is no substitute for hands-on experience, so begin with simple tasks to become familiar with basic procedures and to develop confidence. As with most learning experiences, the 'step principle' applies: when you think your efforts are leading nowhere, by sticking to the task you will suddenly find yourself stepping up onto a higher level of awareness and understanding. If, at first, you do not find it exciting, you will soon change your thinking as you begin to see the computer's potential to help you enhance your world of landscape photography beyond belief. In practically any given outdoor situation, seeing with the heart, seeing with the eye, and seeing with the camera may reveal three entirely different fields of view. Equipment, from film format to filters, may make a considerable difference. The question of timing, from seconds to seasons, may further dramatically alter your interpretation. However, introducing the computer to your photography may make the biggest change of all.

your photographs: from camera to computer

Before we can start to apply the enhancing techniques covered by this book, we need to know how to get the photographs we want to enhance onto the computer. For those of us with a digital stills camera, or digital video camera with a stills option, it is simple to transfer photographs directly to the computer, as the manufacturer has included the necessary technology.

With negative or slide film it is not quite so simple. If you use a lab to develop and print your photographs, a flatbed scanner is the best DIY option. Alternatively, the lab can scan the photographs for you when you have them developed. They will put them onto a CD, and all you have to do is place the CD in your computer and load the images into the editing programme. Another option is to buy a dedicated slide scanner so that you can scan your images, from both slides and negatives, at your own convenience. Slide scanners have an optical resolution of up to 4000 dpi (dots per inch) and can produce top-quality prints up to A3 size. In the long run, they are the best option for anyone considering using a non-digital camera for the foreseeable future. Alternatively, a professional firm can scan your negatives or slides for you using a drum scanner. This will probably give you the best-quality results overall, but at a price.

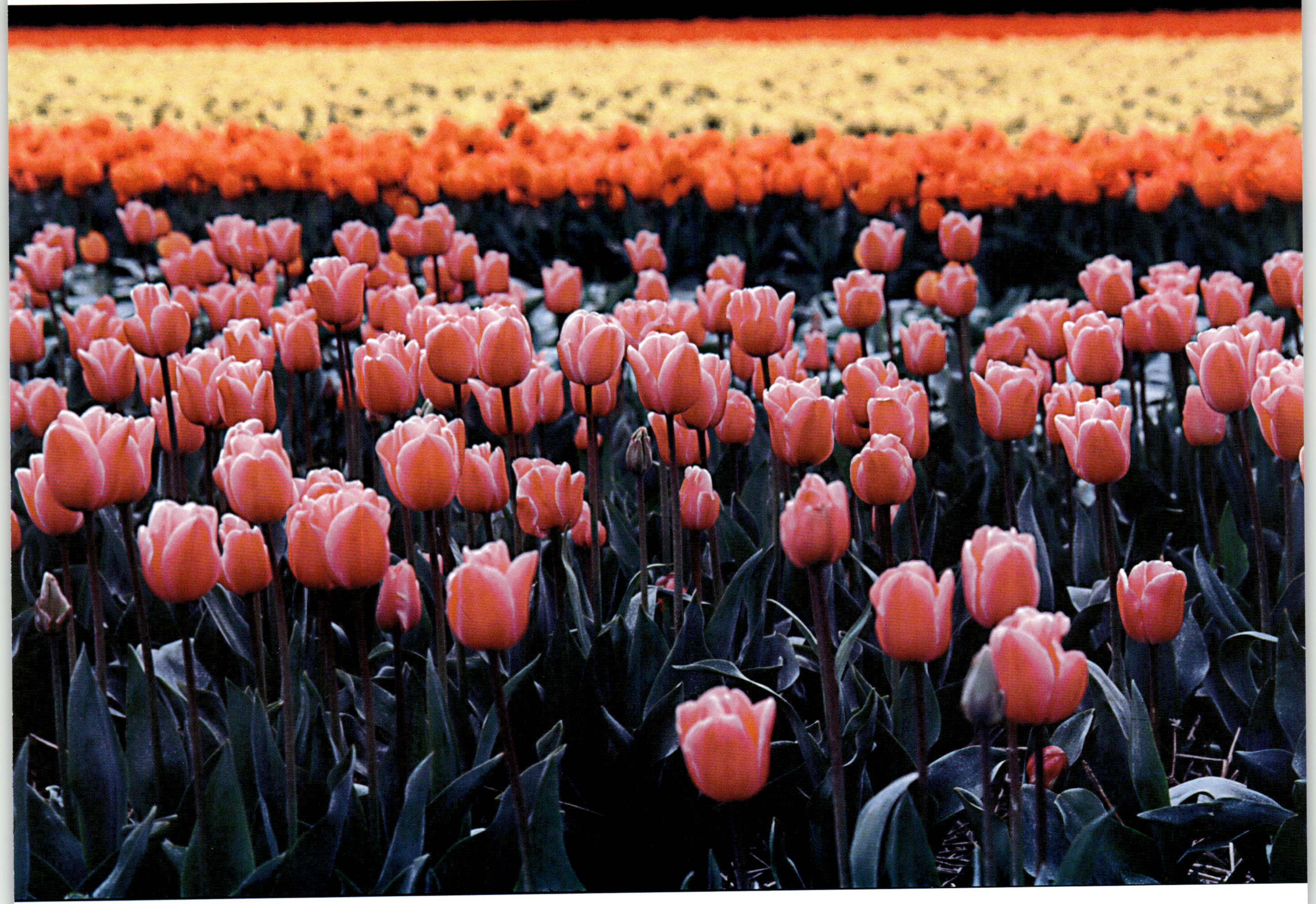

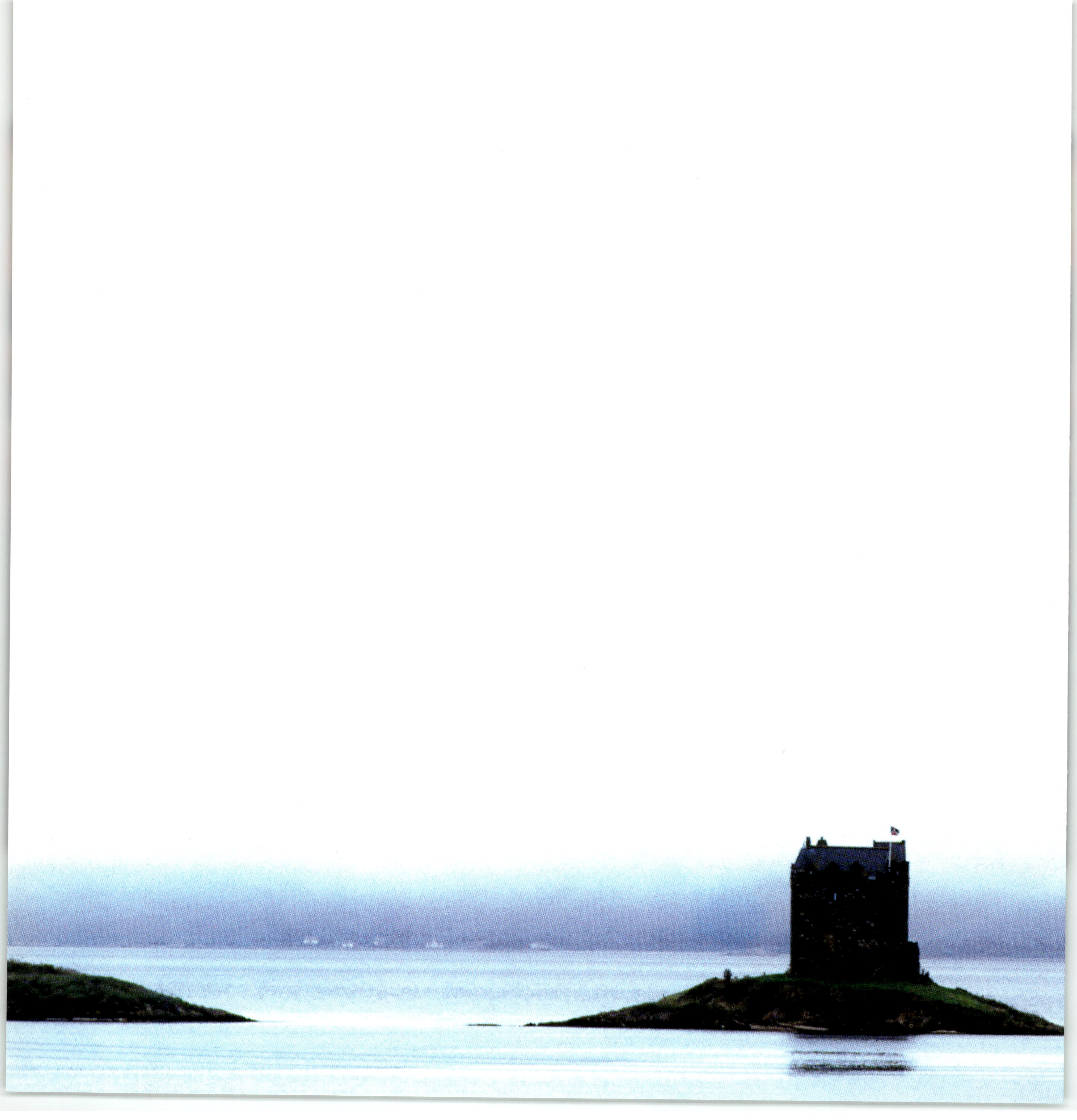

The techniques covered by this book can be applied to both PCs and Apple Macs. The relevant hardware (i.e. scanners, etc) and software (i.e. computer programs) are available for both platforms, and the projects only use the mouse in combination with the pull-down menus. (The alternative is to use keyboard shortcuts, but these vary from one platform to the other.) In those instances where keyboard keys are used, any Apple variations are placed in square brackets. Another variation between the two involves the mouse, since the Apple has just one mouse button, while a PC has two. Where the instructions indicate a click on the right-hand mouse button (on a PC), Apple users should hold down the CONTROL button and click the mouse. The left-hand mouse button on a PC has the same function as the Apple's single mouse button.

The photographs in this book are enhanced using Adobe Photoshop, but other image-editing programs have similar functions and commands.

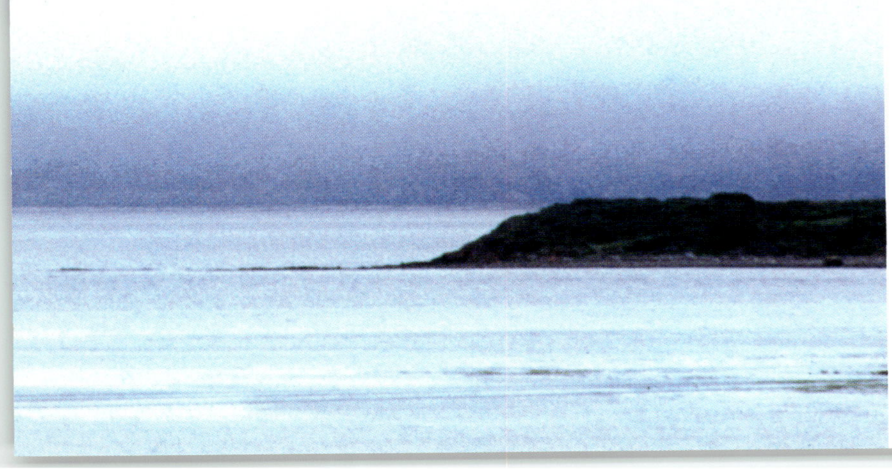

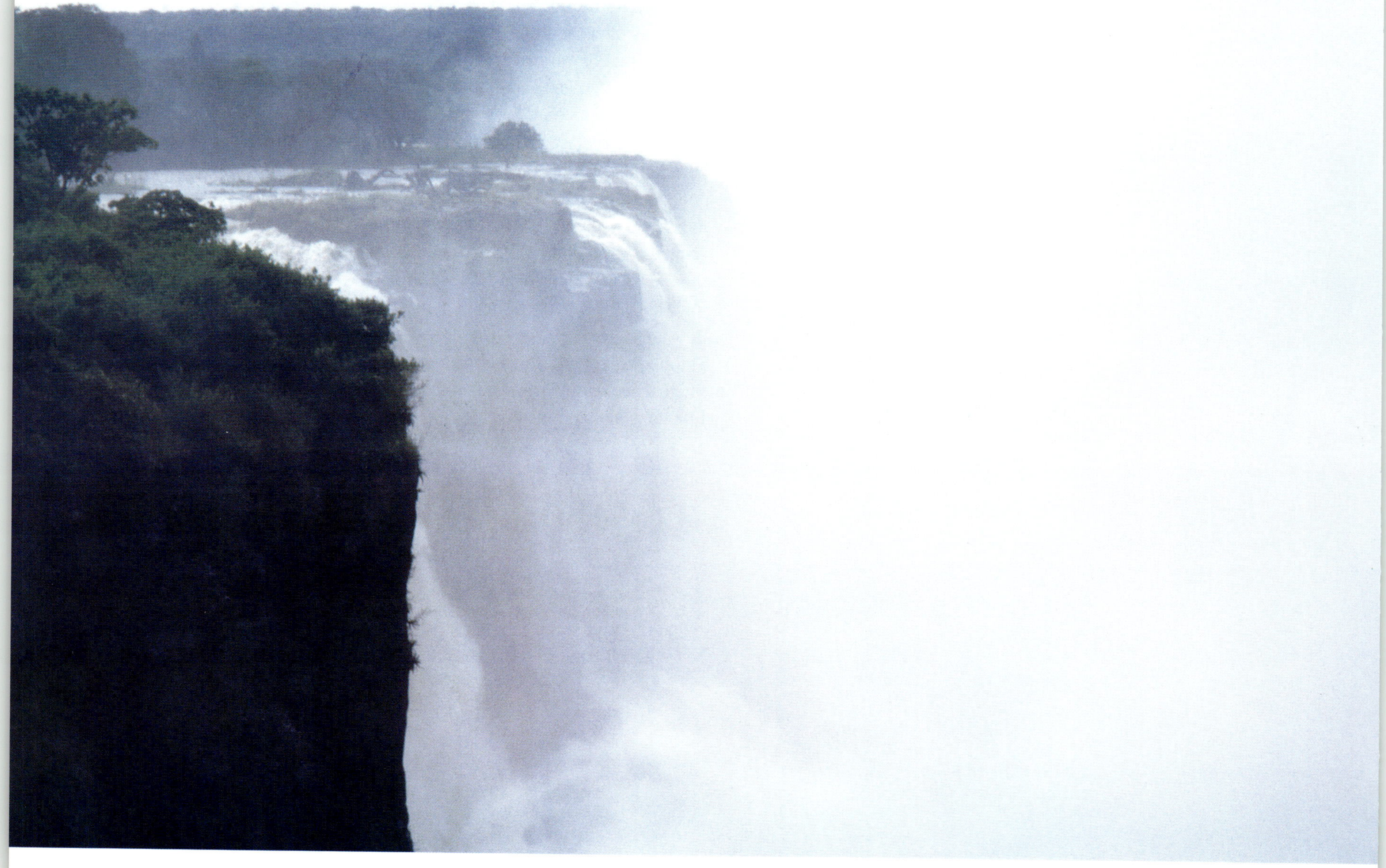

Using our image-editing program we load a photograph onto the computer screen by, first, clicking the left mouse button on FILE. We select OPEN and a small window appears (fig. 1) enabling us to locate our photographs, for instance in our directory MY DOCUMENTS/MY PICTURES. Finally, we choose the image we wish to work on.

We never work on an original photograph so that, if we make a mistake, we can restart with no permanent loss. To make a copy we go to LAYERS/DUPLICATE LAYER (fig. 2), or we pull the BACKGROUND bar in the layers menu over the small icon (second from the right) at the bottom of the window (fig. 3). Save your work at regular intervals, then when something does go wrong, not everything is lost at once.

With our image on the screen before us, we are ready to begin...

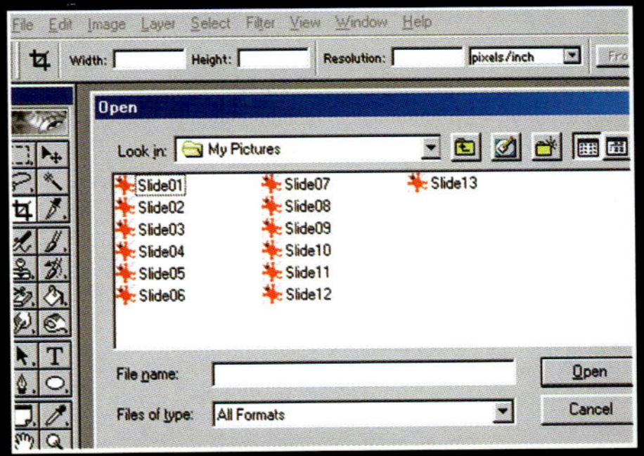

Fig 1

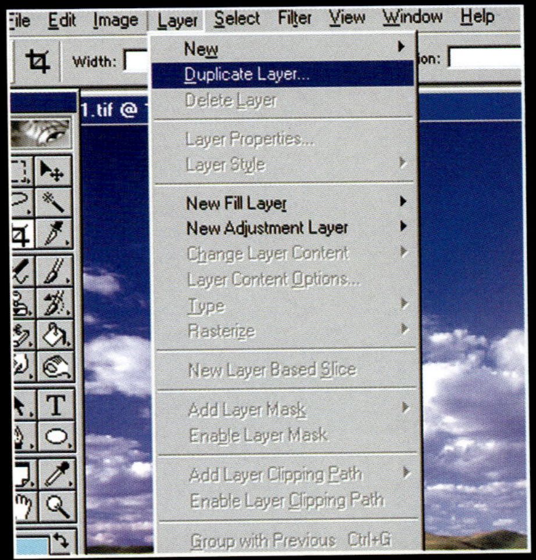

Fig 2

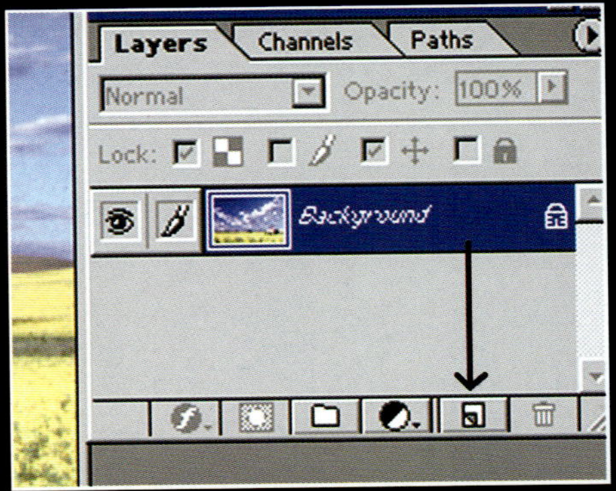

Fig 3

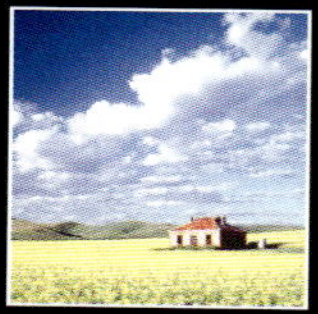
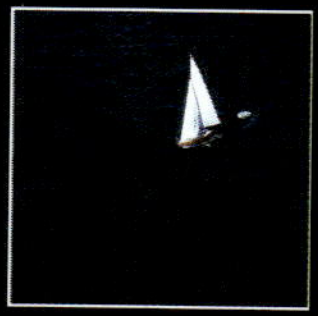
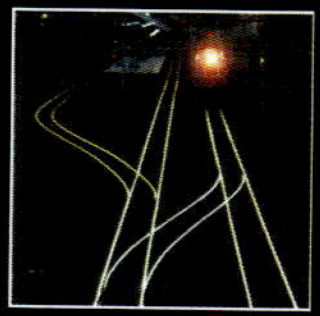
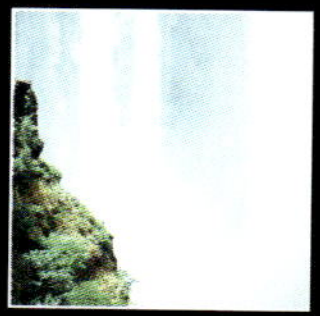
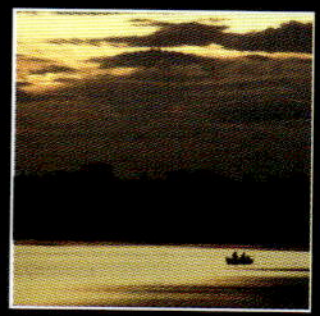
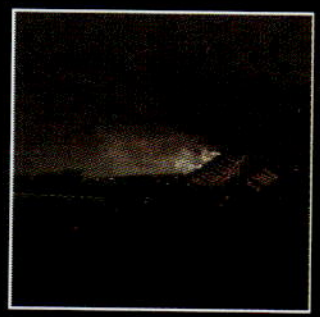
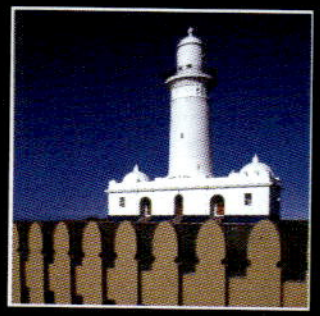
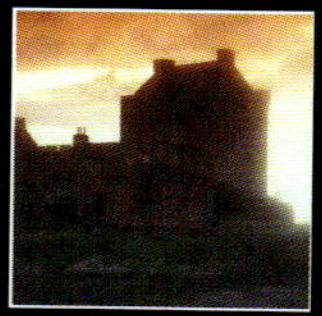
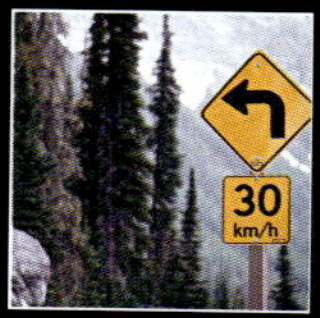
30
km/h
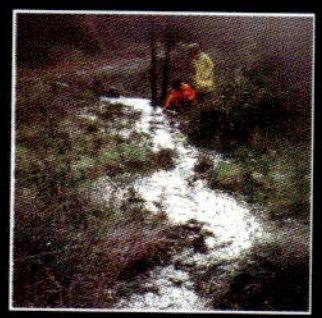
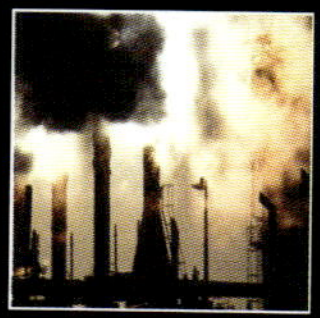
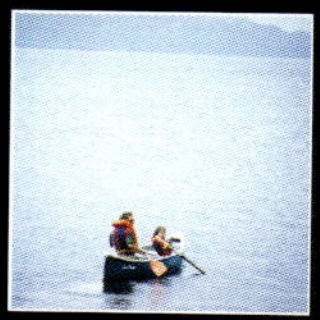
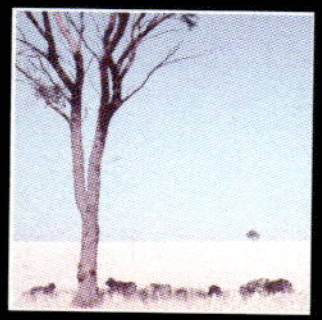
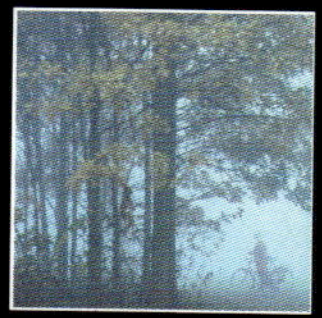
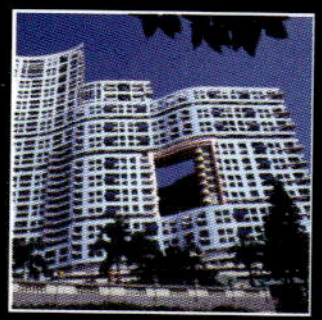
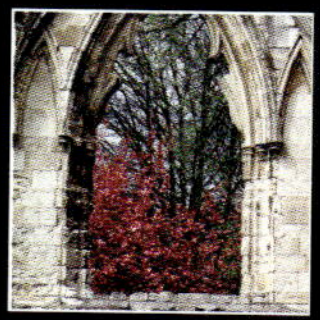
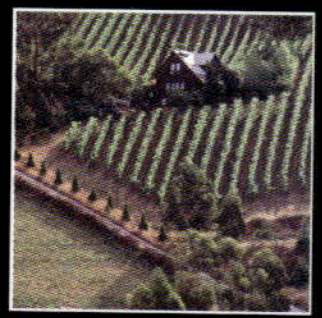
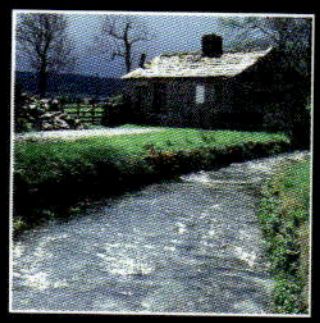

the projects

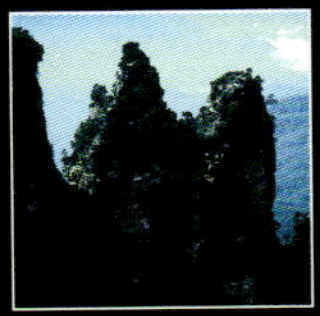
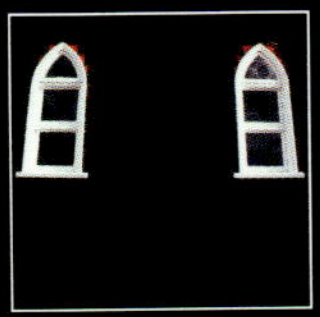
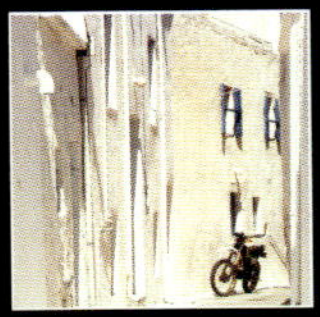
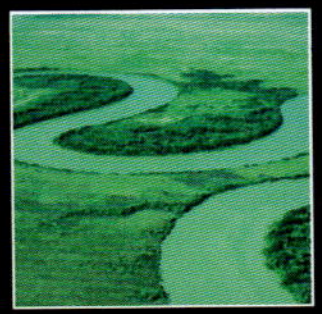
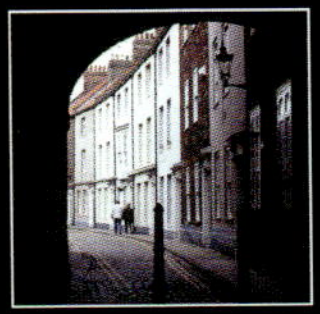
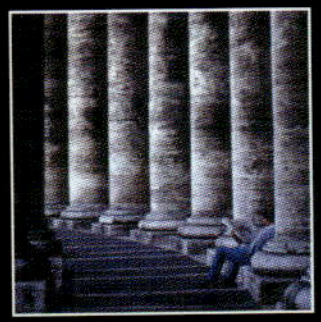
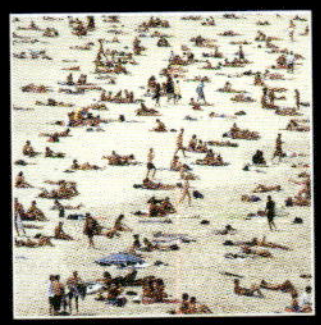
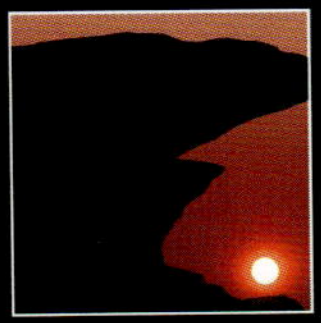
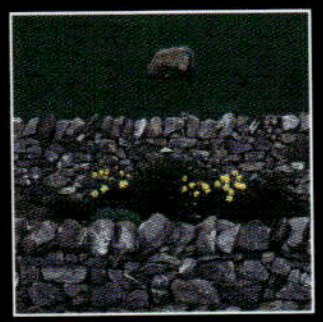
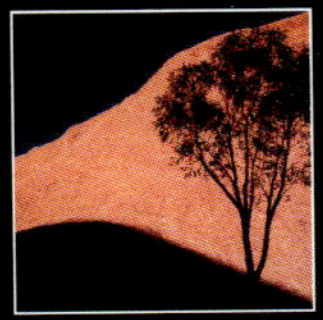
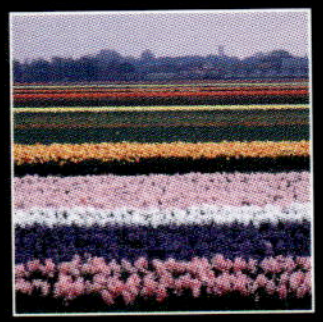
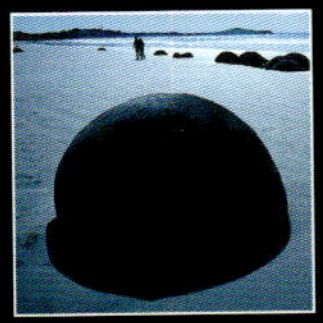
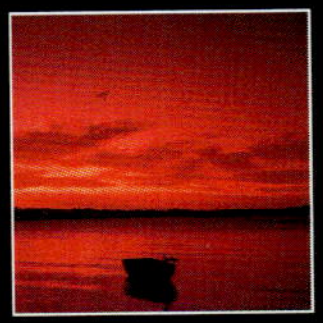

project 1

bringing colour to life

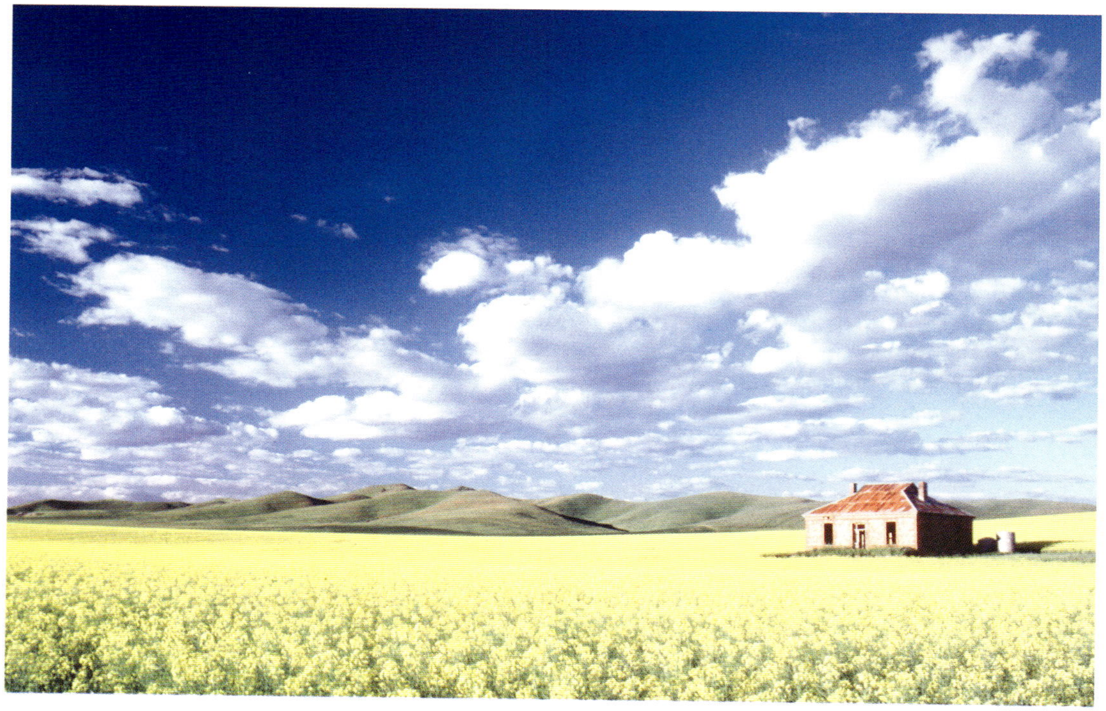

Fig 1.1 *House at Burra* lacks much of the colour I remember when visiting the scene.

ADJUST/LEVELS

When you discover a landscape that inspires you to take out your camera and make a photograph you may be influenced by some factors that are not immediately apparent. It is only when your finished print or colour slide is returned from the camera shop or laboratory, and your excited anticipation gives way to disappointment, that you start to realize the extent of the problem. Sometimes it even seems possible that the lab has made a mistake or sent the wrong photo. However, if the processing is not to blame and camera and film are performing correctly, why do so many landscape photographs fail to please?

Fig 1.2 Using ADJUST/LEVELS revives the colour that was lacking in the original image of this rural landscape.

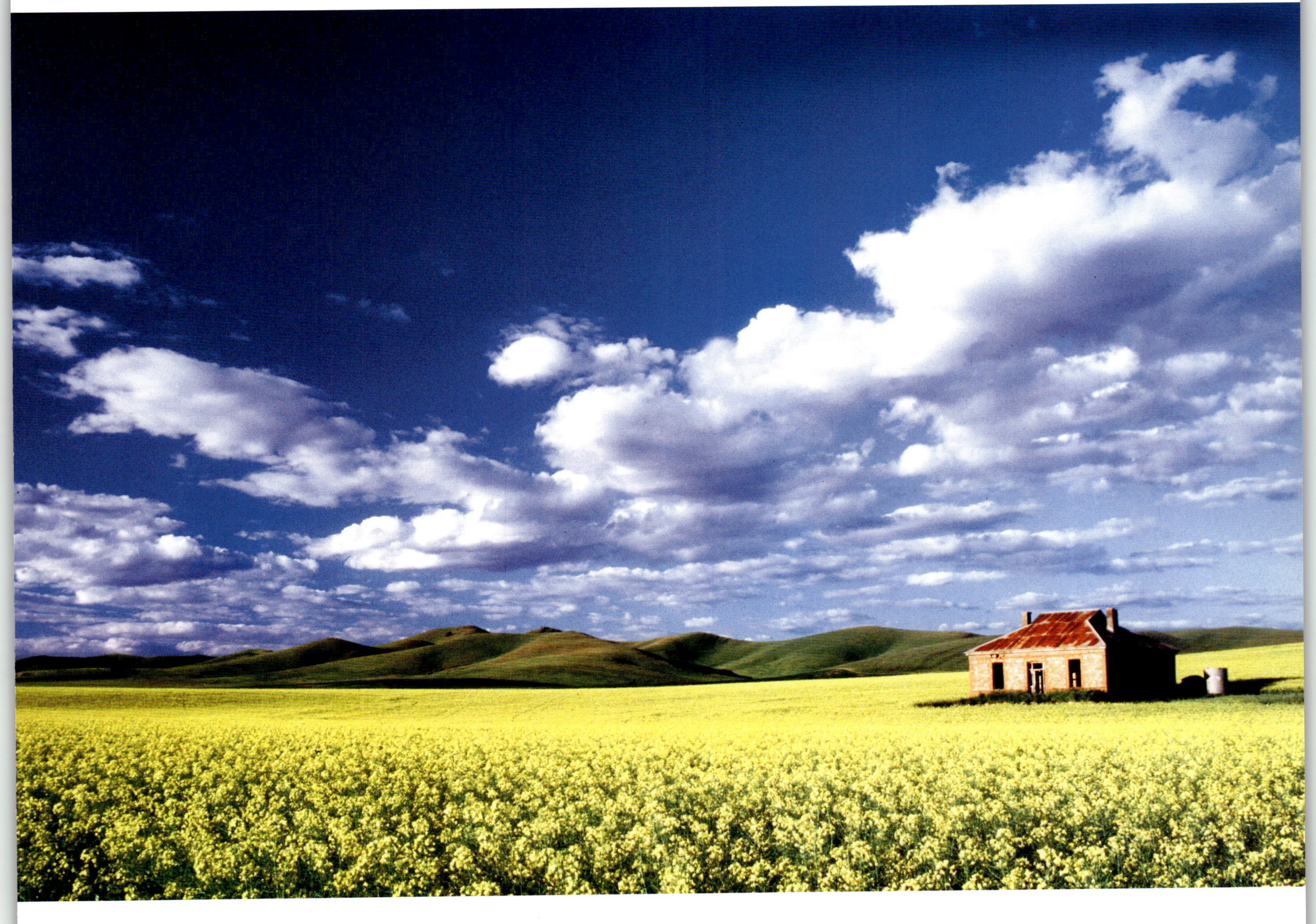

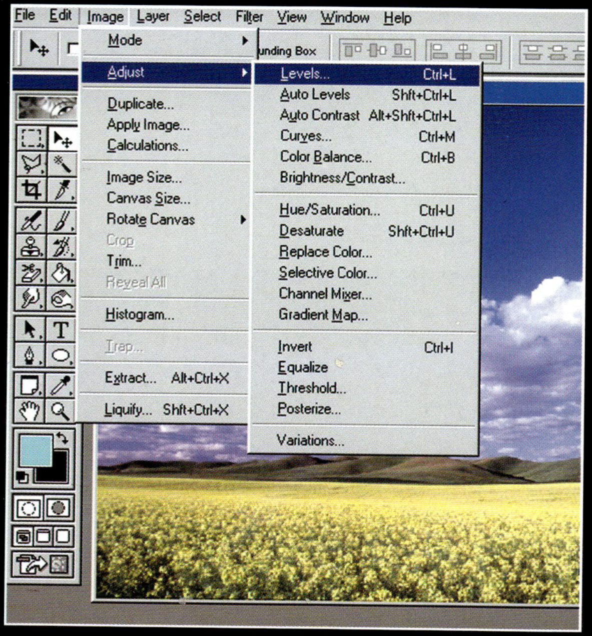
File Edit Image Layer Select Filter View Window Help
Mode
Adjust
Duplicate...
Apply Image...
Calculations...
Image Size...
Canvas Size...
Rotate Canvas
Crop
Trim...
Reveal All
Histogram...
Trap...
Extract... Alt+Ctrl+X
Liquify... Shft+Ctrl+X
Levels... Ctrl+L
Auto Levels Shft+Ctrl+L
Auto Contrast Alt+Shft+Ctrl+L
Curves... Ctrl+M
Color Balance... Ctrl+B
Brightness/Contrast...
Hue/Saturation... Ctrl+U
Desaturate Shft+Ctrl+U
Replace Color...
Selective Color...
Channel Mixer...
Gradient Map...
Invert Ctrl+I
Equalize
Threshold...
Posterize...
Variations...

Fig 1.3

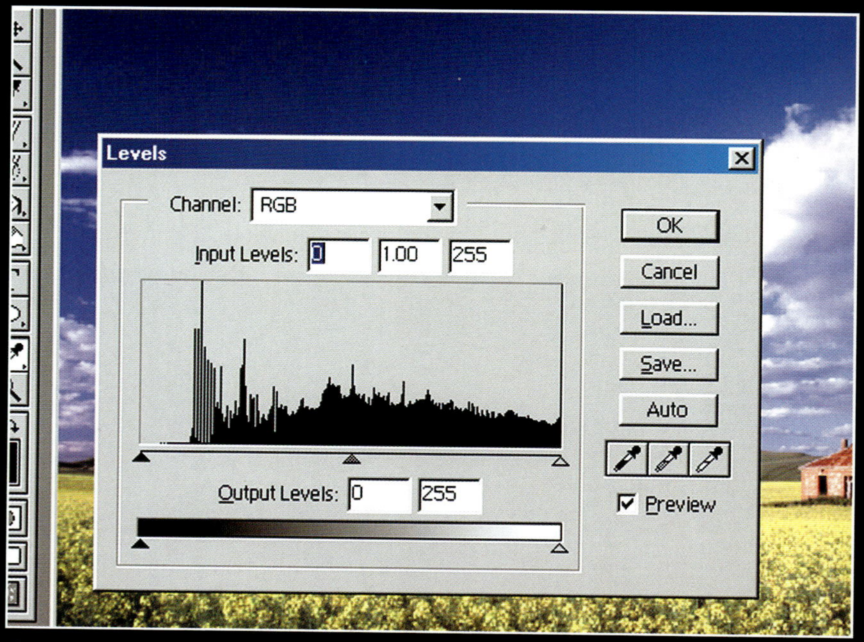
Levels
Channel: RGB
Input Levels: 0 1.00 255
Output Levels: 0 255
OK
Cancel
Load...
Save...
Auto
Preview

Fig 1.4

Most amateur photographers operate on an emotional level, and our senses can change our response to a situation. We feel the warmth of the sun, hear the whistle of the wind, smell the sweetness in the air, and then we take a photograph. In addition, our present-tense situation is often coloured by past-tense experience as we make our subjective selection. The camera, on the other hand, holds no such emotions as it goes about its objective and impartial task.

I felt that the sheer distance covered to reach *House at Burra* (fig. 1.1) and the difficulties involved in getting there were sufficient reasons in themselves for me to photograph once I had arrived. Jumping out of a crowded car increased both the pleasure of the experience and the impression of wide-open space. Unfortunately, the colour of the resulting photograph did not match my mood of the moment, particularly when viewed more objectively later on. In spite of the rush of feelings at the time of shooting, this should have been the time to apply cool technique and clear thinking so that the experience could be enjoyed in the longer term.

The choice of a 24mm wide-angle lens helped convey the feeling of space and gather in the cloud formation, but in spite of my enthusiasm the resulting photograph lacked the bright colour I remembered so well. To return to a scene and shoot a photograph again, though often desirable, is not always practical. This was the case here – from where I write, Burra is on the other side of the world. A more effective solution was to turn to the computer.

The use of a polarizing filter when the photograph was taken could have deepened the blue sky, given greater contrast to the white clouds and enriched the yellows and greens to produce a much stronger image. All of this can now be achieved on the computer, simply by using the IMAGE/ADJUST/LEVELS technique (so-called because these are the headings of the options used).

First, we click with our left mouse button on the IMAGE pull-down menu. We select ADJUST and then choose LEVELS (fig. 1.3) on the second menu to appear. Underneath our chosen option we see AUTO LEVELS. This option instructs the computer to do for us, automatically, what we are about to do for ourselves. However, using this technique would not give us direct control in the development of our picture.

When we click on LEVELS a new window appears (fig. 1.4) containing a graph with three sliders directly below. These can be used to influence the tonal values of the image, which consist of SHADOWS, MID-TONES and HIGHLIGHTS. The graph indicates how different colours are used in our image. The extreme left of the graph represents black and the extreme right, white. We can see from the graph there is no indication of any black but there is a lot of white. A glance at our image confirms this. To enhance the colours we simply move the left-hand slider (holding down the mouse button as we do so) to where the curve starts. This makes the available black in the image darker. With PREVIEW switched on, the effect on the image is shown immediately. By moving the left-hand slider to the right, the shadow cast by the house has become much darker and the sky has developed a deeper blue. Now we move the middle slider carefully to the right until we are satisfied with the intensity of yellow.

At the bottom of the LEVELS window is a bar showing colours from black to white. Above it OUTPUT LEVELS show as 0 and 255 (black is 0 and white is 255). When we use a program such as Photoshop in RGB (Red-Green-Blue) mode, all colours are identified by three numbers, as all colours are a combination of those levels of red, green and blue. For example, in *House at Burra* the yellow below the left hill is R: 194, G: 182, and B: 119. Thus anyone following these simple steps can recreate this precise colour.

When compared with the original, the computer-enhanced image (fig. 1.2) is 'perfect' because it portrays the scene exactly as I remembered it.

project 2

emphasizing the details

ADJUST/CURVES

For a photographer to make the most of his or her photography, whatever their level, there must be a plan – from the setting up of long-term goals down to the compositional fine-tuning of a photograph. And yet every photographer must be flexible because, in reality, nothing is guaranteed to turn out as we expect. I also believe that, if the spark of creativity is not to be extinguished and freedom of thought and expression are to be encouraged, there must be space for spontaneity at every stage of the process.

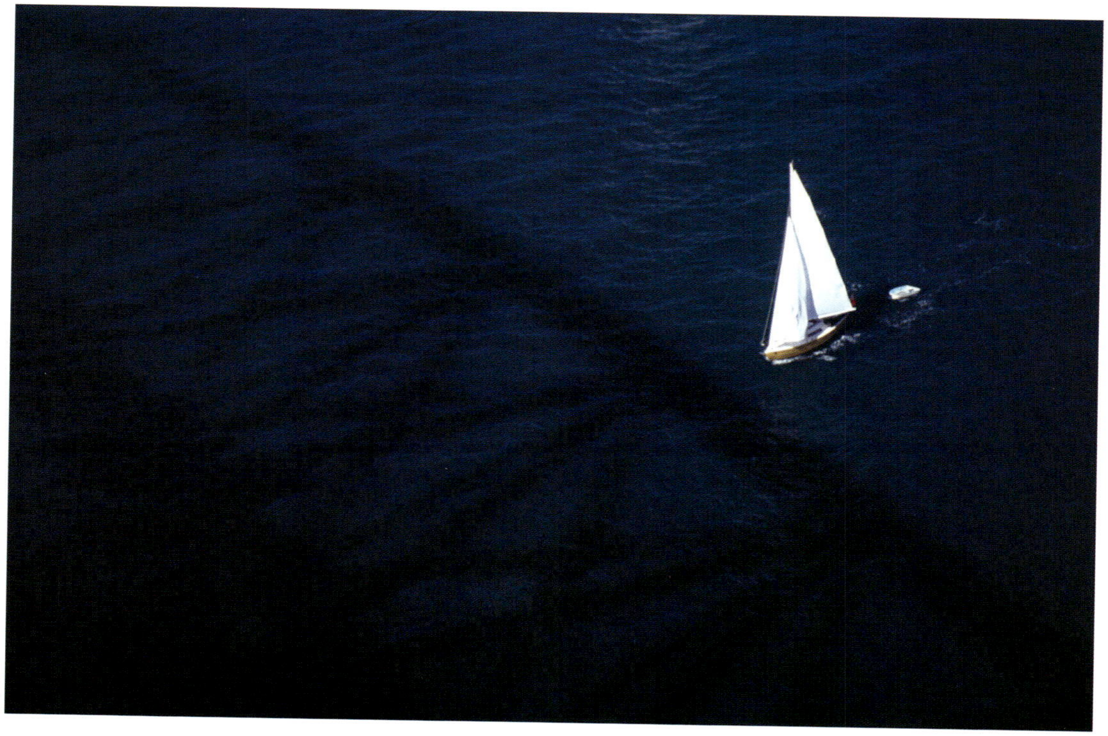

Fig 2.1 *Bridge Shadow* does not reflect the symbolism I had intended at the time of exposure, and I am disappointed on seeing the result.

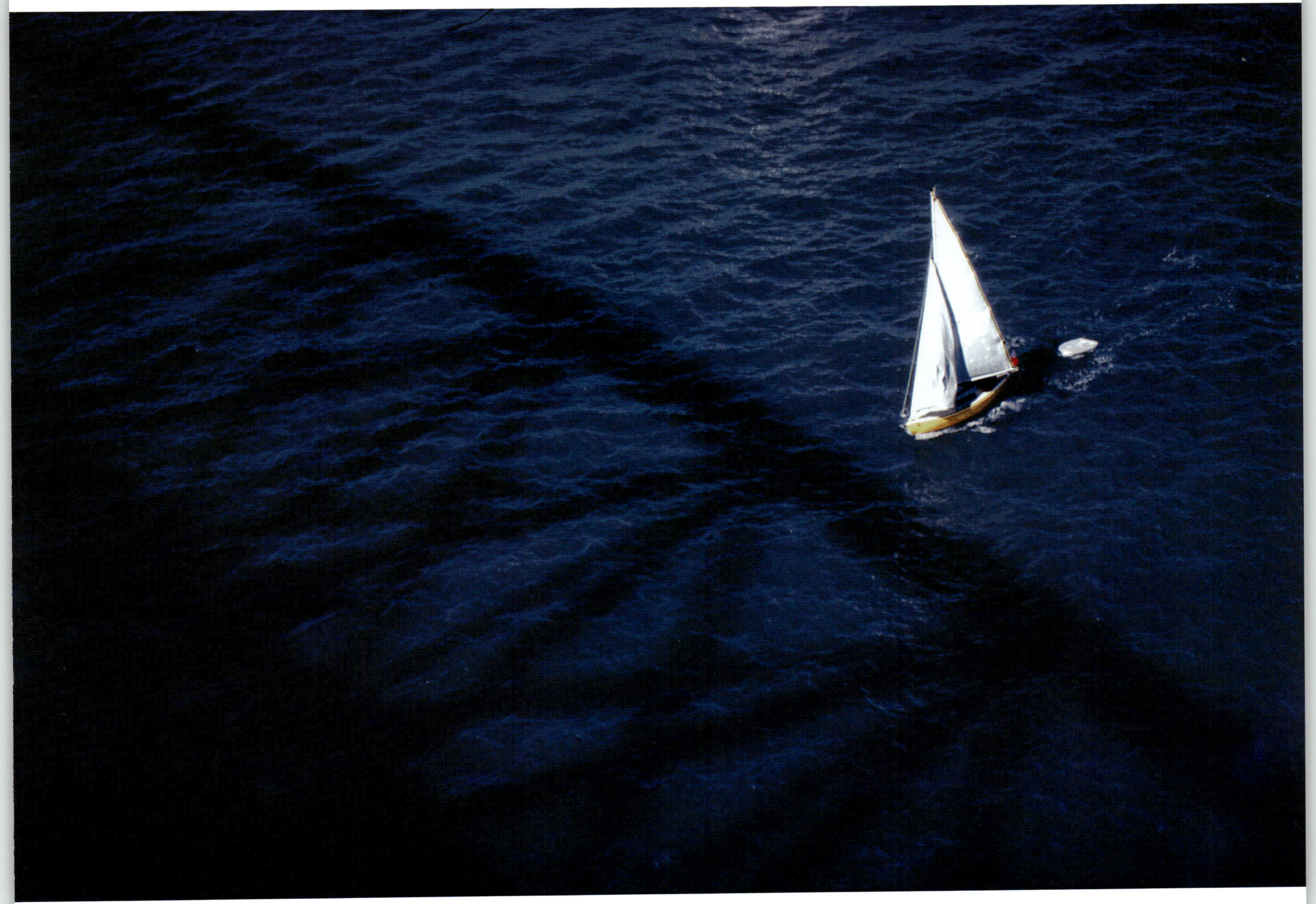

Fig 2.2 I was able to reinforce my interpretation and salvage this image using the ADJUST/CURVES technique.

Bridge Shadow (fig 2.1) is a good example of how a photograph can come about as a result of an unanticipated opportunity. On this occasion, my original plan had been to photograph the hustle and bustle of Sydney's inner-city life. Despite my familiarity with the area, I noticed a stairway leading upwards that I had never seen before. On impulse, I decided to take it. After a long climb I found myself, to my surprise, high above the crowds and about to set foot upon the walkway of Sydney Harbour Bridge.

The contrast between my previous environment and this new location was tremendous, and, suddenly released from the city's hold, I felt as free as a bird. However, it is one thing to enjoy a feeling and something else to encapsulate that feeling in a photograph. Having moved onto the bridge to look at the possibilities, I noticed the bridge's shadow on the water. It suggested a creative approach to a well-known landmark – a much more original perspective than could have been found from my intended location. Moreover, the composition (land-free and devoid of bridge supports) helped to convey my sense of freedom. Adding the yacht helped to reinforce this impression much more accurately than one of the crowded ferries that cross the harbour.

When my photograph returned from the lab, the result was not quite as I had hoped. The shadow of the bridge was not as prominent as I would have liked, the sails of the boat did not show the detail I had expected, and the blue of the water was almost black. It was left to the computer to throw me a lifeline.

For this image we use IMAGE/ADJUST/CURVES (fig. 2.3). Here, rather than three, there are sixteen points to influence the tonal value. When using curves it is possible to work with percentages or tonal values (i.e. the 0–255 scale). To change between the two, click on the two little triangles in the bar located under the graph. Many photographers seem to prefer to work in tonal values, so that is what we use here.

Changes can be made to the photograph by manipulating the 'curve' in the graph (fig 2.4). The photograph's highlights are influenced by the upper part of the curve, and the shadows by the lower part. When we click our mouse on a part of the curve, the input and output values in the left corner indicate our position. Moving this point affects the image, and using the PREVIEW option enables us to see changes immediately. By selecting additional points on the curve, we can make further changes as required.

This option needs careful handling, plus some experience, but it is a very effective aid when adjusting a picture. In this instance, we push the curve up and down until we achieve the right result (fig. 2.2).

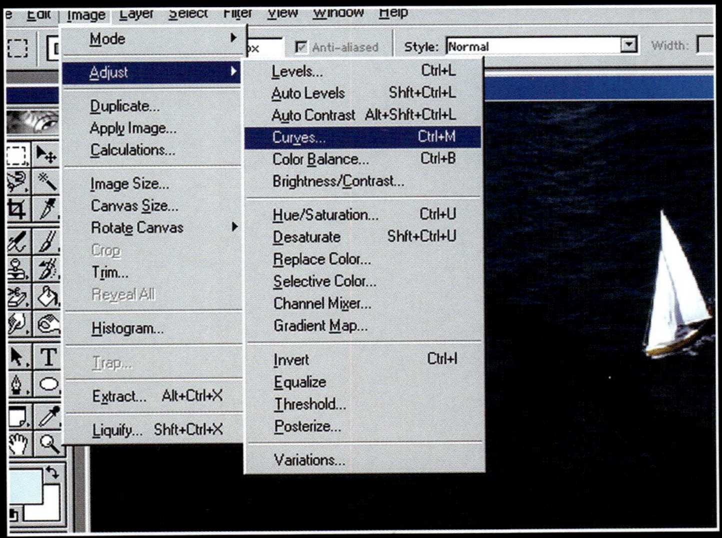
Image
Layer
Select
Filter
View
Window
Help
Mode
Adjust
Duplicate...
Apply Image...
Calculations...
Image Size...
Canvas Size...
Rotate Canvas
Crop
Trim...
Reveal All
Histogram...
Trap...
Extract... Alt+Ctrl+X
Liquify... Shft+Ctrl+X
Levels... Ctrl+L
Auto Levels Shft+Ctrl+L
Auto Contrast Alt+Shft+Ctrl+L
Curves... Ctrl+M
Color Balance... Ctrl+B
Brightness/Contrast...
Hue/Saturation... Ctrl+U
Desaturate Shft+Ctrl+U
Replace Color...
Selective Color...
Channel Mixer...
Gradient Map...
Invert Ctrl+I
Equalize
Threshold...
Posterize...
Variations...
Anti-aliased
Style: Normal
Width:

Fig 2.3

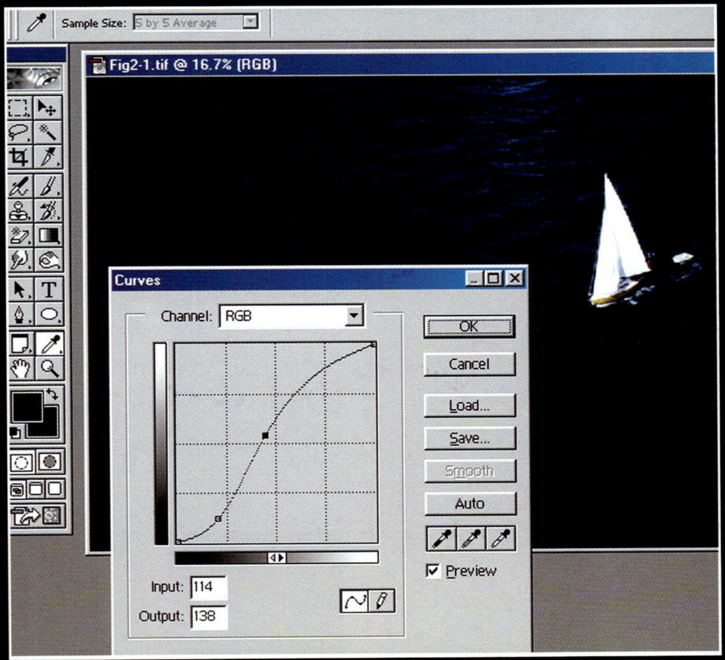
Sample Size: 5 by 5 Average
Fig2-1.tif @ 16.7% (RGB)
Curves
Channel: RGB
OK
Cancel
Load...
Save...
Smooth
Auto
Preview
Input: 114
Output: 138

Fig 2.4

project 3

enhancing contrast

ADJUST/BRIGHTNESS-CONTRAST

There are many enjoyable reasons for entering international photographic salons. For instance, after the close of a salon each entrant receives an eagerly awaited catalogue illustrated with the salon's award-winning entries. The catalogue selection

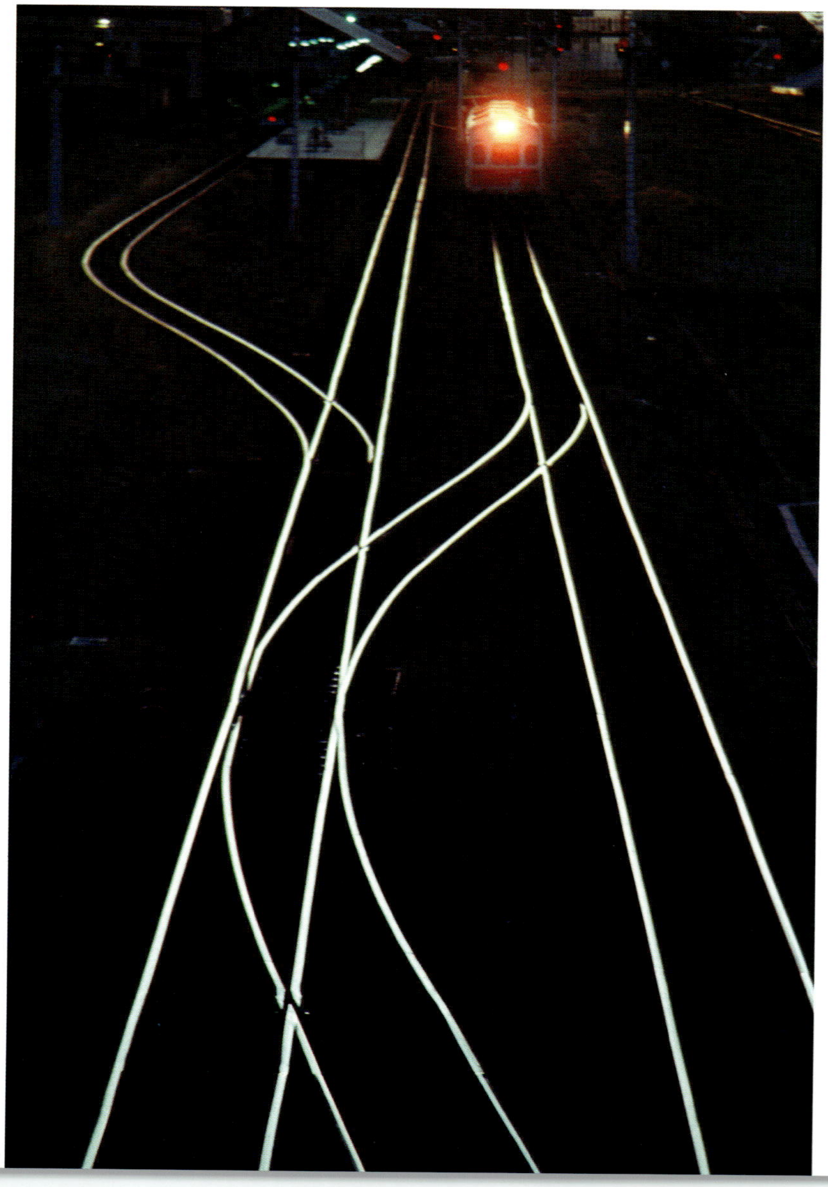

Fig 3.1 Rapidly failing light made this simple composition a difficult prospect.

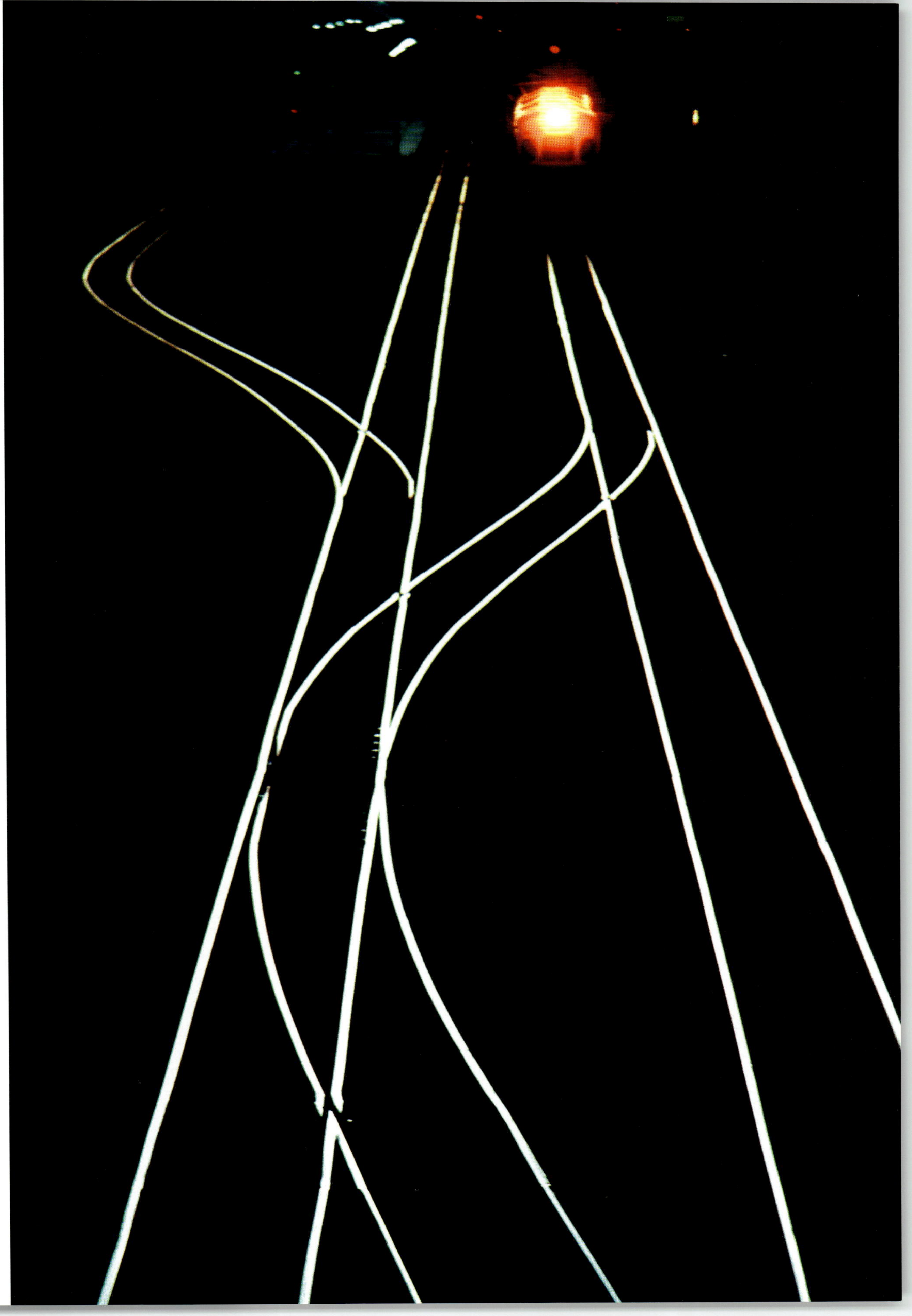

Fig 3.2 ADJUST/BRIGHTNESS-CONTRAST compensates for a difficult lighting situation.

often represents some of the most outstanding contemporary photography in the world. One of the most dramatic photographs I recall seeing in one of these catalogues was a landscape composition featuring a train. The photogenic era of the steam train had long passed, but as a result of seeing that one stunning image I went off with my camera in pursuit of trains.

I have never discovered a train image close to the one I remember so well from the salon catalogue, but I have enjoyed the journey, and the inspiration gained from that single salon image has kept me on track in the search for my own 'perfect' railway landscape.

Rail Track (fig. 3.1) was photographed from a footbridge, just as a train was about to pull out from the station. My interest had been aroused initially by the tracks, which brightly reflected the lingering remains of daylight and stood out in marked contrast from the descending darkness. Unfortunately, when I received the processed transparency, the contrast was not as dramatic as I had hoped. Lights from the platform and surrounding station, which at the time of taking the photograph

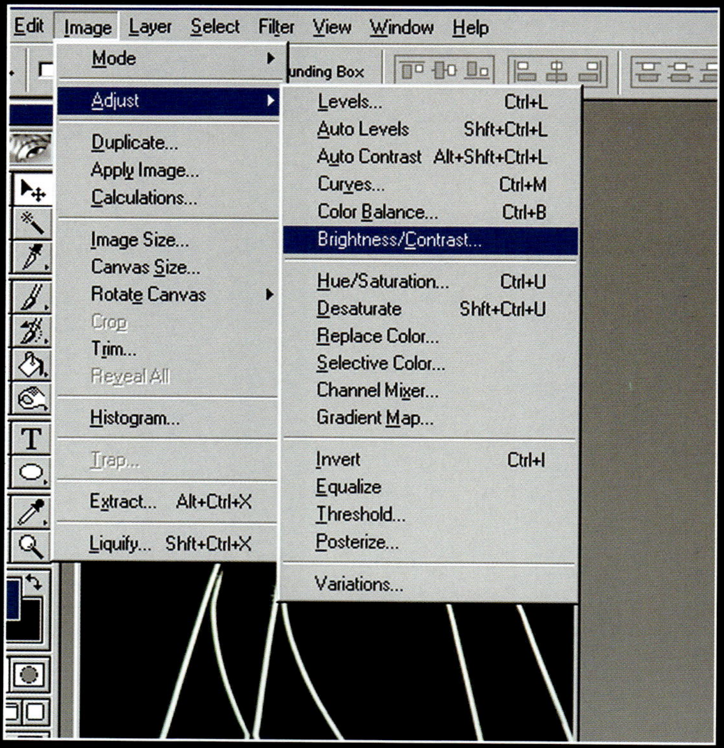

Fig 3.3

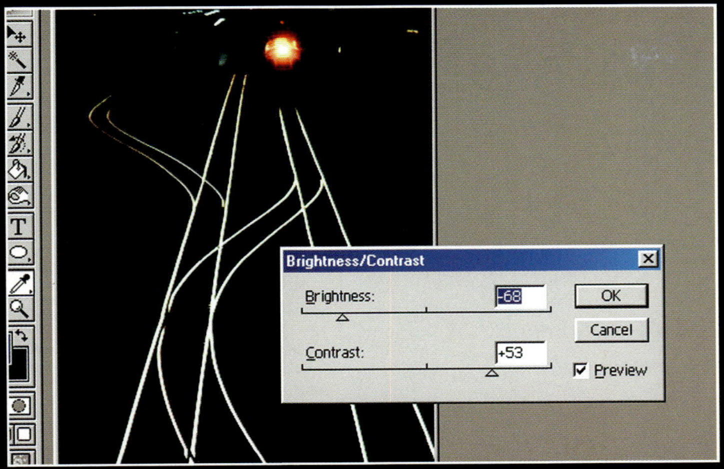

Fig 3.4

had gone unnoticed, now appeared more prominent. They created a distraction and further lessened the impact of the rails. Photography affords us the pleasure to please oneself and, although a magazine editor used this original image to illustrate an article of mine on twilight photography, I remained disappointed with my efforts.

Given such a rapidly changing light situation it would have been wise to bracket exposures, but in this instance it was not an option if I was to capture the departing train in my composition. Fortunately, the benefits of bracketing can be achieved in hindsight through the computer.

Rather than making adjustments to colour, as in the previous projects, this photograph requires an enhancement technique to increase the contrast between light and dark. To alter the contrast of a picture, we go to IMAGE/ADJUST/BRIGHTNESS-CONTRAST (fig. 3.3) and click with the left mouse button. The screen that appears in front of us (fig. 3.4) shows two sliders; one for brightness and one for contrast. These can be moved to alter the image, and, as usual, the results are instantly visible when the PREVIEW option is active. The best results can be achieved through experimentation, although in this case values of –68 for brightness and +53 for contrast created the desired effect (fig. 3.2).

project 4

changing the format

CROP, ADJUST/LEVELS

I bought my first camera, a Kodak Coloursnap, on impulse while in a local chemist's shop in the picturesque town of Dornie in western Scotland. It was the only camera in the store. Amid such scenic splendour my photography turned, quite

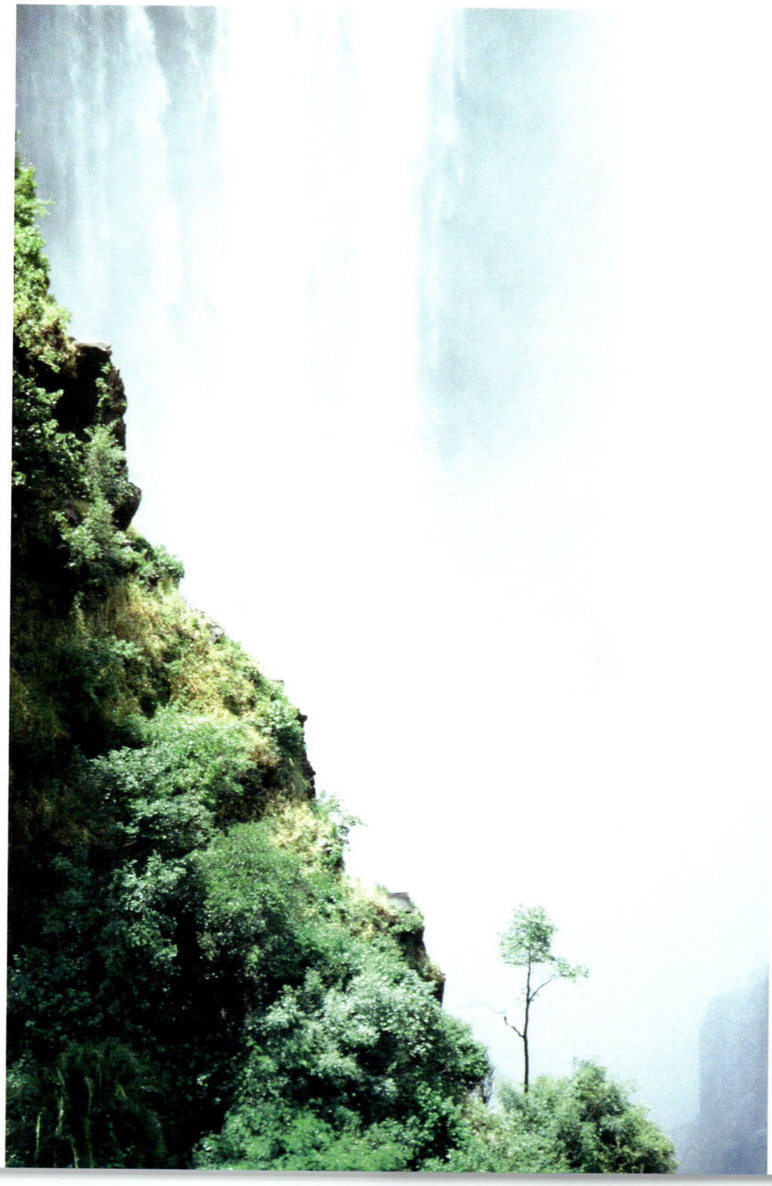

Fig 4.1 Zimbabwe's Victoria Falls presents a real challenge to photographers.

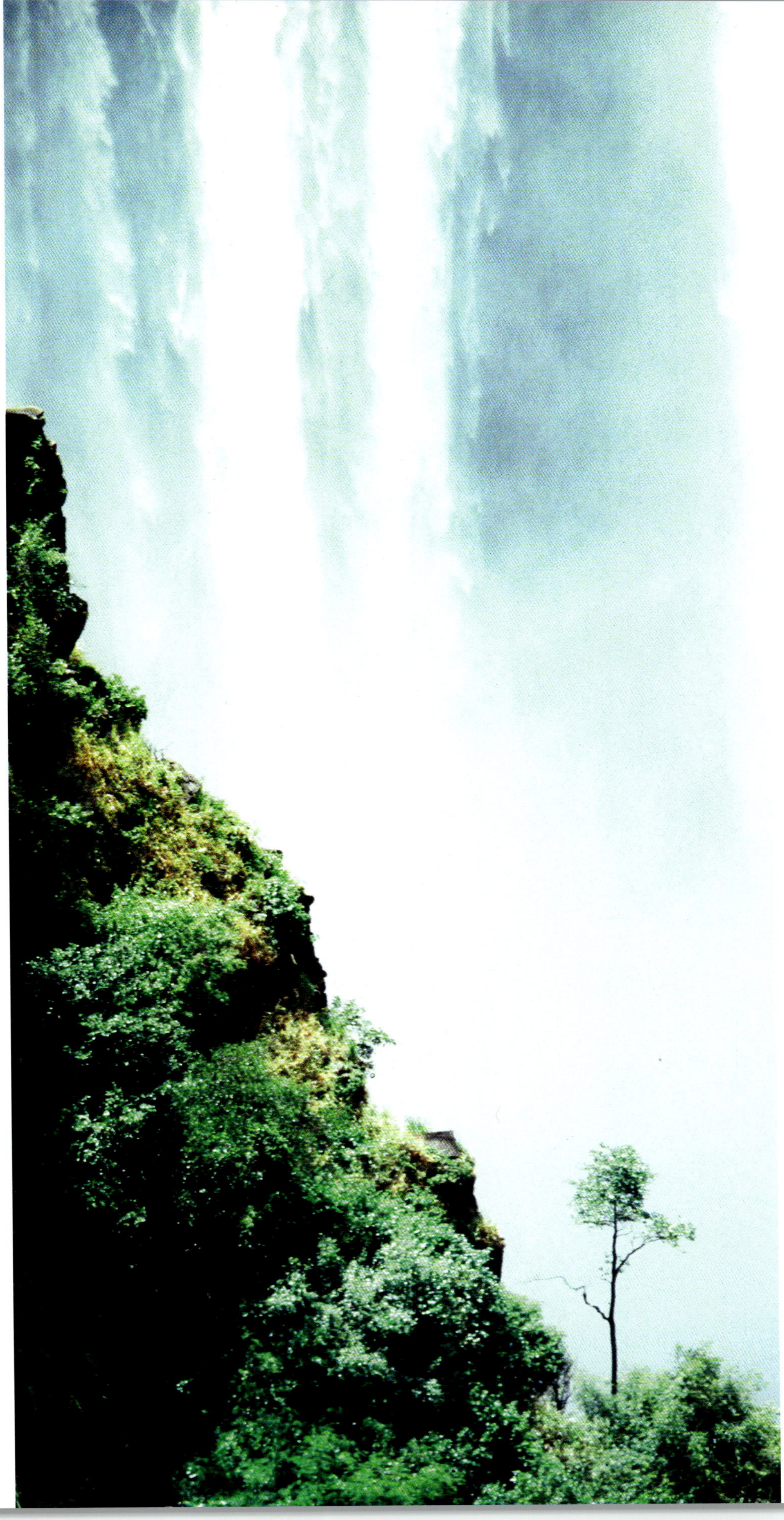

Fig 4.2 Cropping to the core of a picture can show less but say more.

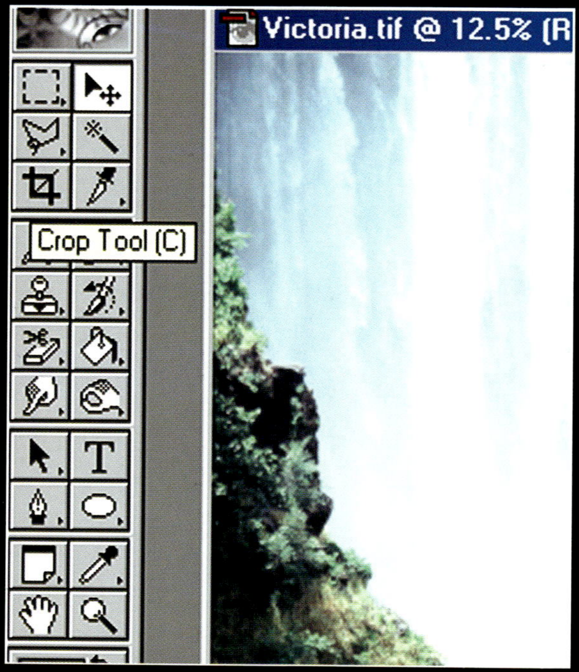

Fig 4.3

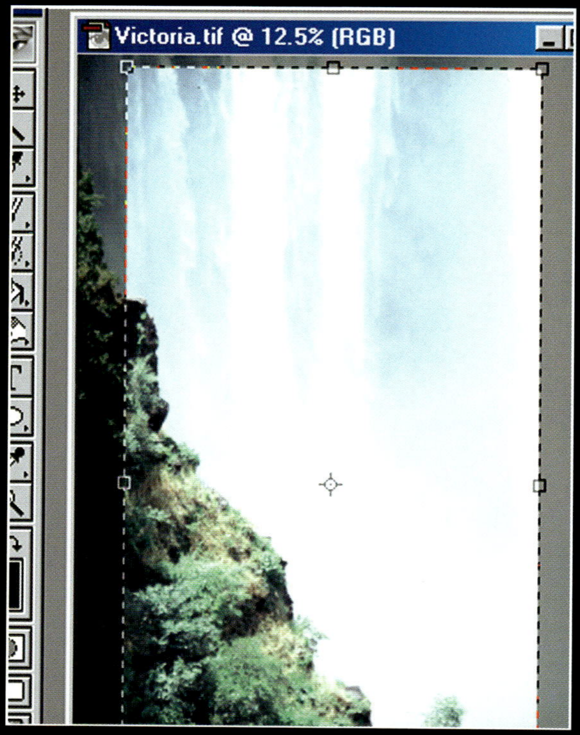

Fig 4.4

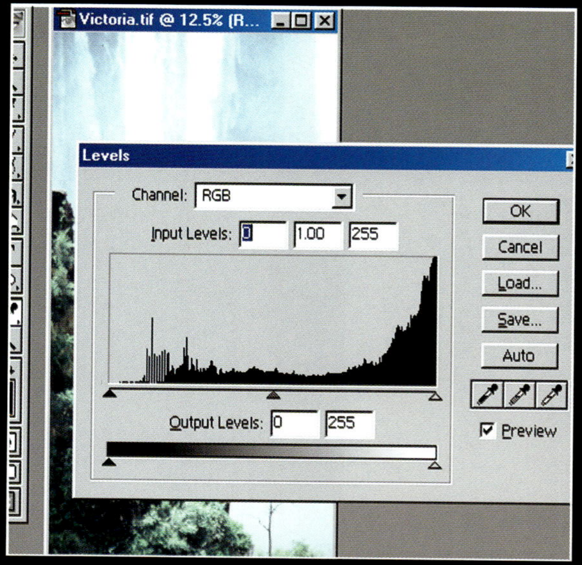

Fig 4.5

naturally, to the landscape of panoramic mountain ranges, wide lochs and broad islands. It was equally natural to me at the time to make each exposure with my camera held comfortably in the horizontal, landscape position.

It was not until I visited a zoo and tried to photograph a giraffe that I found my camera worked equally well when turned on its end. It helped me to frame tighter, thus adding to the impact of my photograph. I then found that if I masked off either side of my giraffe portrait, the impact was further increased.

We all have our favourite place in which to photograph, and *Victoria Falls* (fig. 4.1) is mine. As a tourist, I approached my visit with such high expectations that I might easily have been disappointed, but this did not happen. In retrospect, to try to impart my experience with words is nearly impossible, and to try to show you with one photograph, even worse. This is not to negate the value of words or photographs. It does, however, speak volumes for the wonderful world in which we live and the privilege that is ours as landscape photographers.

The immense power of Victoria Falls is truly amazing, inspiring a sense of awe in visitors. Long before you actually reach them, you hear them – there are even reports that the noise has caused windows to shatter over six miles away. A subtle change in the direction of the breeze can turn a heavenly mist into a fog from hell, and, in moments, a sunny walk along a harmless ridge can be transformed into something far less enjoyable.

My only disappointment was failing to photograph the experience adequately. I wanted to convey my on-the-edge, unnerving and ear-splitting experience. By comparison, the resulting picture suggests a stroll in a park with a waterfall in it. It needs to get closer to the action, to bypass the safety barriers, transcend the passive setting and give exclusive value to the size and power of the falls. To close crop this vertical format using the computer is a step in the right direction.

Once we have decided the area of our original image we want to retain, we use the CROP tool from the toolbox (fig. 4.3) to crop the picture. We place our mouse cursor in one corner of our imaginary new frame and drag it, with the left mouse button held down, to the opposite corner.

If, at first, our selection is still not right, we have the choice of changing the final cut. Our chosen section is now surrounded by a darkened area, which is the part of the picture we want to discard (fig. 4.4). All around the chosen area you can see little square boxes. These can be moved to adjust our final choice. When we are completely happy with our selection, we double click the left mouse button inside the cropped area and, instantly, we have our image.

To complete our operation we use IMAGE/ADJUST/LEVELS (fig. 4.5) to enhance the image's contrast and increase the colour saturation to the required level (fig. 4.2).

project 5

cropping for impact

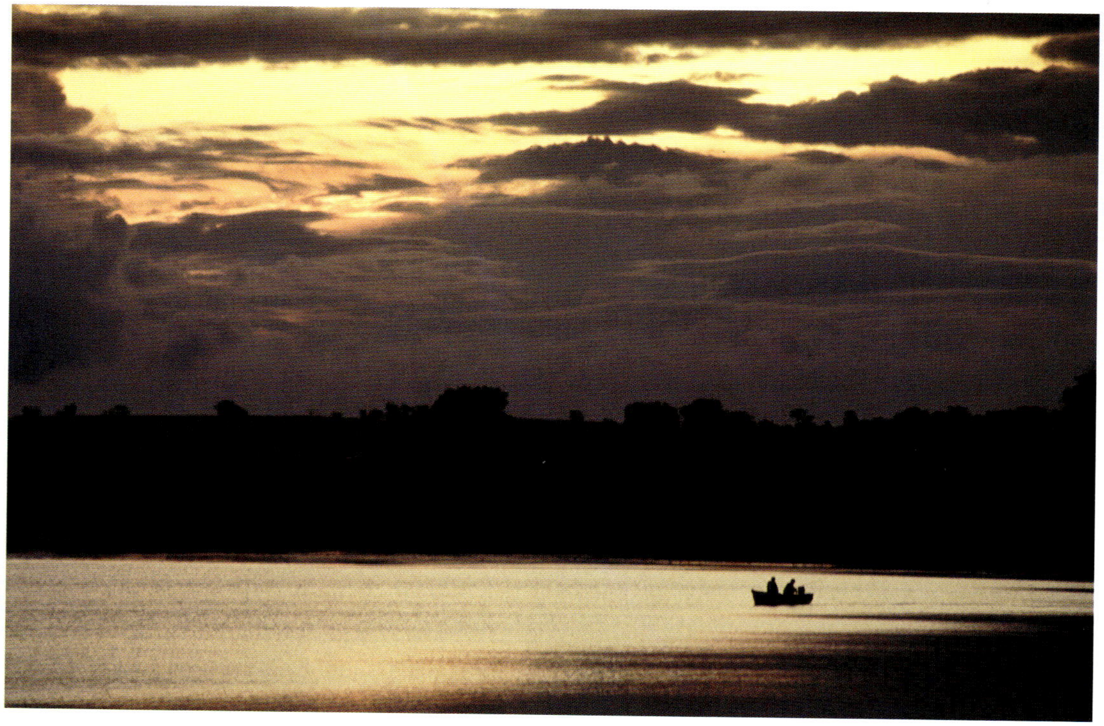

Fig 5.1 *Boat on Lake* illustrates that perfect landscapes do not 'just happen'; first, obstacles must be overcome.

CROP, ADJUST/CURVES

I learned at an early stage in my photography to pay attention to the background. I became conscious of checking that intruding telegraph poles and lamp posts did not appear from nowhere in my images, that offending cars did not obstruct my compositions, and that distracting highlights, whenever possible, were removed from my field of view before I made an exposure. This prepared me for my later commissioned photography, as I learned to weigh up options, consider new angles and vary viewpoints. I accepted that problems, large or small, were there to be overcome.

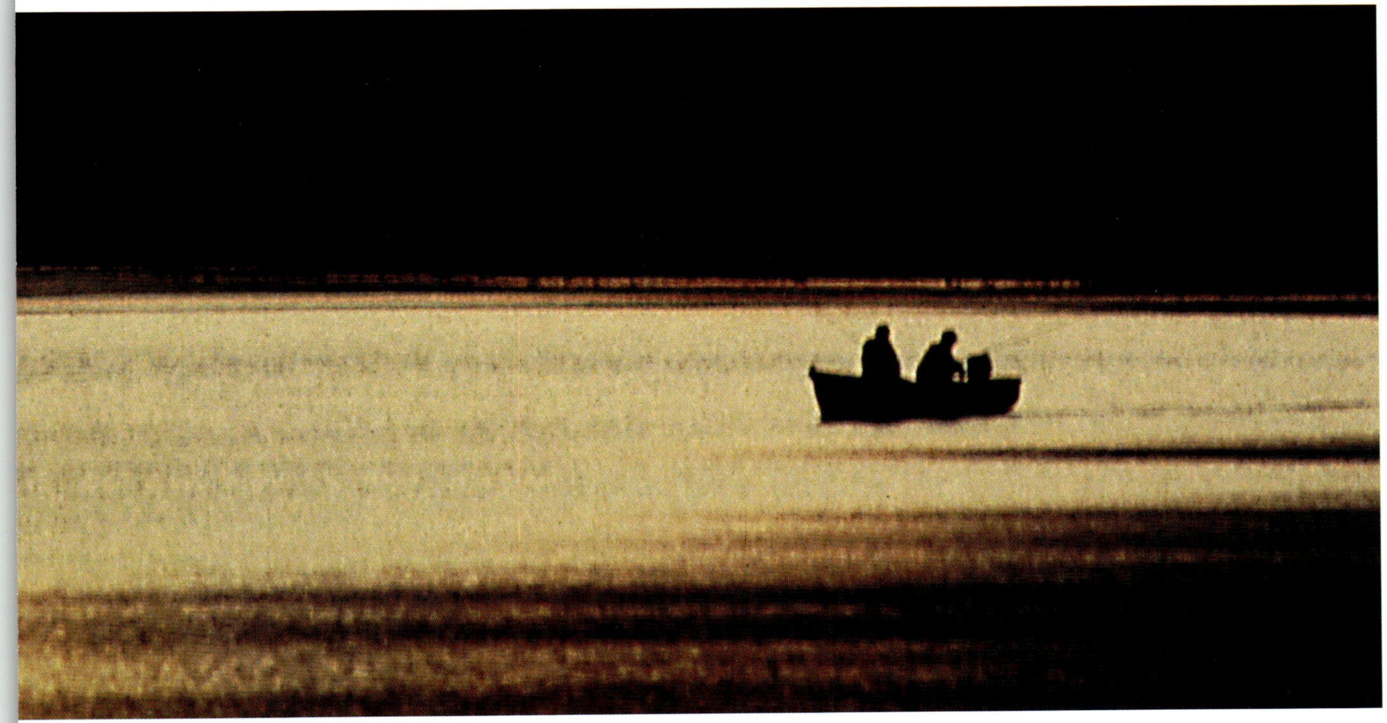

Fig 5.2 Varying problems are removed effortlessly using different enhancing techniques.

I also came to understand that any one problem had a number of solutions waiting to be discovered and that this process could bring unexpected benefits. On one occasion, when photographing in New Zealand, every landscape at which I pointed my camera appeared to be filled with rough-hewn telegraph poles, and my day's photography seemed to be heading nowhere. As I found it impossible to shoot around the poles, I decided to make a feature of them and write about the experience. The result was an article later published in a magazine.

One subject throws out its challenge to me repeatedly: boats. Whenever I wish to photograph one, a stretch of land will appear in my field of view without fail, cutting my composition in two and interrupting the entire flow of my photograph. The occasional cliff top may provide a suitable vantage point from which to photograph, a mist may obscure all but the required boat, but these are the exceptions.

When I came across *Boat on Lake* (fig. 5.1) unexpectedly, I knew I had only moments in which to photograph. The silhouette of the boat against the reflected colour of the sky first caught my attention, and in attempting to record the scene I relied heavily on the available but quickly disappearing light. I was aware of my usual landmass problem, but could do nothing about it at the time.

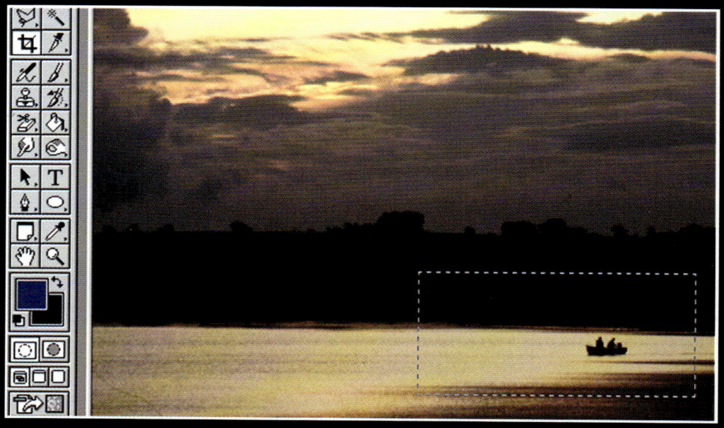

Fig 5.3

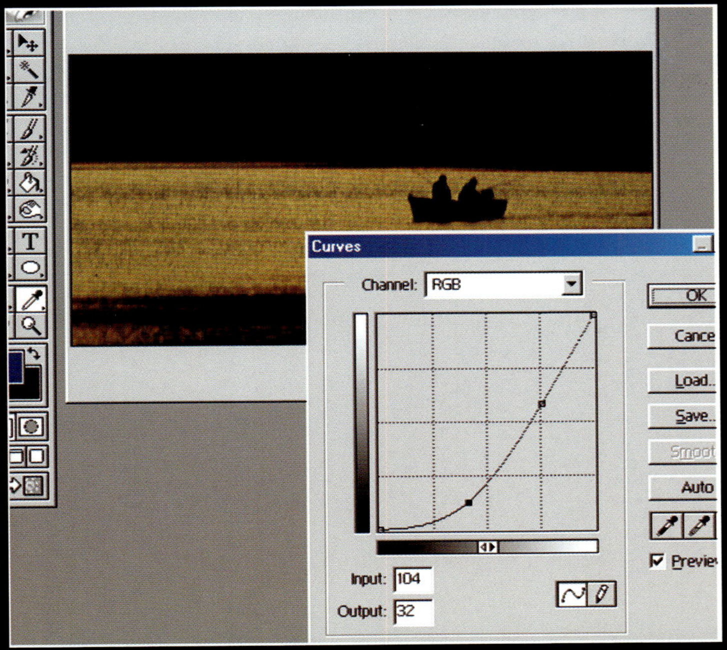

Fig 5.4

Changes are easy to make in hindsight using a computer, but how much change do we desire? Each project in this book is designed to enhance an existing photograph using basic techniques, not to change it radically or turn it into something it is not (no matter how easy that might be). One of the surprising things about enhancing a photograph is the choice of options available. We will look at one of these options in addressing the problem of the intruding background: cropping.

As in Project 4, when we use the CROP tool the most important consideration is deciding which part of the picture we wish to retain in order to create the strongest composition. We click on a starting point with the CROP tool, and then pull the cursor across to the opposite corner, covering the area of the photograph that we want to keep (fig. 5.3). Helpfully, we have the option of moving the cropped area, which, though darker, remains visible at this stage, thus making it easier to decide exactly what to include. Once the final selection is made, we double click on the chosen area to complete the crop.

Be careful when you use only a small part of the original. We started with about 8.8 million pixels and now approximately 1 million remain. Consequently, there is little room in which to enlarge the end result, if we wish to do so, without losing image quality.

To adjust the colours we use the IMAGE/ADJUST/CURVES (fig. 5.4) option, as before (see Project 2, page 20), to optimize our image (fig. 5.2).

project 6

touching out unwanted details

Fig 6.1 Here, the dramatic light highlights some equally dramatic distractions.

EYEDROPPER, PAINTBRUSH

Lookout points provide a ready-made, often idyllic, scene for landscape photographers. One of my favourite views looks out over a coastal town; a view in which a clear blue sky meets a deep blue ocean against a backdrop of sweeping golden beaches that climb to lush banana plantations on the hillsides of a subtropical mountain range. And yet, frustratingly, my photographs of this view so often fail to please.

Fig 6.2 The PAINTBRUSH tool deftly removes any distracting highlights.

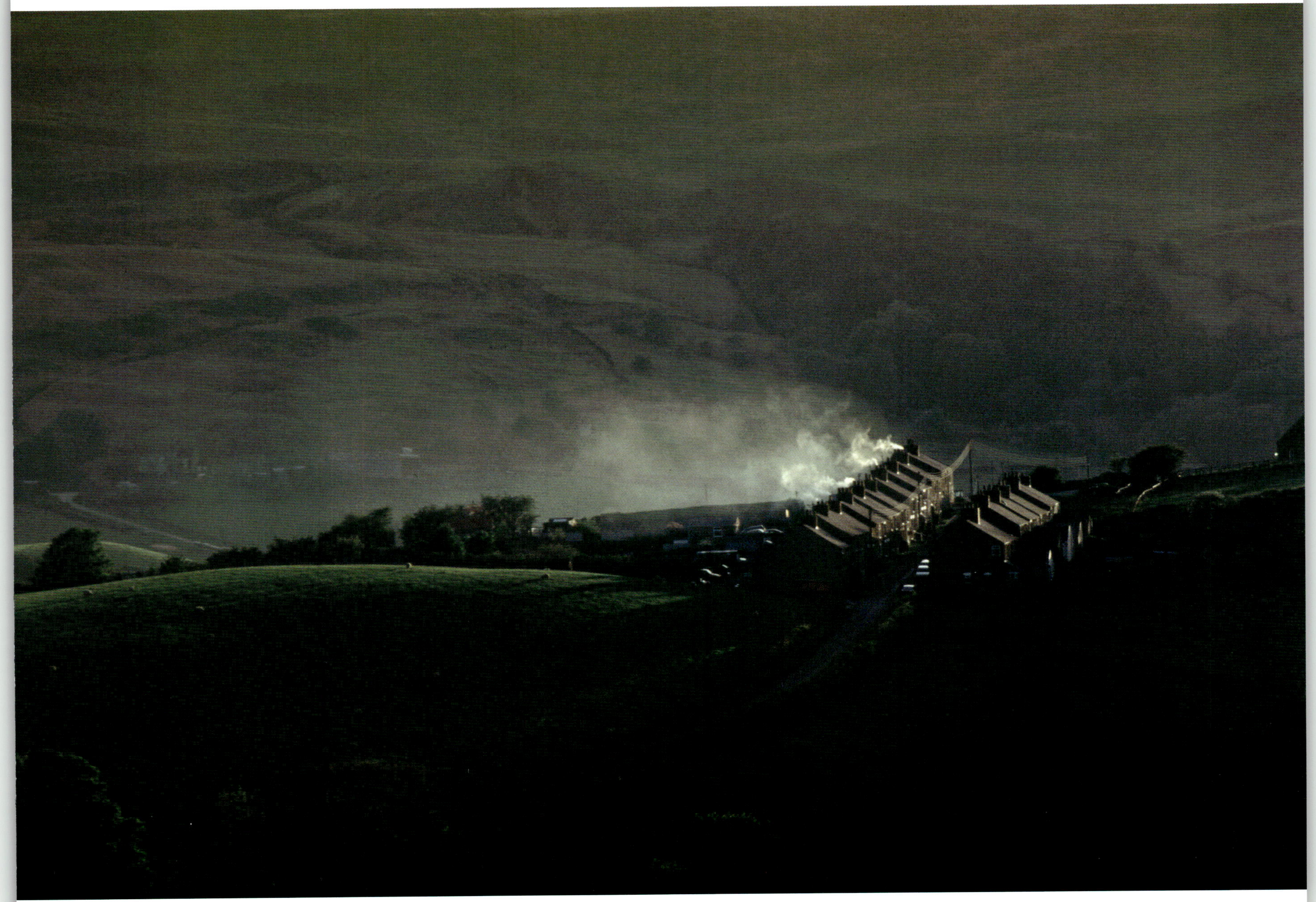

My advice to you is to look out for lookout points. Take in the view, soak up the atmosphere, but don't expect too much of it to be caught on film. Perhaps one of the most obvious reasons why photographs taken from lookouts can fail to impress is that of timing – we tend to visit them in the middle of the day when the lighting is flat. Also, most lookouts offer panoramic views that even a panoramic camera cannot begin to cope with. A breathtaking view can swamp a photograph – it is often hard to find a focal point because there may not be one, and any detail is likely to be too far away to be of interest. To make matters worse, light-sensitive film picks up atmospheric haze over distance, which the human eye may not be able to see.

Why did I photograph *Last Light* (fig. 6.1) from this lookout in the Yorkshire Dales, UK? Perhaps the question can be answered best in the light shed by some of the points just made. Here the timing is perfect, capturing that magic time of day a little while before sunset. The light area, which contrasts with the dark mass, provides a strong focal point for the composition. Even the atmospheric haze, accentuated by the smoke, is a feature here rather than a fault.

To visualize a scene at the point of photographing it is to be aware of how the camera is going to record the scene and how it will eventually emerge as a finished print or colour slide. This is a skill that only develops with experience. When we enhance an image using a computer, it is just as important to visualize the end result, to decide what it is that we wish to alter and stay focused on that, not least because there are so many options available. In the case of *Last Light*, the dramatic play of light across the landscape creates some unwelcome distractions, which can now be removed by the computer.

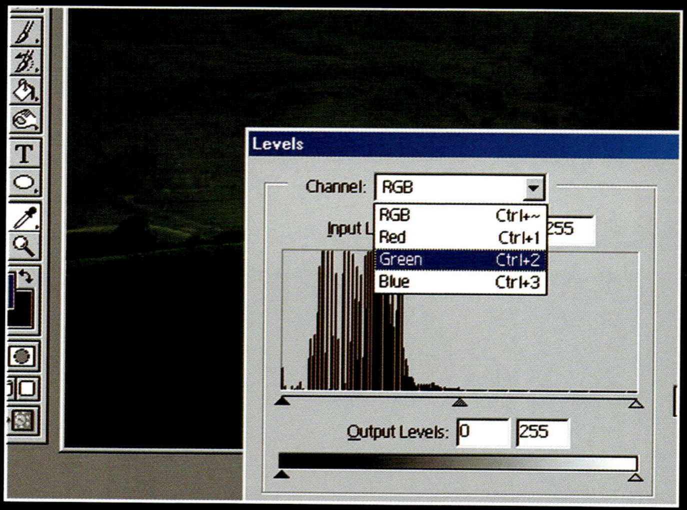

Fig 6.3

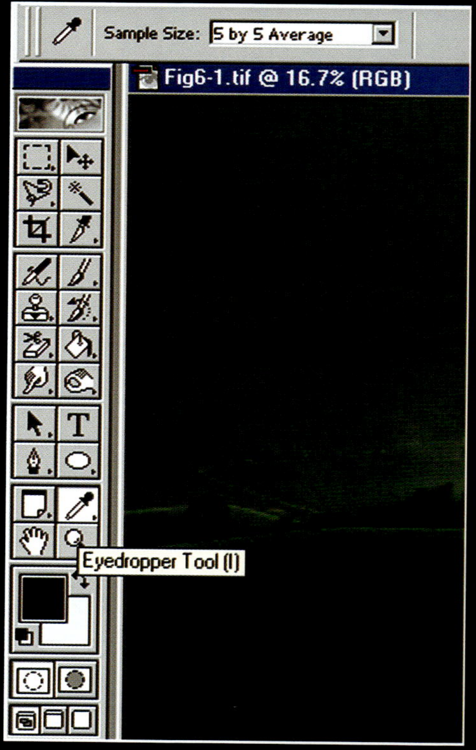

Fig 6.4

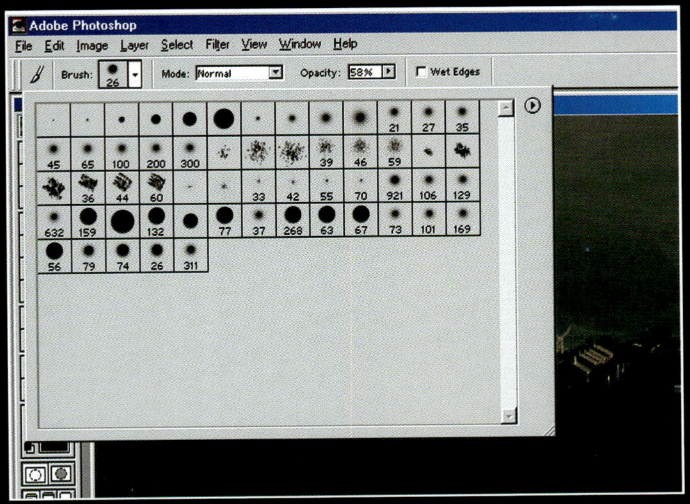

Fig 6.5

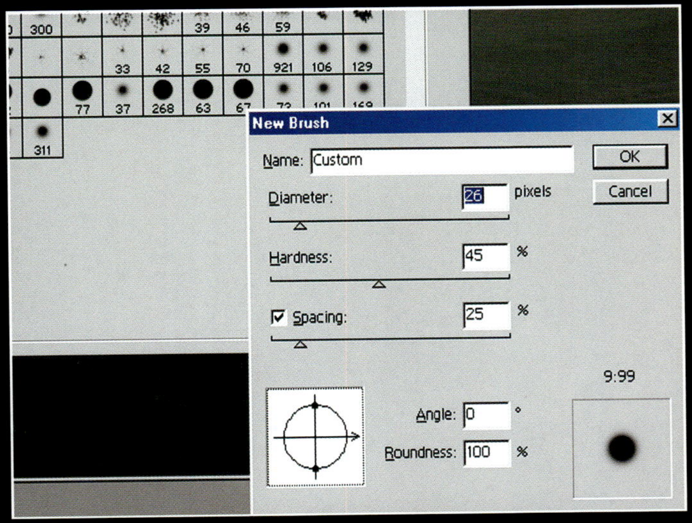

Fig 6.6

Our first step is to use the IMAGE/ADJUST/LEVELS technique (see Project 1, page 16) to improve the balance of light and colour. To add more green, we change RGB in the CHANNEL box to GREEN (fig. 6.3) and use the slider to add more to the picture. The image improves immediately, though the unwanted elements in our composition remain a distraction.

First to catch our attention for removal is the caravan to the right of the row of houses. We activate the EYEDROPPER tool from the toolbox (fig. 6.4). The tool options appear on the bar immediately above the working area. By selecting a SAMPLE SIZE of '5 by 5 Average' we overcome any slight colour fluctuations. The EYEDROPPER is brought close to the dark area around the caravan and we click the left mouse button to provide the foreground colour. We click close to the area we want to remove to ensure the colour we use is in harmony with its surroundings.

Then we paint over the caravan with a PAINTBRUSH from the toolbox. We adjust size and hardness of the brush by clicking on the triangle to the right of the BRUSH window in the tool options bar (fig. 6.5). If none of the existing paintbrushes is suitable, we can create a new one by clicking on the small triangle on the far right of the paintbrush palette. This opens the NEW BRUSH window (fig. 6.6), where we can select the properties most suited to our needs. We also have to decide on the OPACITY of the paintbrush, and in this case use 100% so that the caravan is completely covered over. Now all we have to do is paint over our chosen area. It is that simple. We repeat the exercise on other unwanted highlights until we are satified, and the image is complete (fig. 6.2).

project 7

re-painting

MAGIC WAND, PAINT BUCKET

You may be surprised to learn what I consider to be the most noticeable difference between amateur and professional photographers. It is not the choice of equipment. Many amateurs own a range of equipment the professional cannot

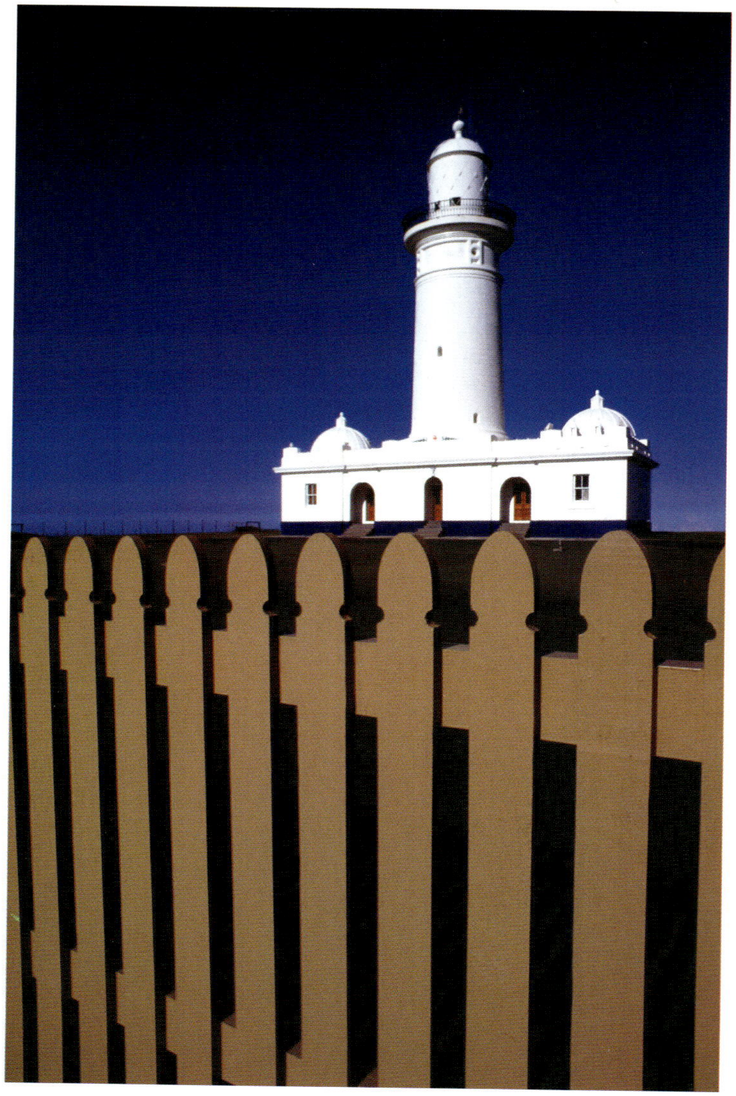

Fig 7.1 A local council's coat of paint suddenly upsets my carefully planned lighthouse composition.

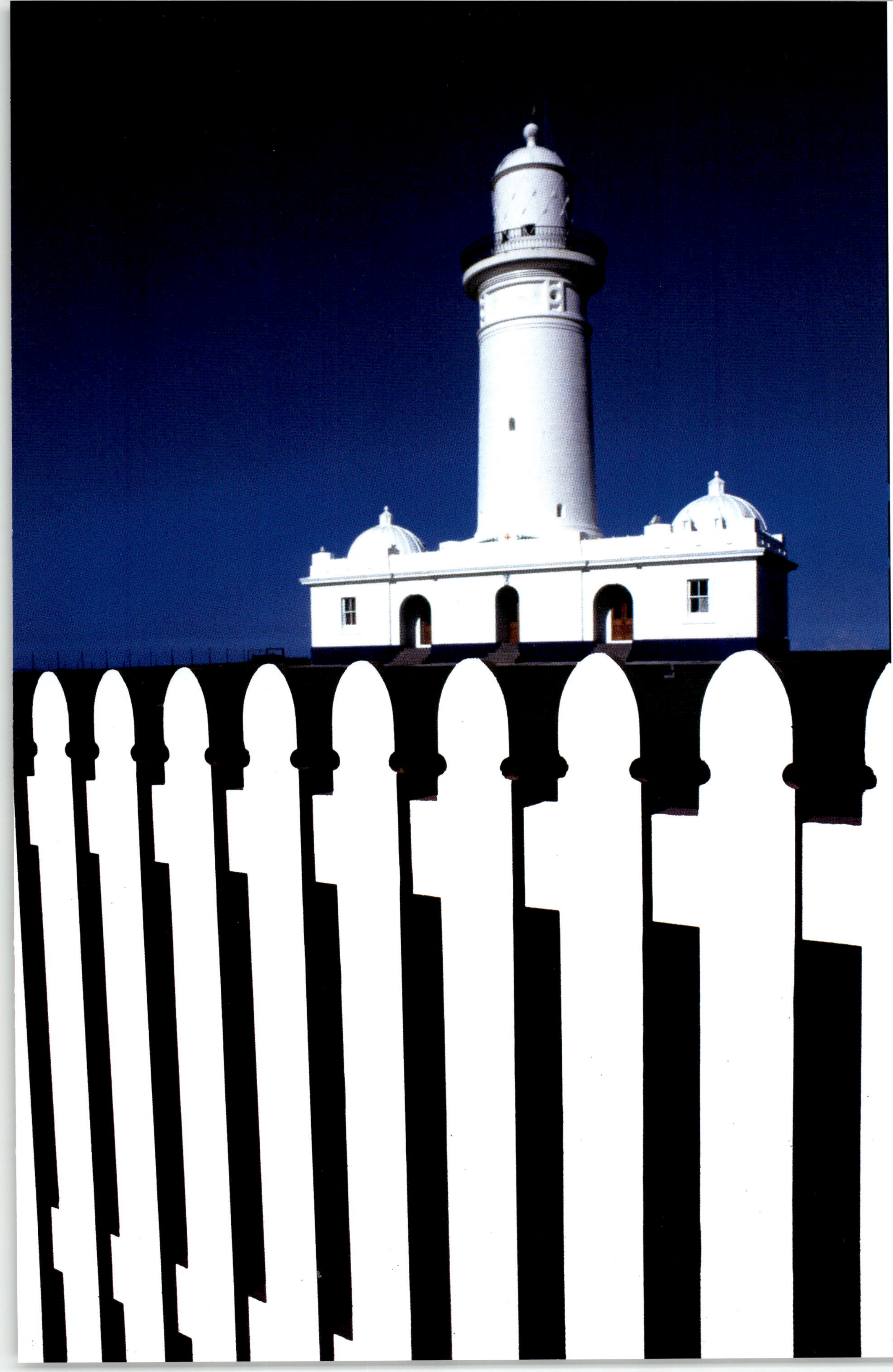

Fig 7.2 What was 'corrupted' is soon corrected using the MAGIC WAND and PAINT BUCKET tools.

afford to buy – an assertion borne out by flicking through most photography magazines and seeing who the pages of advertising are targeted at. Nor is the major difference time or opportunity. The amateur, though possibly restricted on occasions, has time at his disposal to shoot what he wants, when he wants to; he has no client breathing down his neck or editor dangling dreaded deadlines in front of him. Neither is talent always the main difference. In my opinion, the difference is planning.

Amateurs might be lucky on occasion and find themselves in the right place at the right time with just the right lens attached to their camera, but a professional would quickly lose face if they made the mistakes that amateurs make repeatedly. How often does an amateur check in advance the position of the sun in relation to a subject they want to photograph? Can you imagine a magazine photographer embarking on a foreign assignment before doing his or her homework? Of course, things can and do go wrong, but this is further reason for employing a more professional approach and planning a shoot down to the finest detail.

When I photograph a lighthouse, I want, on the one hand, to reflect some of the history and the romance associated with lighthouses – the crashing of waves on rocks, the light in the darkness guiding ships to safety. On the other hand, I see few lighthouse photographs (including my own) that reflect the feeling of danger and deliverance. Of course, there is a good reason for this – unless the photographer is on the point of being shipwrecked with a lighthouse beaming out above them, the shot is taken out of context. *Lighthouse Fence* (fig. 7.1) portrays something of this conflict symbolically: the lighthouse stands in a position of glory, and the photographer in a position of safety behind a fence.

It is also a location I visited a number of times to ensure that as much as possible worked in favour of my finely tuned and thoughtfully planned photograph. In spite of all this, fate intervened and I found that the fence had been re-painted to a different, and less suitable, colour. However, when our planning breaks down the computer can help to repair the damage.

First of all, we select the parts that have to be re-painted digitally. Since the colour of the fence is not being used in any other parts of the picture, we can use the MAGIC WAND tool (fig. 7.3). When we activate it on the toolbar, we see that the arrow cursor changes to a wand. We go to one of the slats on the fence and click on it. A rotating dotted border (known as 'marching ants') appears enclosing one of the slats (fig. 7.4), but since we want to paint all of them we must add to our selection. We do this by holding down the SHIFT key while we click on the remaining slats of the fence.

If another colour in the picture matches the colour we have chosen to change too closely, the MAGIC WAND will add it to the selection as well. If this happens, we go to EDIT/UNDO to erase the last step, or use the HISTORY palette to step back. If this becomes a problem, we can adjust the sensitivity of the MAGIC WAND (to any figure between 1 and 255) using TOLERANCE in the tool options bar (fig. 7.5). A low figure indicates little colour variation, and vice versa.

Now we decide on the colour of paint. We click on the square with the foreground and background colours (fig. 7.6) and a palette appears from which we choose our colour. The cursor changes to a small circle, which we click on the colour we want to use (fig. 7.7). Now all we have to do is activate the PAINT BUCKET tool (fig. 7.8) in the toolbox and click on the slats to change them to the colour of our choice. By changing OPACITY on the tool options bar (fig. 7.9) we can influence the density of the layer of paint that is being applied to the slats. Leaving this at 100% obtains the result as shown in our completed image (fig. 7.2).

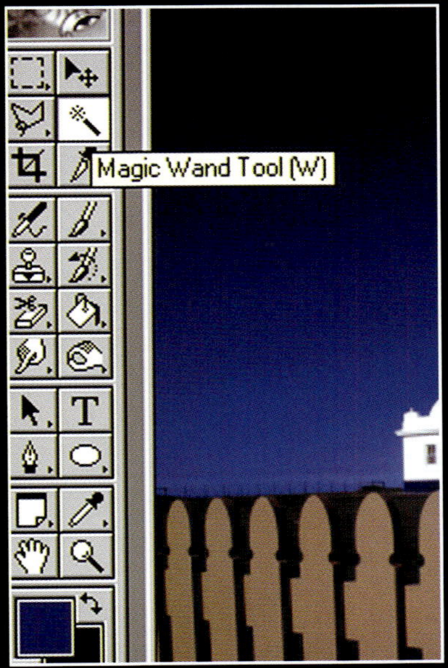

Fig 7.3

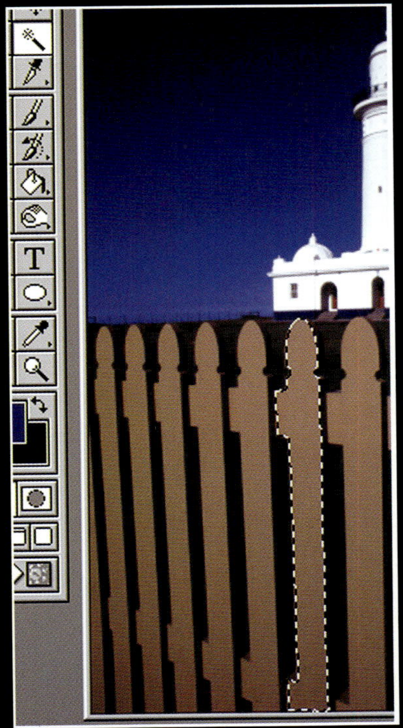

Fig 7.4

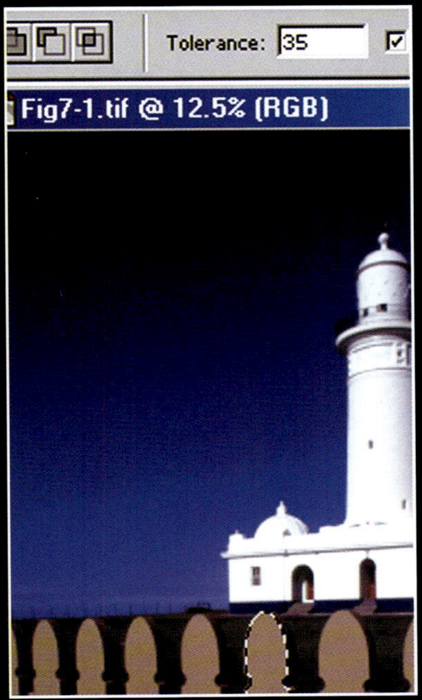

Fig 7.5

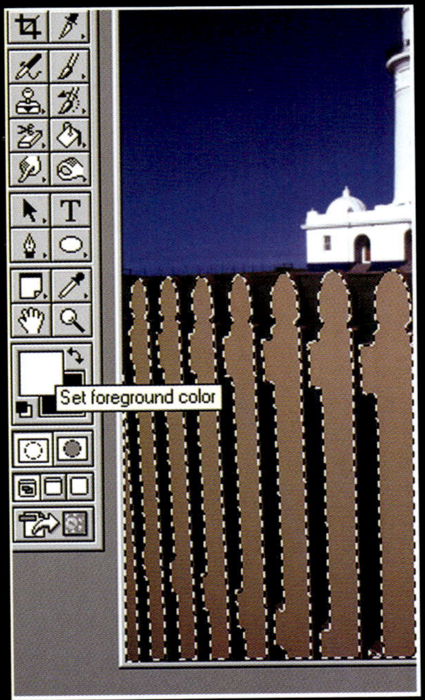

Fig 7.6

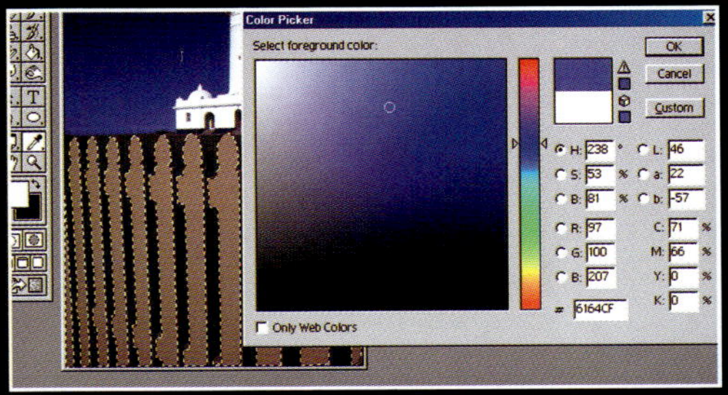

Fig 7.7

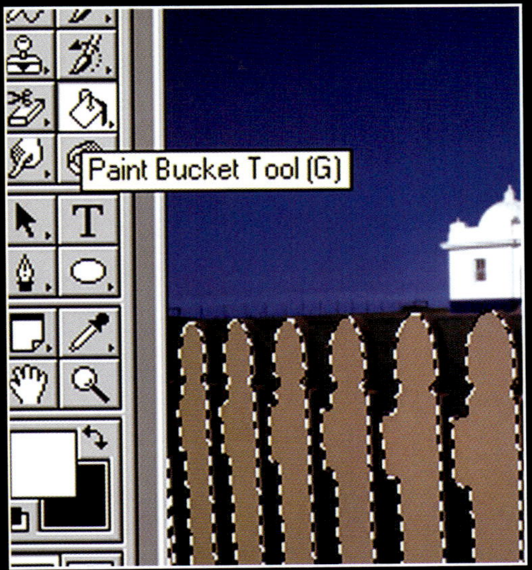

Fig 7.8

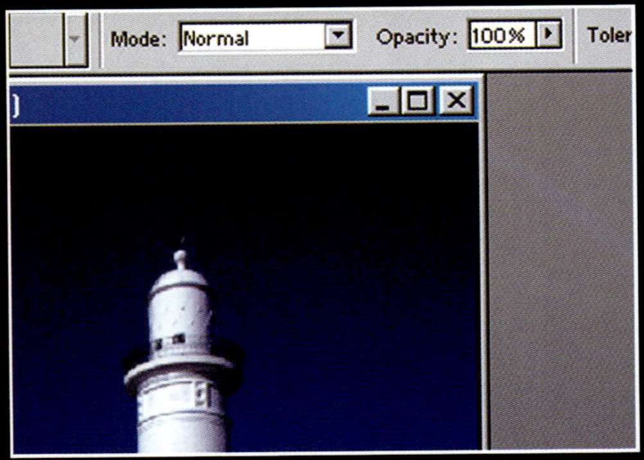

Fig 7.9

project
8

lightening shadows

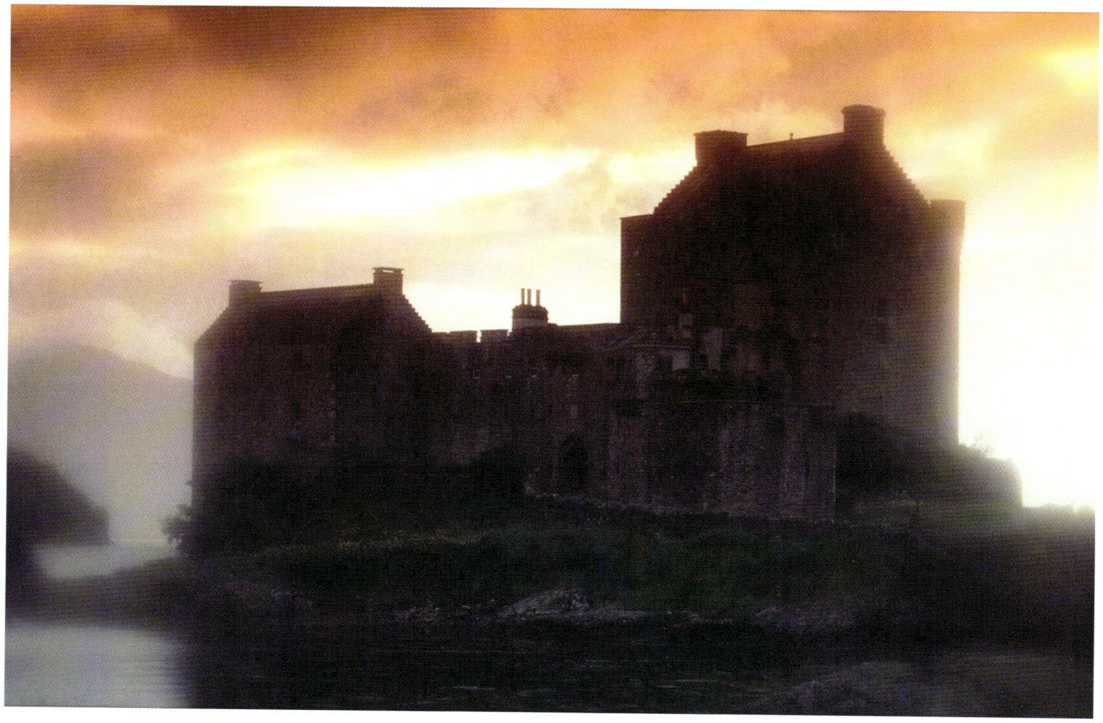

Fig 8.1 The detail of Eilean Donan Castle is lost in shadow.

LASSO, BRIGHTNESS-CONTRAST

The more you learn to see like your camera, the more successful your photography will be. I have alluded to 'camera vision' in other projects, but here I wish to address it more directly. When compared with our own vision it would appear that the camera's ability to 'see' is very limited. For instance, the human eye can enjoy seeing detail in highlights and shadows at the same time, while the camera cannot. Many photographers become frustrated with this apparent limitation of their camera's ability. A better alternative would be to invest a little time in learning to understand how a camera 'sees'. In fact, this understanding is one of the keys to getting ahead in photography.

Fig 8.2 Shadows have been a perennial problem for photographers when shooting towards the sun. Today, simple computer techniques can be used to get round them.

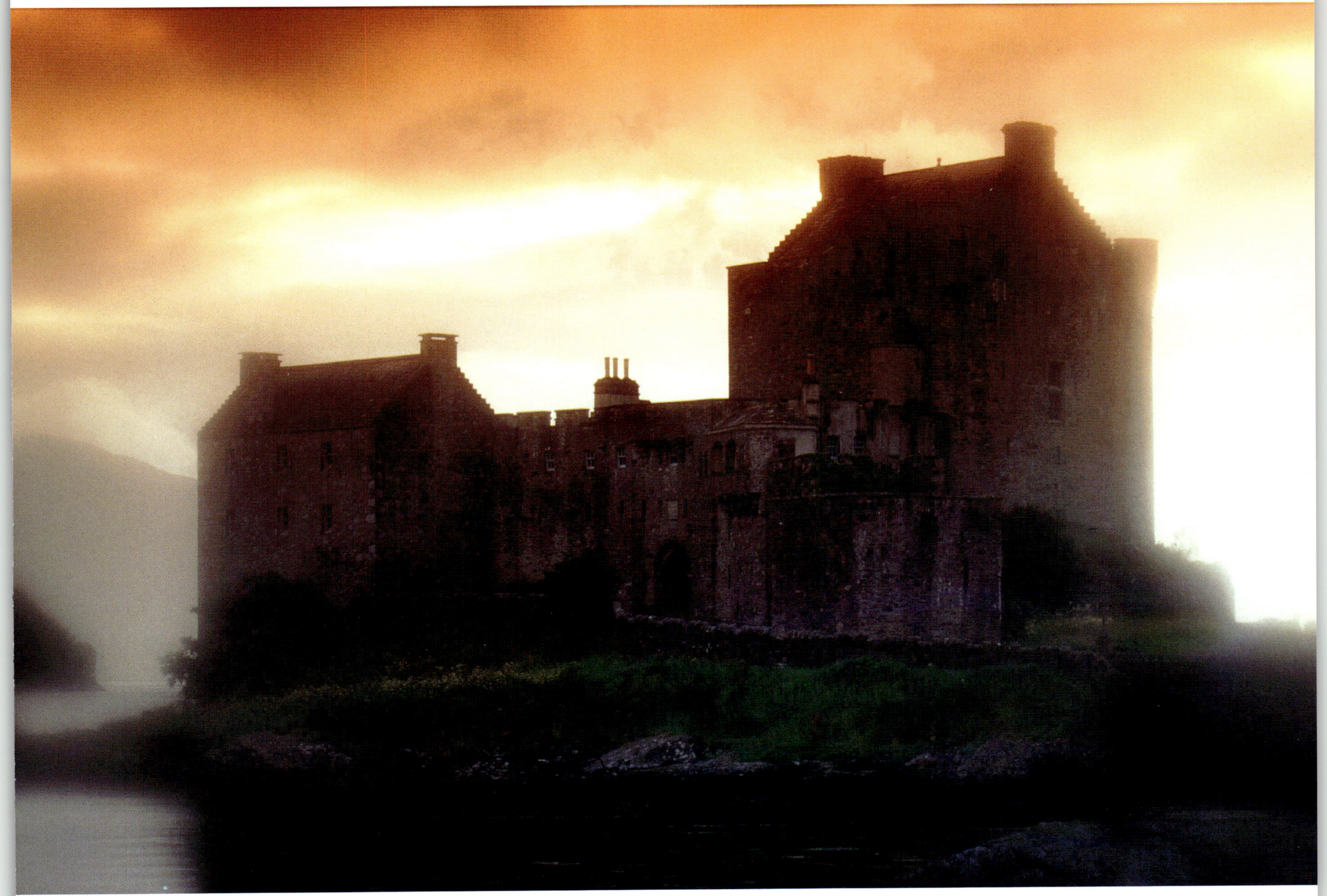

Having taken a picture there on my first ever roll of film, I enjoyed a special nostalgia as I approached Eilean Donan Castle, in Scotland, for the first time in 35 years. It had been raining non-stop for six days, but just as I arrived the clouds ahead parted to reveal the setting sun beyond the island of Skye. The sky exploded into magnificent colour, made all the more dramatic by the darkness from which I had emerged.

Of course, it is one thing to bask in an exhilarating experience and another thing entirely to photograph it. Amid such fast-moving light conditions decisions have to be made quickly or the moment will pass. There has to be compromise and there may be sacrifice, just as the decision to use a standard lens cuts out the photographic options created by a fish-eye or telephoto lens. The choice of an 80–200mm zoom lens affords attractive options, but if I were to dither around changing lenses and adding filters for varying effects I would soon run out of time (and light) and have no options at all.

In *Eilean Donan Castle* (fig. 8.1), my attempt to capture the colour of the sky meant I lost all detail in my main subject. It is a situation that has caused photographers a problem ever since they first pointed their cameras in the general direction of the sun, but it is a problem on which the computer can shed new light.

First, we use the LASSO tool to make our selection of the castle and its setting. This tool comes in three different options, the LASSO, the POLYGONAL LASSO and the MAGNETIC LASSO. The first is a freehand drawing tool that is used to make irregular selections (and requires a steady hand), while the second can be used to make irregular geometric selections. The last is most often used to select areas with well-defined edges. It clings (like a magnet) to these edges to make the selection. Since we just want to make a rough selection, we use the 'freehand' LASSO here.

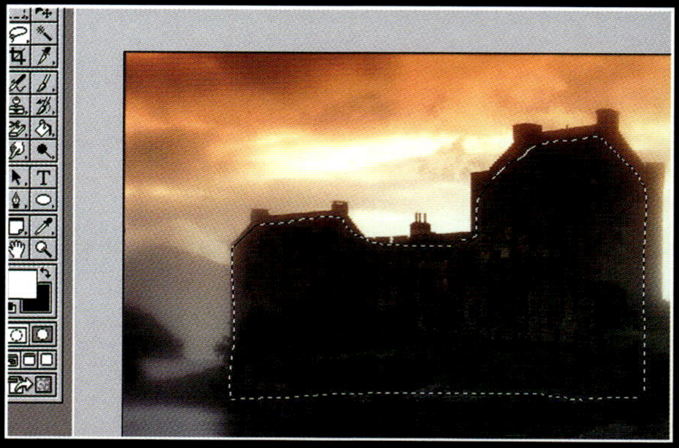

Fig 8.3

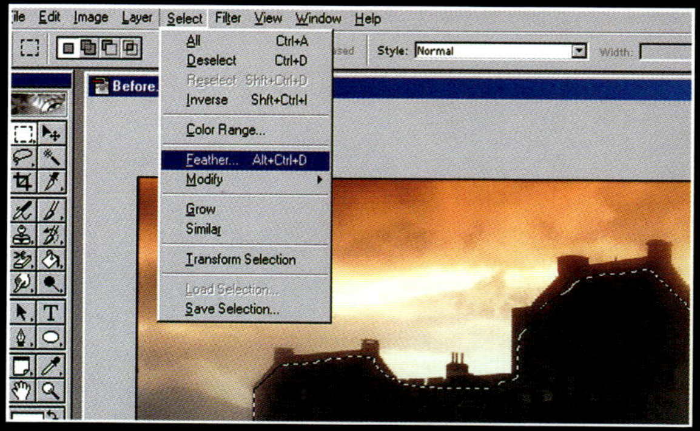

Fig 8.4

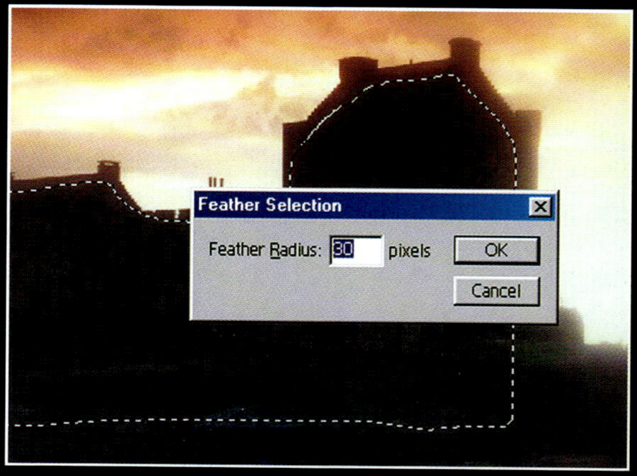

Fig 8.5

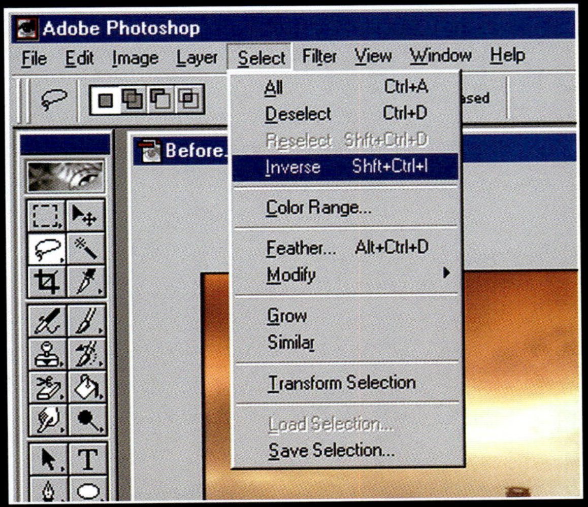

Fig 8.6

Fig 8.7

To use the LASSO, we need to decide on the area that we want to select and then pick a start/finish point. We click our cursor here and, holding down the left mouse button, 'trace' around our chosen area. As soon as we release the mouse button, the marching ants appear around the selection (fig. 8.3).

When they do, we go to SELECT/FEATHER (fig. 8.4) and click the left mouse button. A screen appears on our monitor (fig. 8.5) and we choose an amount of pixels for the FEATHER RATIO. This is to ensure that we get a smooth transition between the treated and untreated parts of our image. Here we choose 30 pixels. If this is not satisfactory we simply go back to our selection and start again.

Now that the selection is made there are a number of ways in which it can be altered. Here we want to make it lighter and add a little more contrast. Consequently, we turn to IMAGE/ADJUST/BRIGHTNESS-CONTRAST. We adjust the sliders until we get the right balance and then click OK. Does our choice look natural? It does, therefore we double click the left mouse button and the ants disappear. If only minor adjustments are required an alternative course is to select IMAGE/ADJUST/LEVELS (see Project 1, page 16). A third option is to choose IMAGE/ADJUST/CURVES (see Project 2, page 20).

If we wish to retain the shadows and change the rest of the image, we follow a slightly different course. We start with the same selection, but go to SELECT/INVERSE (fig. 8.6). A second group of marching ants appears on our screen (fig. 8.7). Our selection is now the area of the image between the two sets of ants. We repeat the earlier procedure, selecting FEATHER if necessary, and lighten or darken our selection accordingly to produce our enhanced photograph (fig. 8.2).

project 9

blurring the background

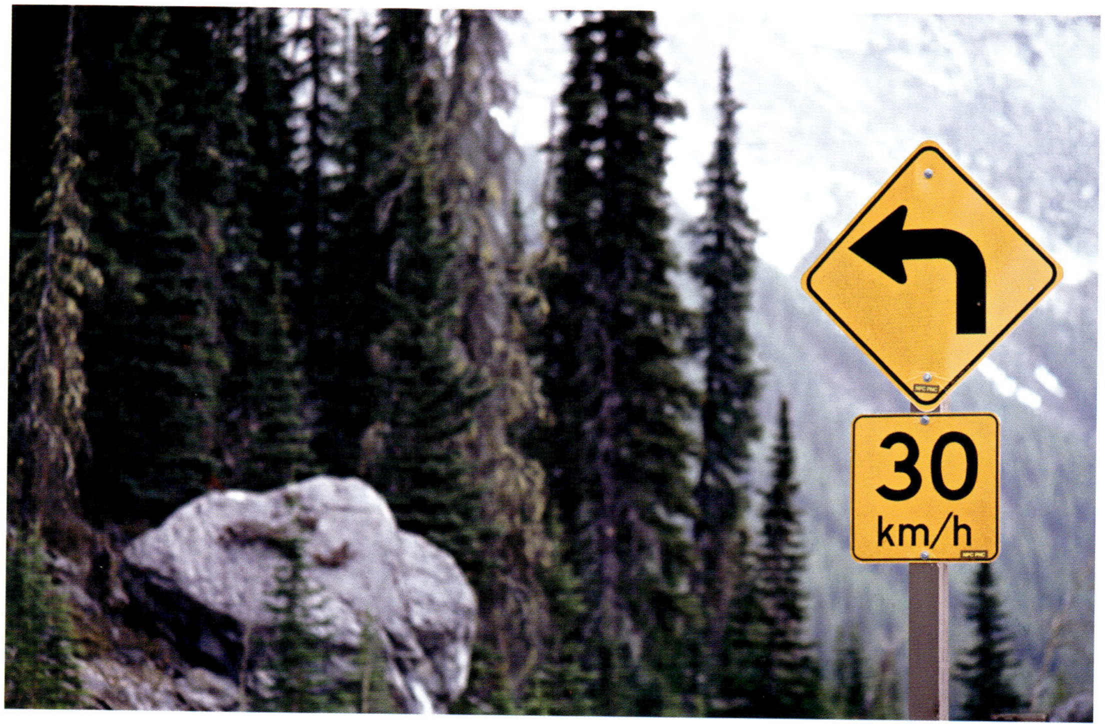

Fig 9.1 *Beyond the Bend* fails to convey the point I was trying to make.

LASSO, GAUSSIAN BLUR

Carrying a tripod, particularly at the end of a long day, can be an inconvenience. However, introducing a firm tripod (and cable release) into landscape photography can have some immediate benefits. Having taken the extra time and effort to set up a tripod, a photographer is more likely to be focused on what they are doing. There will be less inclination to hurry the shot and, with the camera in a fixed position, it is possible to take time in creating a precise composition. In the process, camera shake will be eliminated, and the end result should be a more personally satisfying photograph.

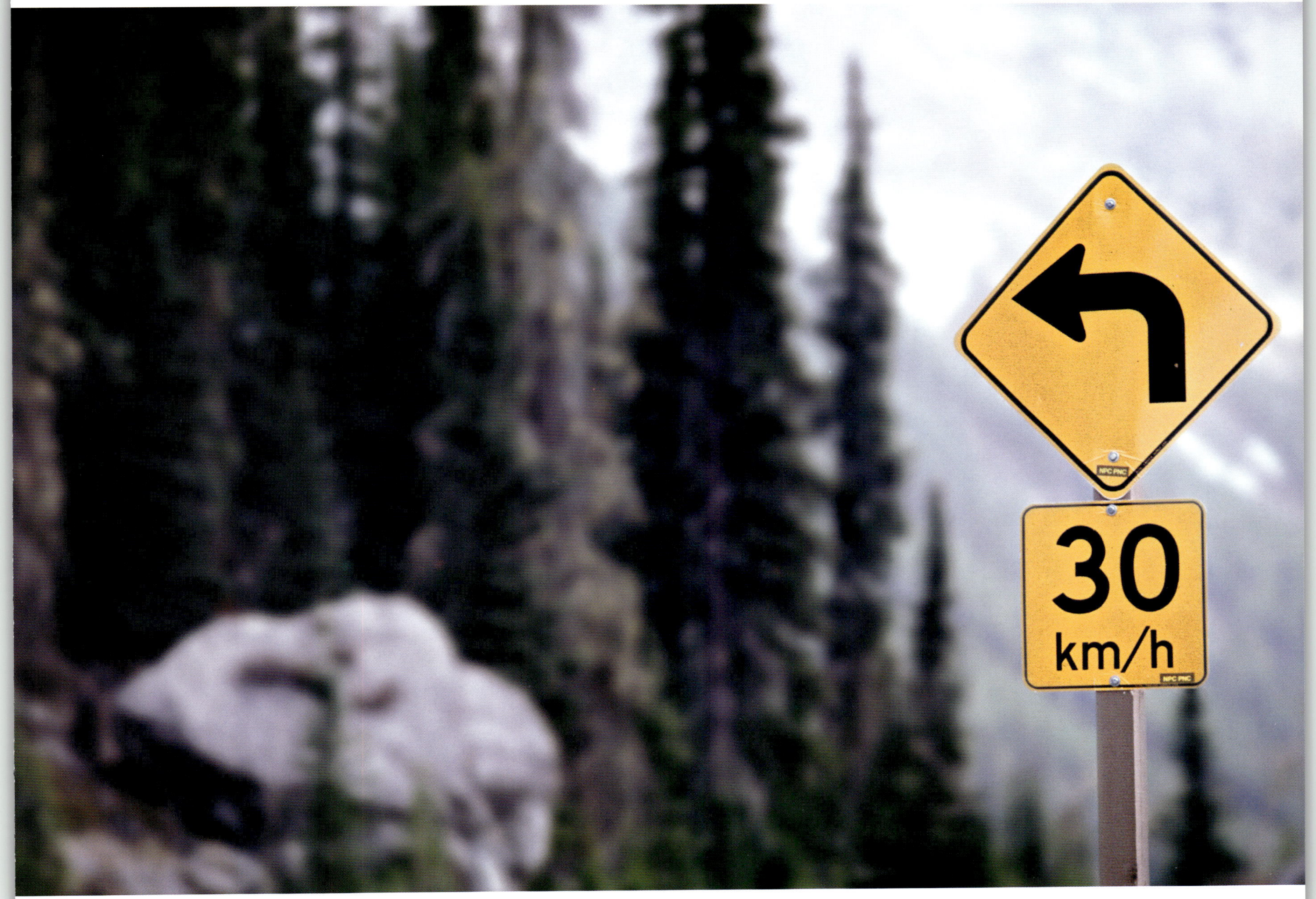

Fig 9.2 By changing the focus, the GAUSSIAN BLUR technique emphasizes the point.

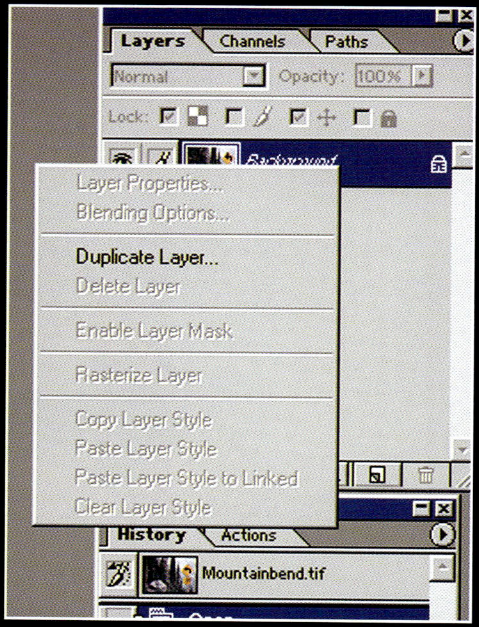

Fig 9.3

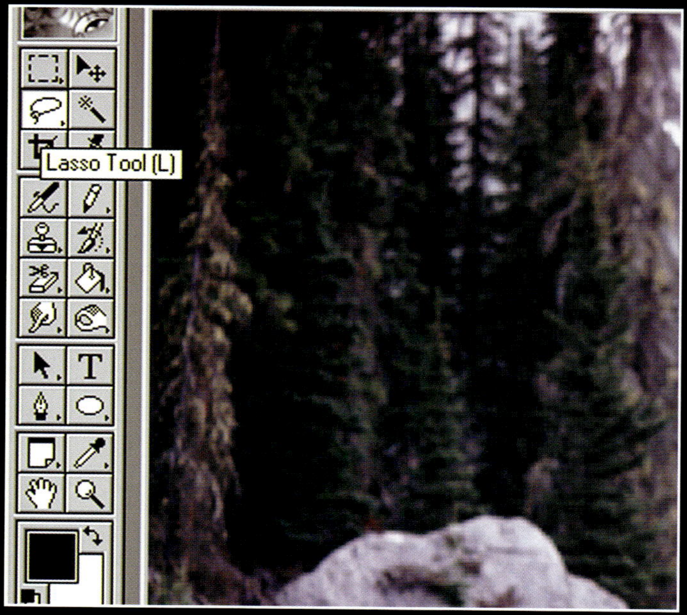

Fig 9.5

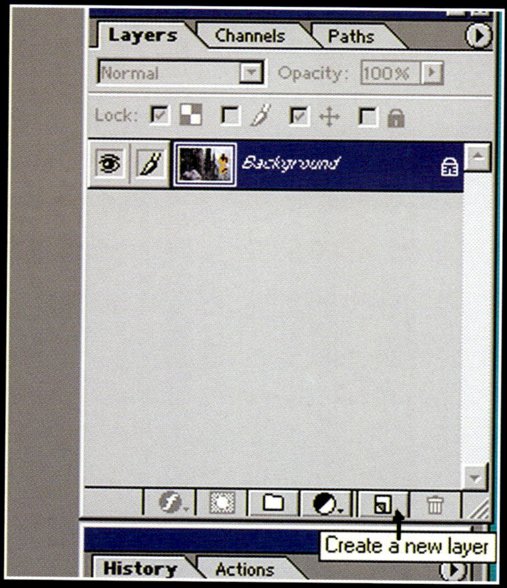

Fig 9.4

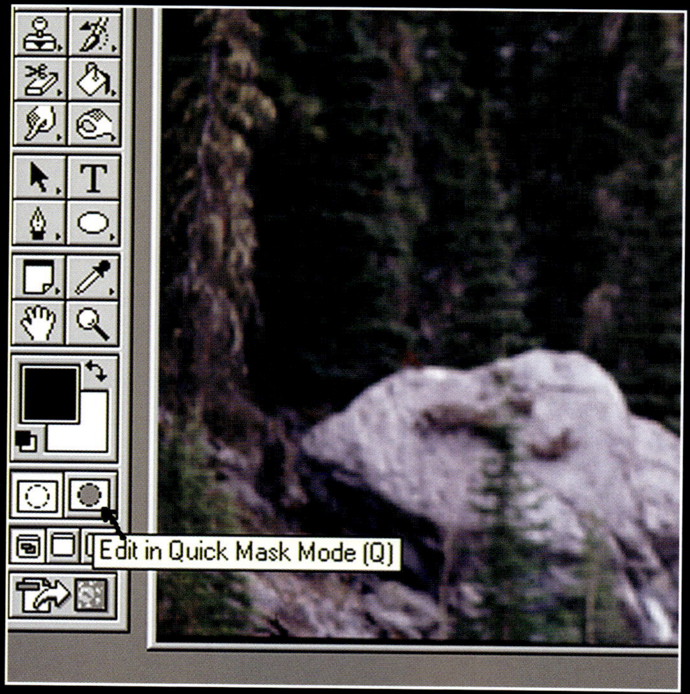

Fig 9.6

Even when I am satisfied with a photograph at the print stage, it does not mean that I forget about it completely, even years later. When given time to think about a photograph in a relaxed situation, the mind can come into play creatively at new levels. With a computer at hand new ideas can be readily incorporated to emphasize the original aim of the composition. The image used in this project has benefited from just such a re-examination. Although my original title, *Mountain Bend*, was adequate, I felt *Beyond the Bend* (fig. 9.1) to be a more creative title. Not only does it describe the enhanced image more accurately, it also better reflects my later thinking.

This shot was taken in a potentially photogenic area of the Canadian Rockies at a time when ferocious weather and treacherous road conditions made driving precarious, and good photography impossible. This road sign shone out through the murk like a beacon announcing that colour was still alive and symbolizing, for me, the journey of the past few hours.

Using a tripod in situations like this is a confidence booster to any photography that may be possible. To show what is visible here with clarity and a good depth of field, despite the conditions, is a tribute to both tripod and camera; and yet this photograph is not meant as a statement about either. I wanted the sign to appear sharp and to the point – that is the reason for warning signs. However, the other elements of the image – the dark forest, the steep mountainside, the remote road – would have conveyed an atmosphere of danger and hostility more accurately if they had been taken out of focus. Once again it remains for the computer to solve the problem.

In the introduction, we suggest you never work on your original picture in case you lose or damage it, and when using this technique it is definitely advisable to make a copy of the original layer to work on. To do this, we click the right mouse button [CONTROL + mouse button] on the blue bar of the background layer (fig. 9.3), or, alternatively, drag the layer to the bottom of the layers menu and over the second icon from the right (fig. 9.4). Either method gives us two layers: the background layer and the background-copy layer.

Having made sure that we are working on the copy layer (i.e. that it is the active layer), we click on the MAGNETIC LASSO tool (fig. 9.5) in the toolbox and draw around the signpost to make our selection (the area enclosed by the marching ants). If completing a selection proves to be difficult, the solution is to select QUICK MASK from the toolbox (fig. 9.6). This option highlights the parts of the picture inside our selection by turning them red, making it easier to spot any errors and allowing us to adjust the area covered. First, we make sure the foreground colour is white and the background colour is black (fig. 9.7) and choose a small paintbrush from the toolbox to work with. Painting white adds to our selection, while painting black over the red areas reduces it. Once we are satisfied with our selection, we click on the icon to the left of the QUICK MASK icon to return to STANDARD mode.

We want any transition between our selection and the surroundings to be smooth, so we click on SELECT/FEATHER. A screen appears (fig. 9.8) that allows us to choose the number of pixels we want to use to soften the edges. We type '2' and click OK. We could use EDIT/CUT to remove the selection to the clipboard for later use. Alternatively, since we want to treat the area outside our current selection, we can use SELECT/INVERSE (fig. 9.9) to change the selection from the one we have to the one that contains the rest of the picture.

The blurred look that we require can be achieved by using FILTER/BLUR/GAUSSIAN BLUR (fig. 9.10). A new screen appears with a + and a – on either side of the figure '100%' (fig. 9.11). The bar at the top of our picture also includes a percentage, and by clicking on the + or – we match these values as accurately as possible. We use the slider underneath the display to indicate the correct amount of blur, and click OK when we are satisfied with the effect.

We click on LAYER/FLATTEN IMAGE (fig. 9.12) to complete the operation (fig. 9.2).

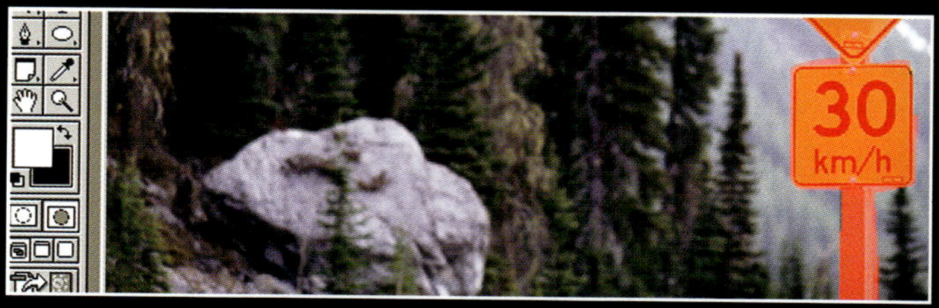

Fig 9.7

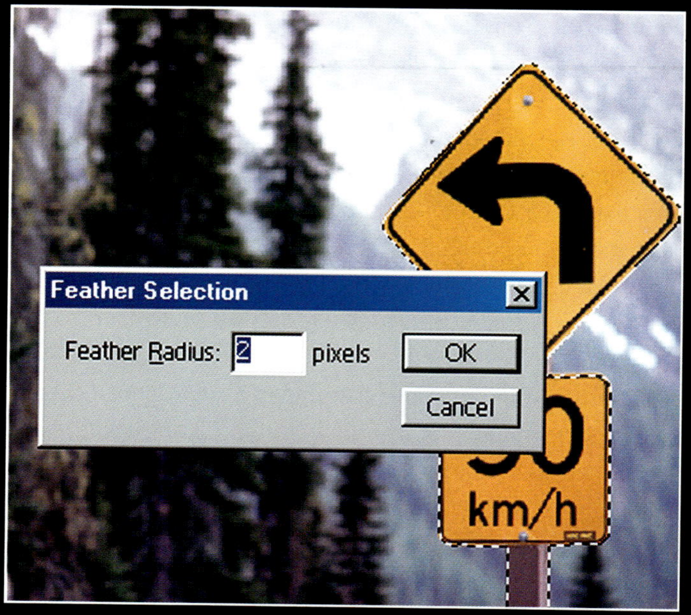

Fig 9.8

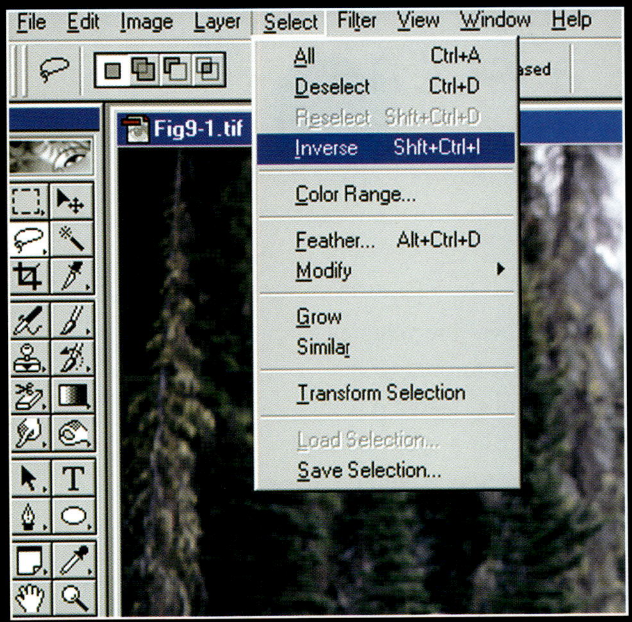

Fig 9.9

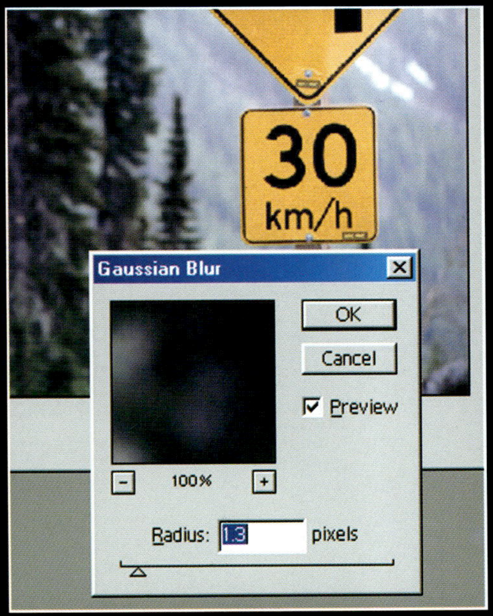

Fig 9.11

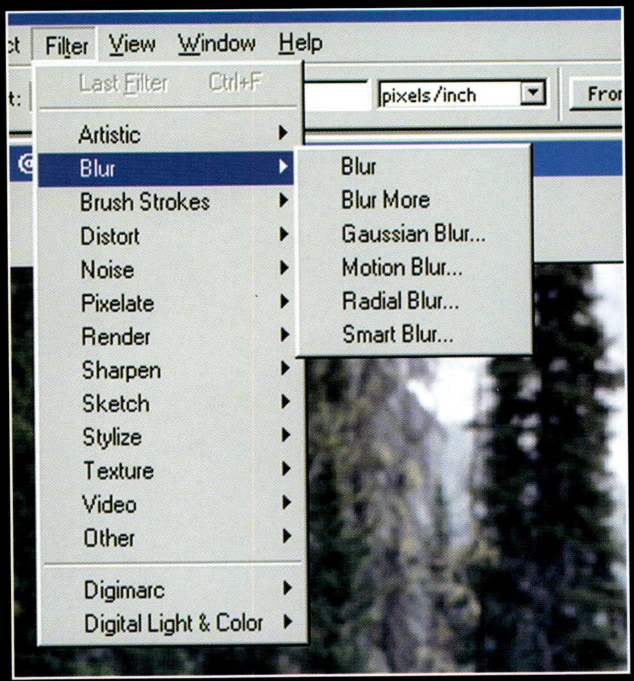

Fig 9.10

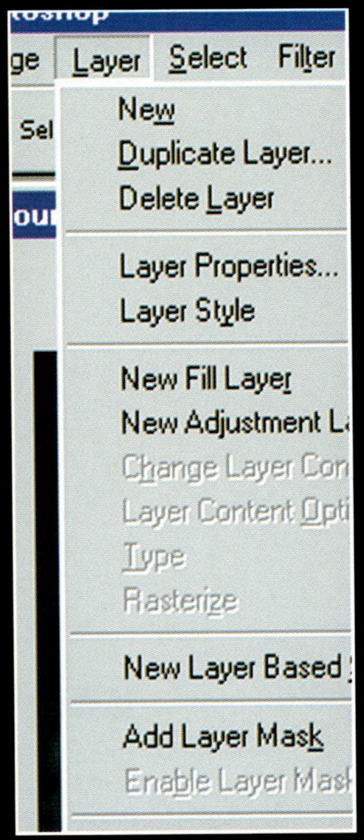

Fig 9.12

project
10

brightening a scene

LASSO, ADJUST/LEVELS

One of the greatest joys I have experienced over the years as a photographer has been having the opportunity to photograph my children as they grow up. Many photographs, taken in a moment – a spontaneous reaction on my part to a spontaneous action of theirs – fill fascinating pages of our family album.

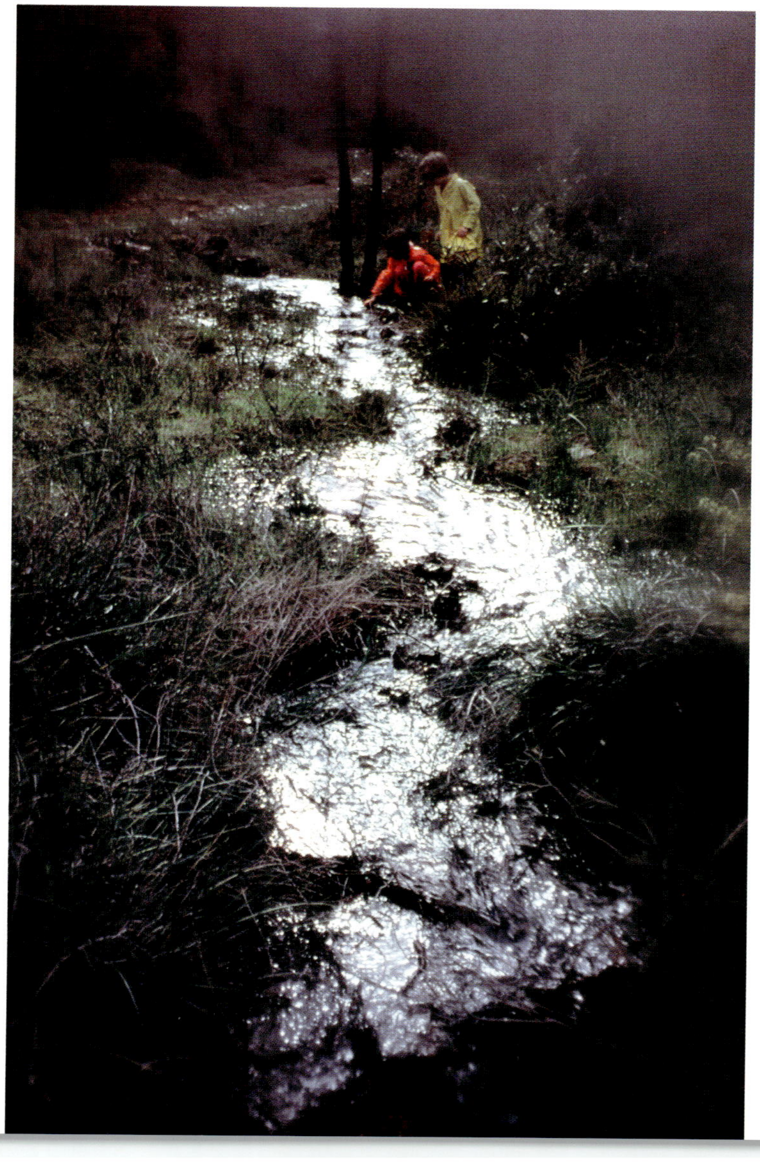

Fig 10.1 In *Children of the Stream* more than a photograph's title is called into question as I 'lose' my children in the fog.

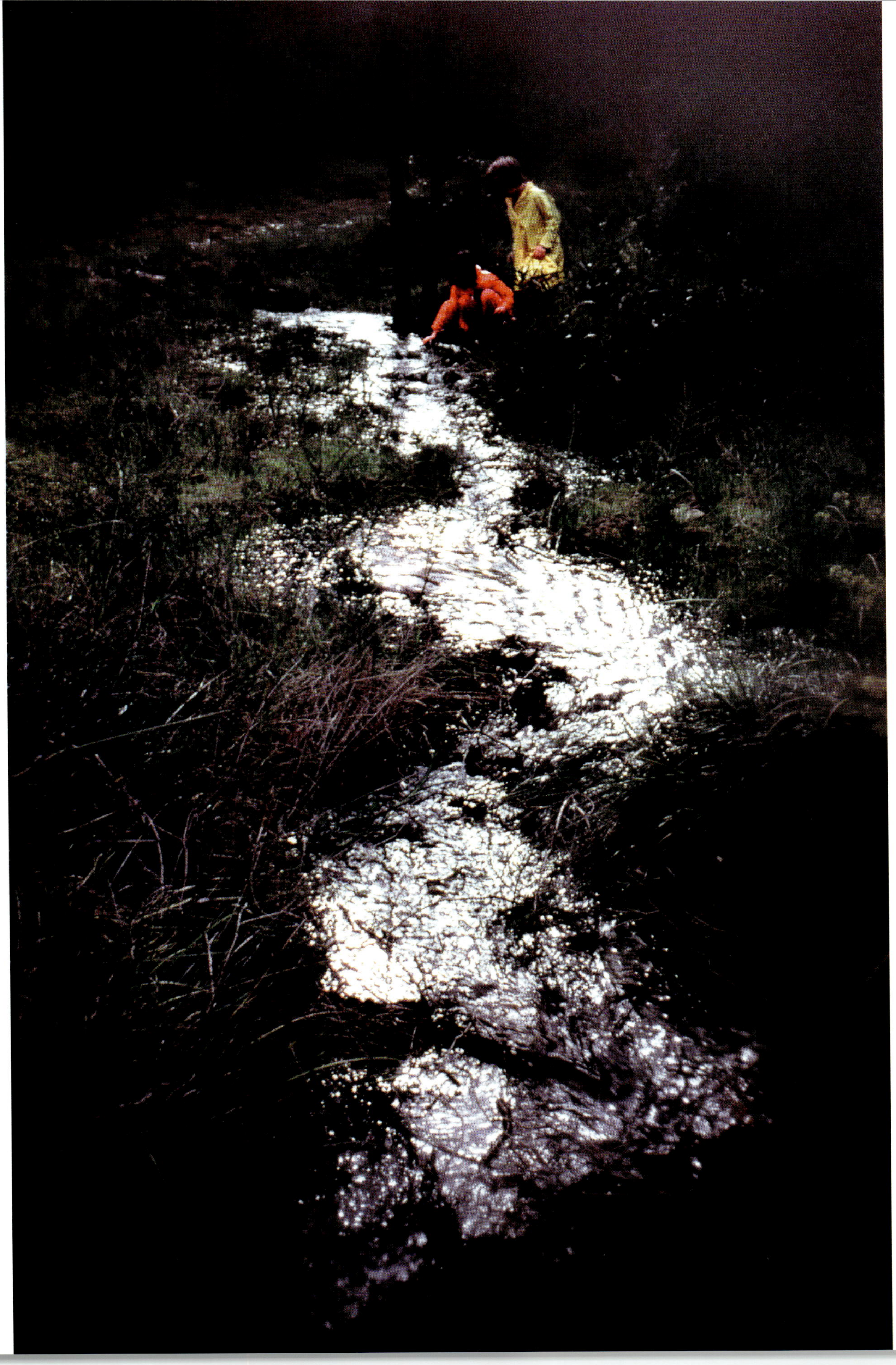

Fig 10.2 As my children emerge from the gloom, we continue to see how practically any photograph can benefit from the computer's intervention.

Perhaps because of my involvement in international salon photography, many of the photographs taken of my children are very different from those seen in most family albums. The shots often included them, for added interest, in a landscape. As a result, they offer a far wider appeal than more traditional compositions.

Children of the Stream (fig. 10.1) was taken in the hills above where we lived at the time. The appearance of the stream varied depending on the season. On this occasion our timing was perfect. Pre-selected rainwear made its colourful contribution to the scene, as did my children who were left alone to do what they do best.

While they explored their world, I explored mine – one of landscape photography. I chose a wide-angle lens and a home-made mist filter when taking this shot. By using the filter I had hoped to increase the atmosphere of the composition. I also wanted to convey the relationship between the stream and my children. I looked downstream to the valley below and beyond. What lay ahead as this rivulet grew into a meandering river? What lay ahead for my children in the twists and turns of life?

As this photograph became a successful salon entry, I gave it its title in the hope that a wider audience would perceive my connection. Beyond identifying it for cataloguing purposes, the value of placing a meaningful title alongside a photograph has often been controversial. In my opinion, the more personal and subjective a photograph, the more it is in need of a title if it is to be understood by a wider, more objective audience. If words can encourage an audience to understand the intended symbolism or deeper meaning of a photograph, the result is a richer experience for all involved.

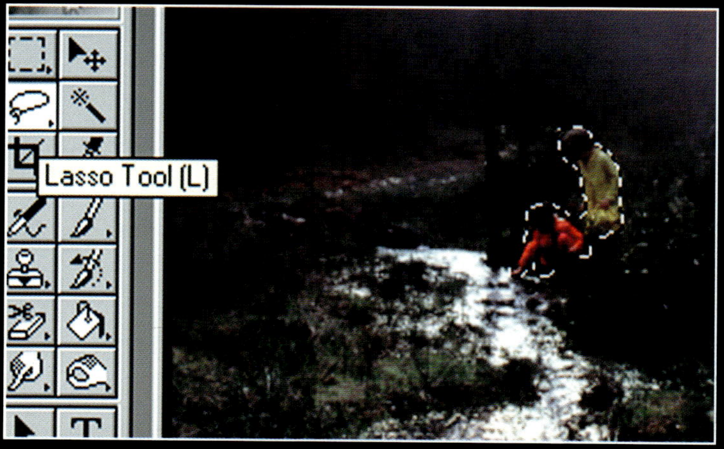

Fig 10.3

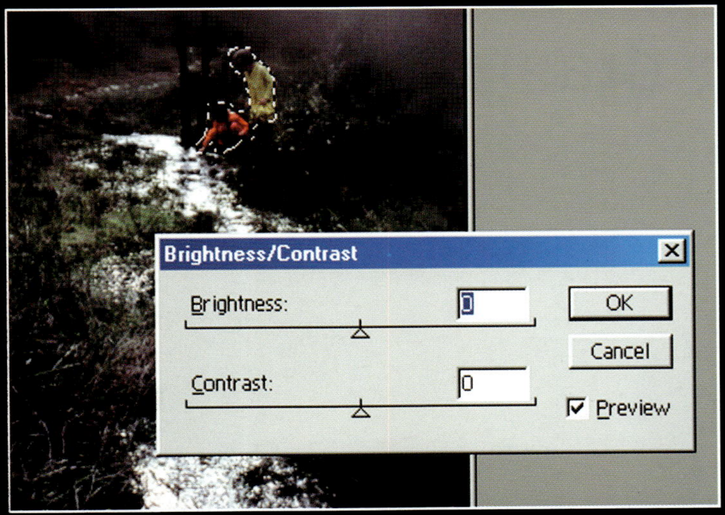

Fig 10.4

However, in this case my symbolism threatens to overpower the photograph. In attempting to create a gentle mist with my filter, I had almost overstepped the mark and obscured the detail in a fog. Fortunately, the computer provides us with the means to rectify the situation. While I am happy with my original photograph (a framed print hangs above my desk), it can be used to highlight not only how simple it is to apply each of these techniques, but also how easily we can enhance specific parts of an image.

To start with we increase the contrast of the image as a whole by using the IMAGE/ADJUST/LEVELS option (see Project 1, page 16). A good result can also be achieved by enhancing the children's colourful rainwear. To do this, we use the LASSO tool (fig. 10.3) and draw around the children to make our selection. Our next move is to use IMAGE/ADJUST/BRIGHTNESS-CONTRAST (fig. 10.4). By adjusting the sliders we obtain the required result.

Finally, we activate the LASSO tool and click anywhere on the image to deselect the marching ants. This technique has helped to lift the 'fog', and the greater contrast that it creates between the photograph's different elements means that the children's clothing now stands out much more clearly (fig. 10.2).

project 11

accentuating drama

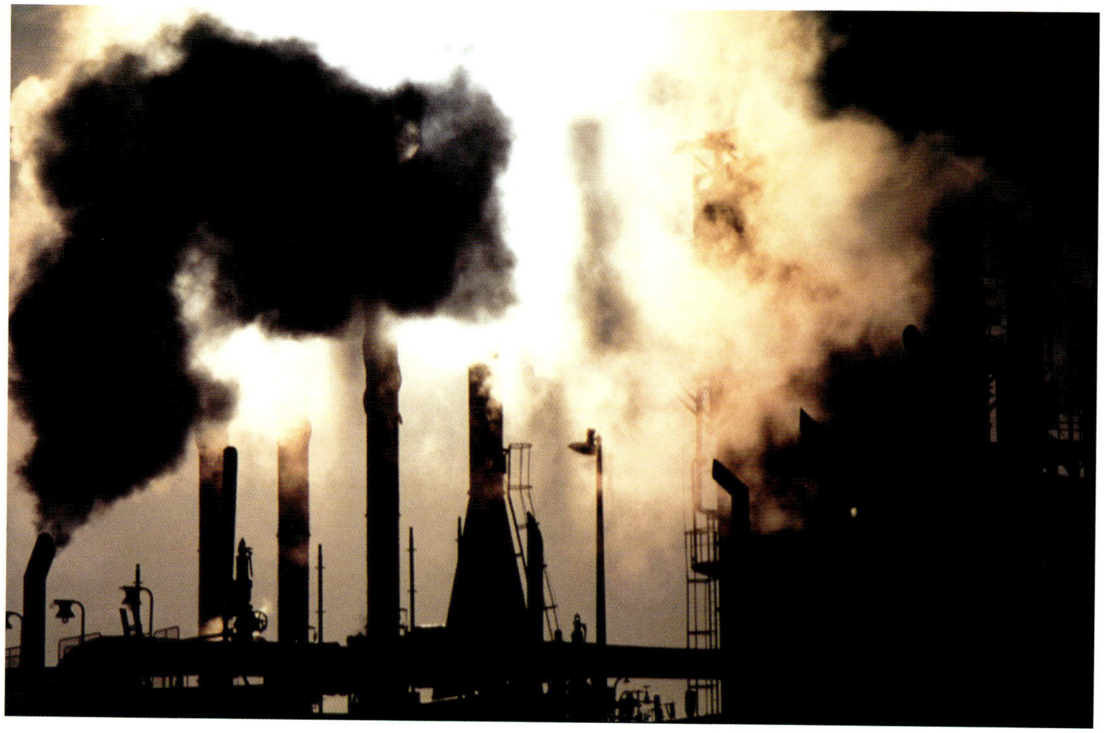

Fig 11.1 This industrial landscape would benefit from a personal approach.

ADJUST/COLOUR BALANCE

Industrial scenes are not to every landscape photographer's taste, but as society's requirements change so does the land, and to ignore the developing industrial landscape is to ignore an ever-increasing source of photography.

Fig 11.2 Our choice reflects a low-key, realistic approach.

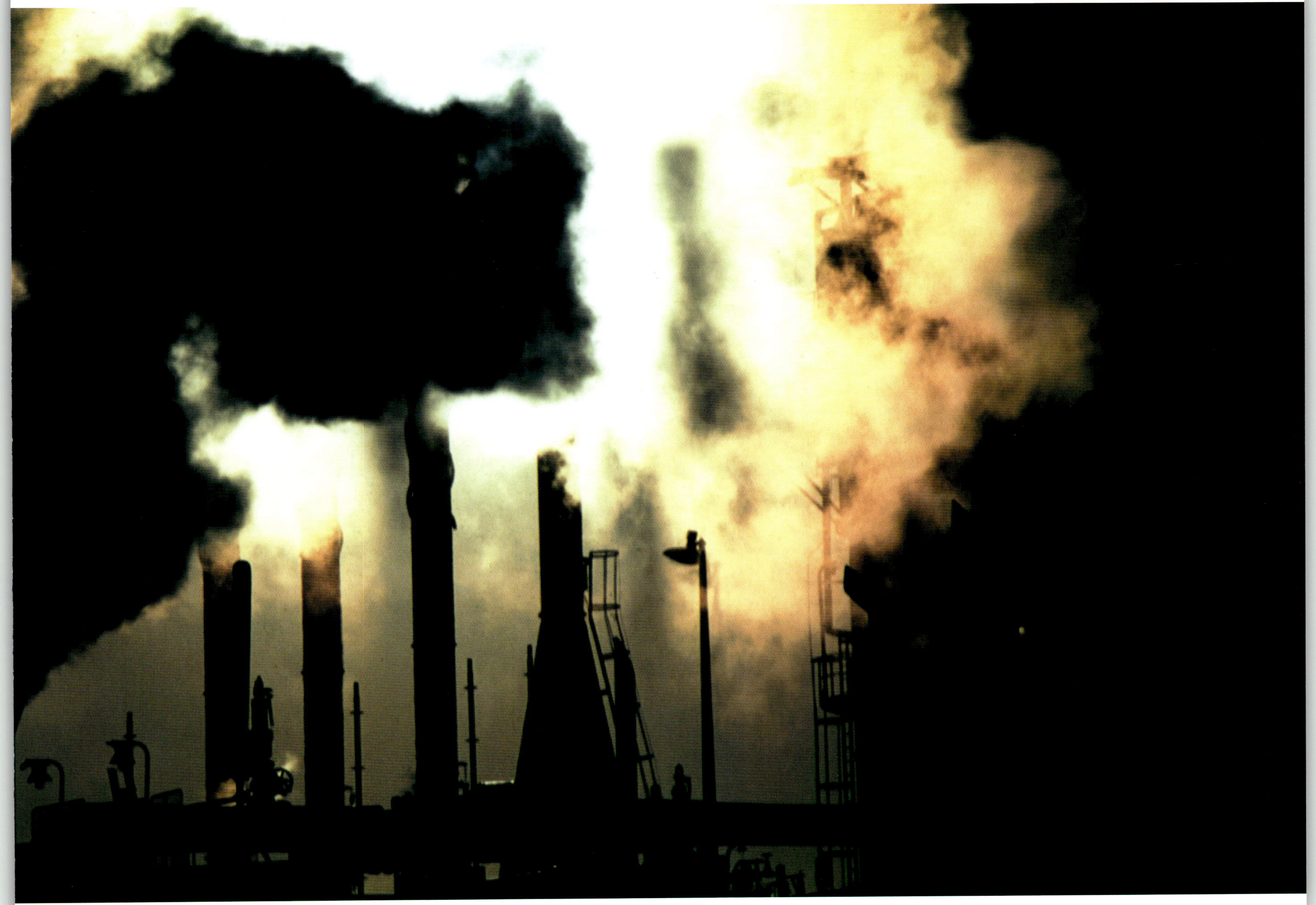

How we see an industrial landscape and the end quality of the photographs we make have much to do with our approach. The most obvious approach to photographing an industrial plant is to link up with a scheduled tour. This offers a good opportunity to get a general overview, but you are unlikely to receive any preferential treatment and, as a result, your photographs may end up being rushed. A further problem occurs with lighting, which is just as important here as when photographing less man-made landscapes. This is because guided tours often seem to operate during the midday hours of uninteresting light, when most professional photographers would prefer to avoid taking landscape photographs.

A better approach is to call in advance and make an appointment to see the manager or public-relations director. It takes a little extra time and effort, but the results make it worthwhile. Making your approach well in advance of your proposed visit has the additional benefit of allowing you time to do your homework and be clear on your aims. Working out the details, such as the direction of the sun at different times of day, can make or break your photographs. To help refine your plans, choose a theme, then follow and emphasize it. When on site, it is important to follow all safety regulations to the letter. Having said that, try to lose yourself in your photography. Afterwards, thank all those involved, and if you promise complimentary prints make sure you deliver.

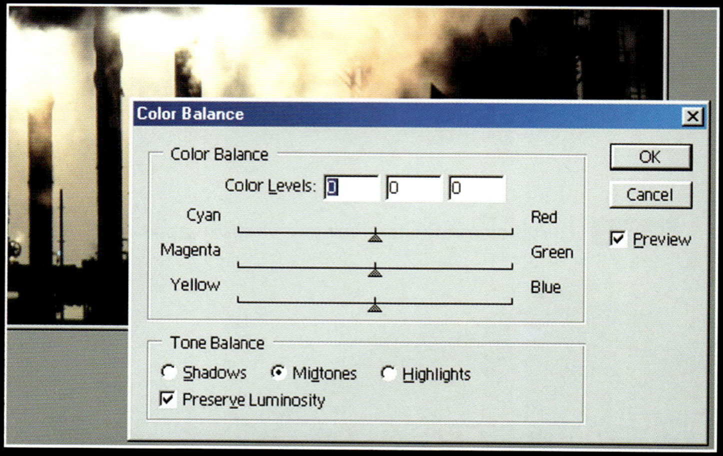

Fig 11.3

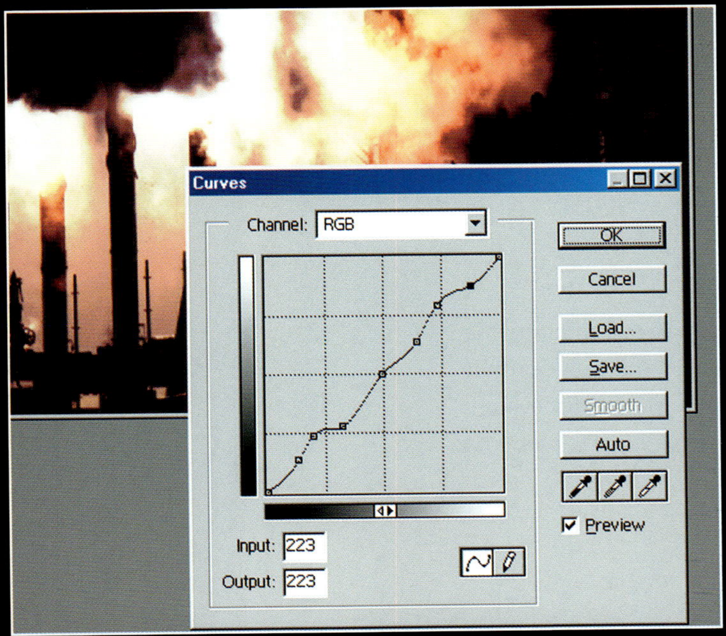

Fig 11.4

In spite of increasing security concerns, I have been amazed and thrilled at the opportunities given to me when I have been open, honest and courteous. Beyond this, I find that a well-arranged personal visit affords more scope to photograph behind closed doors with the freedom of expression I would hope to achieve when photographing landscapes elsewhere.

Industrial Landscape (fig. 11.1) fails to convey the drama of this scene in the way that I had wanted to show it. How can the computer help make up for this shortfall?

For our first approach we turn to IMAGE/ADJUST/COLOUR BALANCE (fig. 11.3), and using the sliders we influence the different colour combinations in SHADOWS, MID-TONES and HIGHLIGHTS. As an alternative, for more detailed control we can use IMAGE/ADJUST/CURVES (fig. 11.4), which has a maximum of 16 reference points to effect change in the image's appearance.

With so many options available, it is easy to enhance the visual interpretation of your subject and to reflect your attitude to industry and industrial landscapes more accurately. We use a low-key approach to illustrate this dramatic setting (fig 11.2).

project 12

straightening the horizon

ROTATE CANVAS

In some photographic circles, much is made of catching the decisive moment in a photograph. Perhaps the true worth of this was devalued for me some years ago when I discovered the true circumstances surrounding the taking of a particular

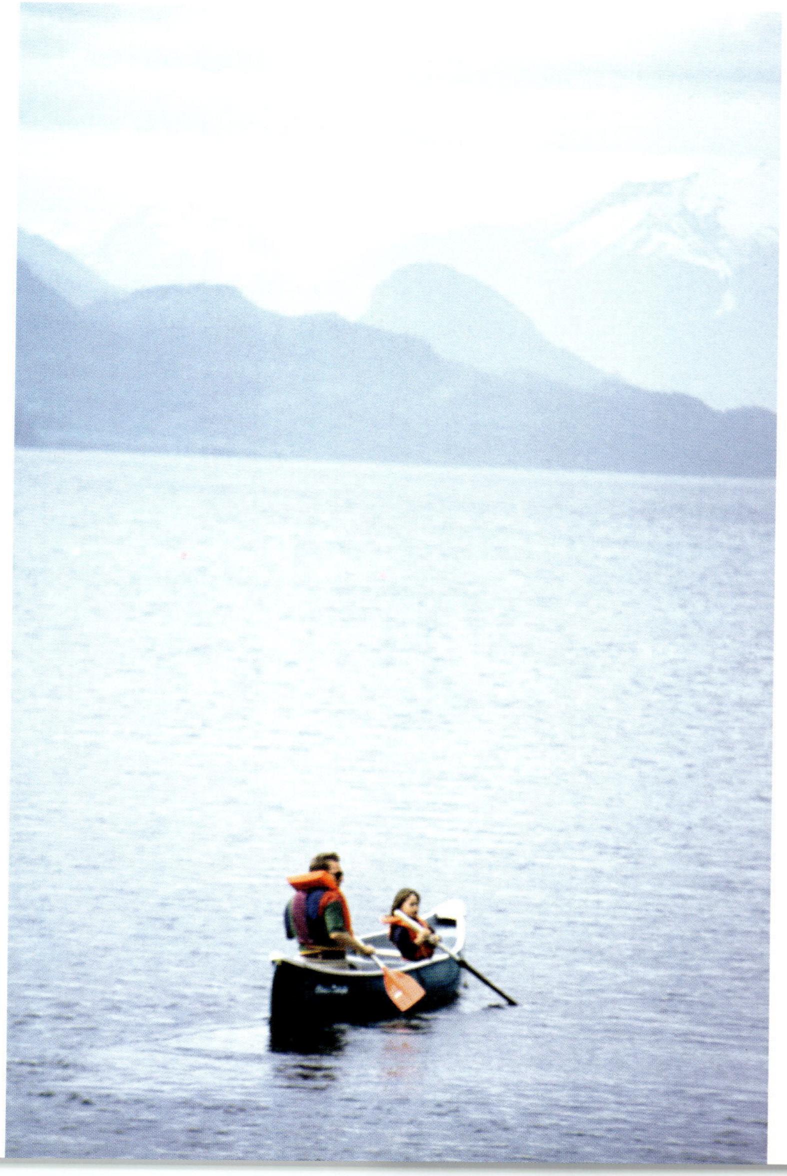

Fig 12.1 The 'decisive moment' of *Canoe* disappears into the distance along with the diminishing subject.

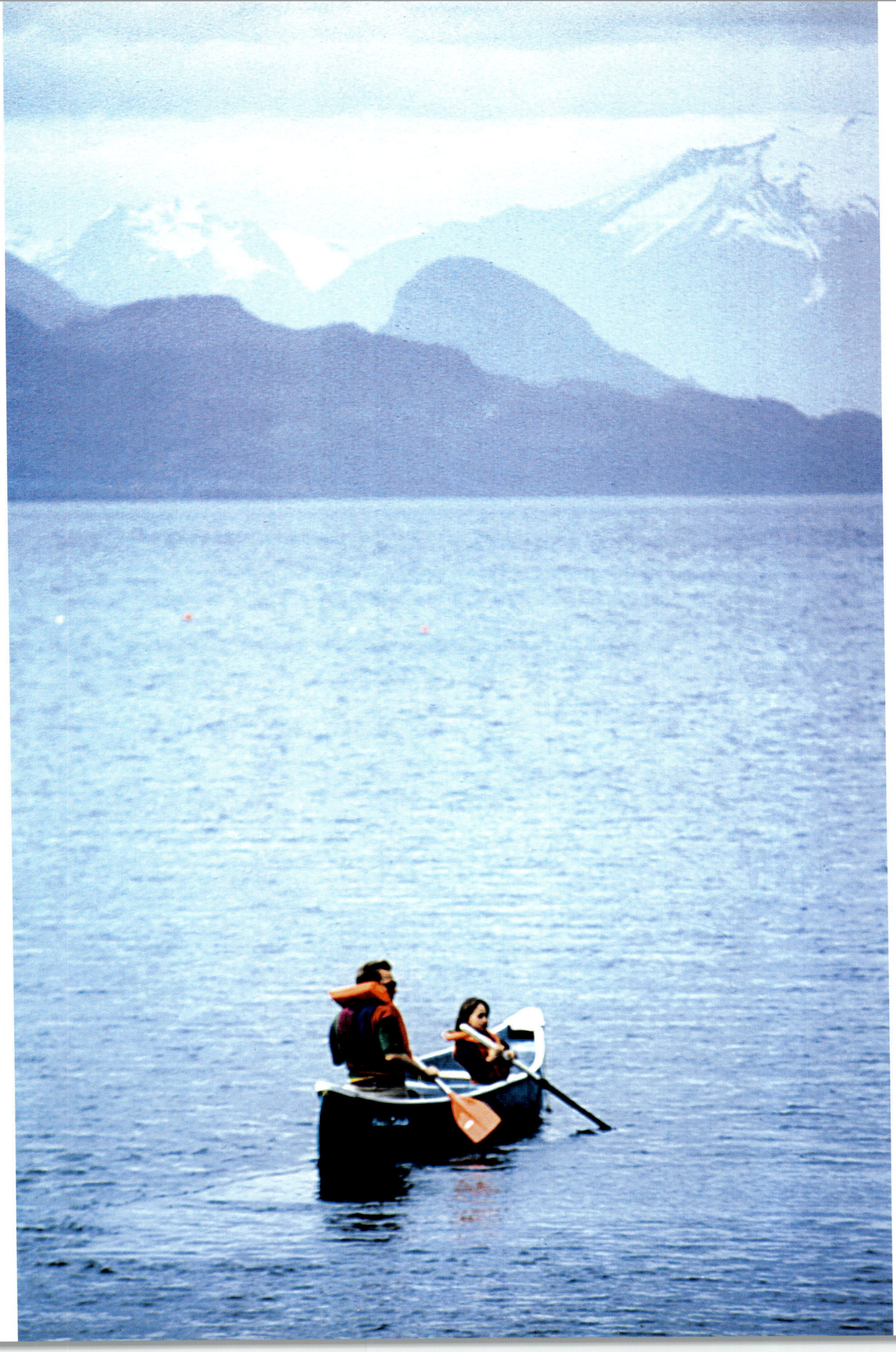

Fig 12.2 As if able to bring back time, the CROP tool recreates a moment that was missed.

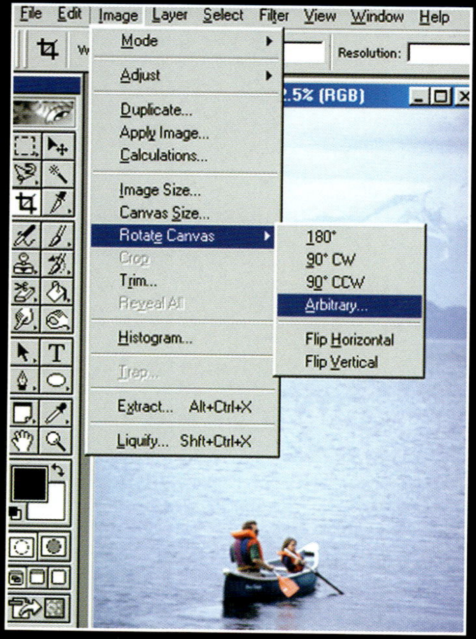

Fig 12.3

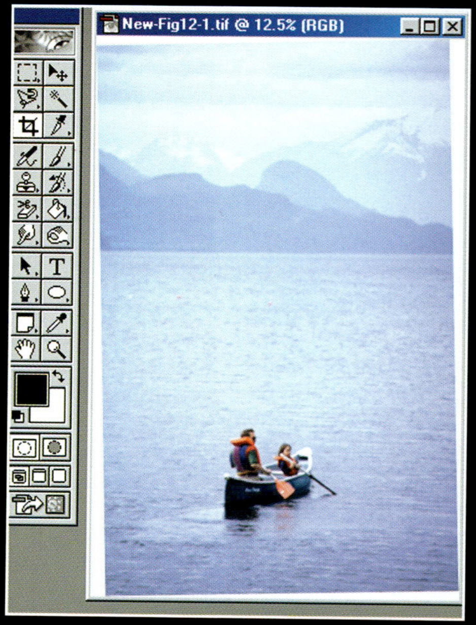

Fig 12.5

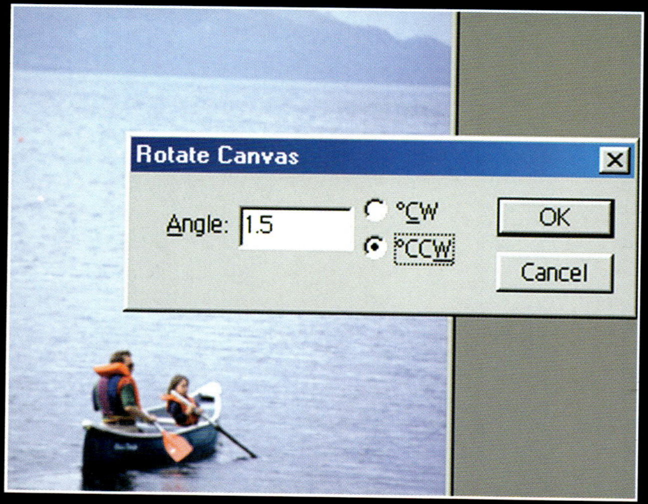

Fig 12.4

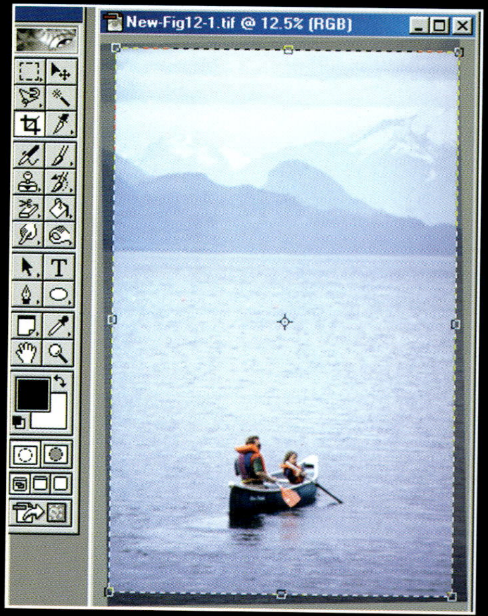

Fig 12.6

photograph, which had been highly regarded because of its portrayal of a decisive moment. Whether the account was true or apocryphal, a report suggested that the whole thing had been staged. Not only that, but to capture the supposed spontaneity of the moment, the photographer had the whole scene re-enacted 14 times.

This is not to deny the importance of timing in a photograph, nor the value of composing a scene inventively, but it did make me wonder about the decisive moment in a sequence of events and whether there can be more than one. Does the decisive moment not depend on one's viewpoint?

Imagine you are photographing a football match hoping to catch the crucial point of the game. We all know that split seconds count when it comes to photographing sports action, but, even here, identifying the decisive moment may be a very subjective act. Not only are a series of events – rather than just a single incident – likely to effect the eventual outcome, but your past experiences are likely to colour your opinions.

Decisive moments are quite different in landscape photography. Sport was far from my mind when I photographed *Canoe* (fig. 12.1), but I could have kicked myself as I let the decisive moment slip away. I had delayed getting out of my car just long enough to see the canoe leaving shore. By the time I had organized myself and got my camera in position, the decisive moment I desired was disappearing into the distance.

For me, the expansive beauty of the setting was a symbolic reminder of the freedom of outdoor photography. This remained, but my focal point was now too far away to make an effective composition. To make matters worse, in my haste to capture what remained of my composition I committed a common error and inadvertently framed the horizon at an angle. Fortunately, both of these problems can be solved as we turn our attention to the computer.

First, we tackle the problem of straightening the horizon. To do this we use IMAGE/ROTATE CANVAS/ARBITRARY (fig. 12.3), and decide how much we wish to rotate the picture to produce a straight horizon. We click OK and a window appears (fig. 12.4) in which we insert the number of degrees required to rotate the image, and choose a clockwise or counter-clockwise direction. We try 2 degrees CCW. Our result shows this is too much. Using EDIT/UNDO we reverse this step and try again. This time we insert 1.5 degrees, which makes the horizon level.

As a result of this correction we notice four white triangles appear on the screen where our image fails to cover the corners of the canvas underneath (fig. 12.5). We remove them by using the CROP tool (fig. 12.6). This also helps to bring the canoe into a more prominent position and tighten the overall composition. To complete the process we use the IMAGE/ADJUST/LEVELS (see Project 1, page 16) and achieve the end result we want (fig. 12.2).

project 13

correcting exposure

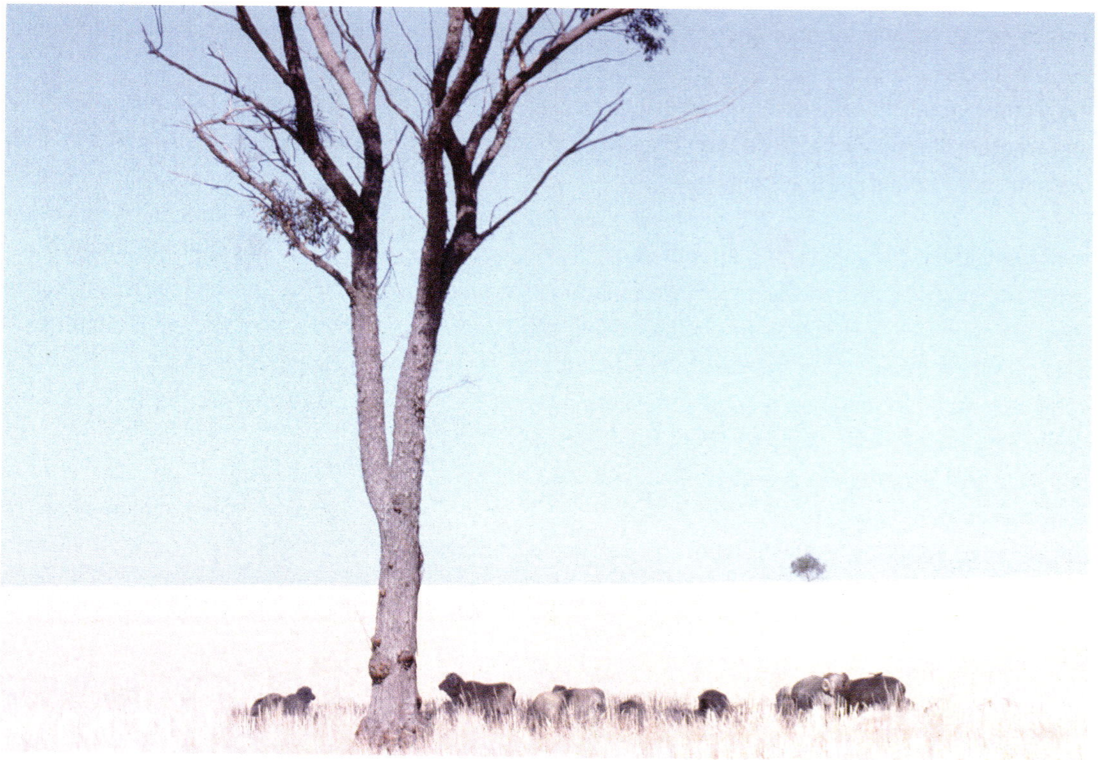

Fig 13.1 In *Midday Sun* a dry sheep scene, over-exposed to reflect the midday heat, is correctly interpreted but, technically, incorrectly exposed.

NEW LAYER/MODE/MULTIPLY

Many years ago I heard a statement by the legendary American photographer Harry Callahan: 'There is only one rule in photography and that is to be good.' It was a statement that I believed in, and I practised and widely endorsed it. Then, years later, I read the same statement in its fuller context: 'There is only one rule in photography and that is to be good – to yourself.'

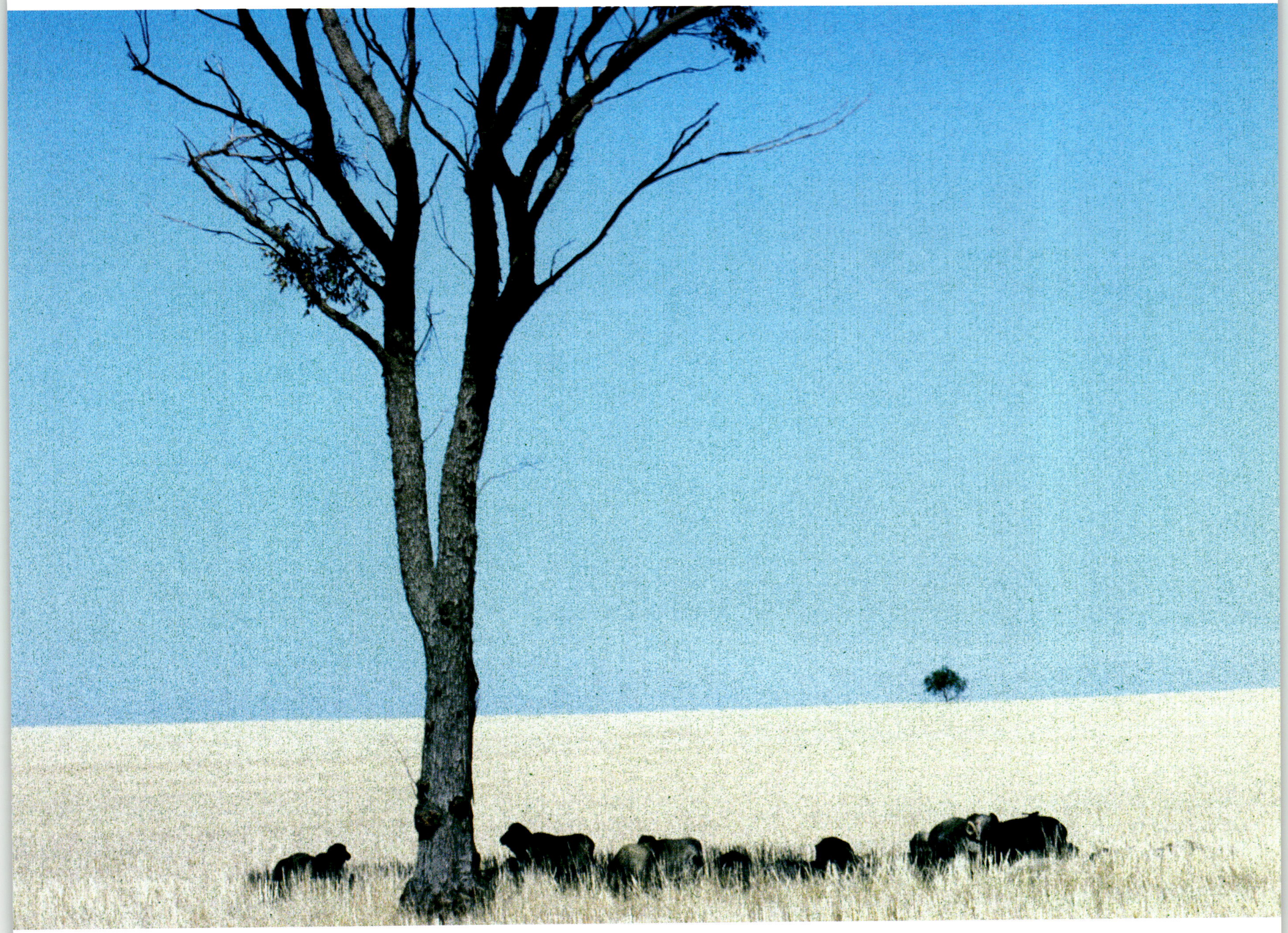

Fig 13.2 A 'correct' rendition is achieved with the application of the MODE/MULTIPLY option.

Too often we follow rules and conventions blindly instead of thinking for ourselves. When photography first became popular, in the late 1830s, many of the practices embraced by early photographers were handed down from the artists and painters of the time – well intended then, but certainly of little consequence now. Other rules were introduced to help cope with the limitations of the materials of the day, such as poor optics and slow films. Again, these are no longer relevant to contemporary photography.

Rules and guidelines have their part to play. In particular, along with the advice and encouragement of others, they help to provide us with a starting point. Once on the move, we should not ignore all that has gone before, but we do need to build upon it and move on. To stay with what we started with is to deny the creative process.

My approach to *Midday Sun* (fig. 13.1) went against photographic convention, but I felt that my execution was appropriate to the situation. In Harry Callahan's terms, I was being good to myself. When I shot it, the sun was high, it was hot, and everything seemed to hover under a heat haze. The sheep sought what shade they could find under a tree. The whole scene seemed to suffer from overexposure in the midday heat, and my photograph was intended to reflect this.

Despite my thinking, many viewers have maintained that the picture is overexposed. Whether it is exposed correctly or not (given the circumstances under which it was taken), this shot can be used to illustrate how the computer can deal with the problems of overexposure. The solution we adopt here is not the simplest one available, but it can be applied to slides that, because of their age or perhaps as a result of incorrect storage, have lost much of their colour.

Once we have loaded the slide onto the computer, we use LAYER/NEW/LAYER to create a new layer (fig. 13.3). When the NEW LAYER screen appears, we click on the little triangle behind NORMAL in the MODE box and choose MULTIPLY (fig. 13.4) to build up the density of the image, and then click OK.

We move back to the background layer and choose IMAGE/ADJUST/LEVELS. Three eyedroppers can be found on the right of the screen. The black one defines black, the next defines middle grey and the right defines white (fig. 13.5). Any colour cast that the image has can be removed by using the middle one. We click on it and find a suitable middle grey in the picture to use as a sample (e.g. a sheep from under the tree). As soon as we click on this the image changes considerably, helping to reduce the appearance of overexposure. By then sliding the left (i.e. black) slider to the right we turn the picture into a more conventionally exposed one (or restore the old, faded slide to its former glory). When we are happy with the results (fig. 13.2), we click OK.

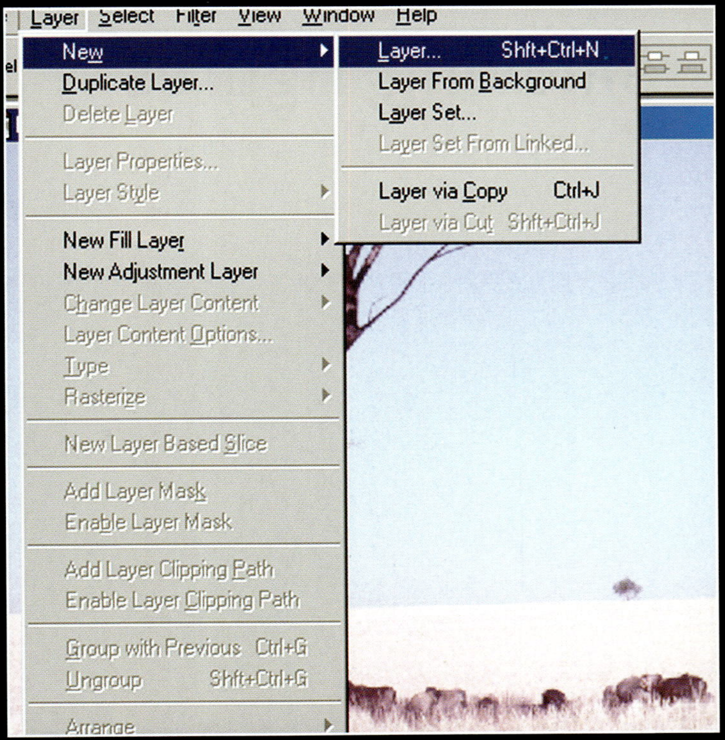

Fig 13.3

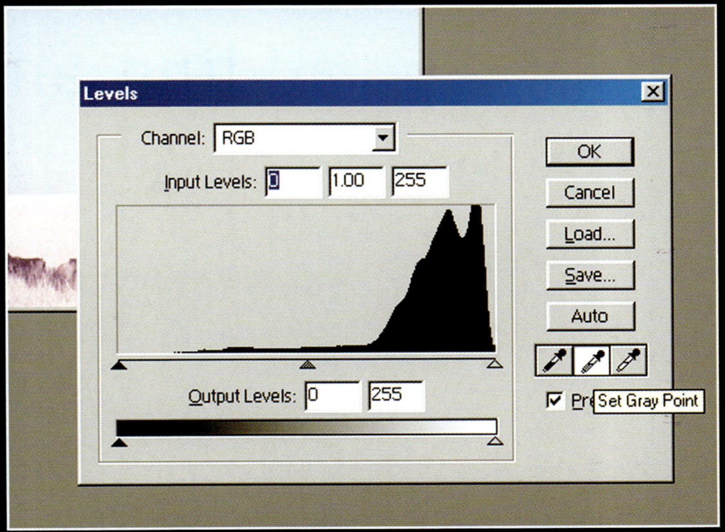

Fig 13.5

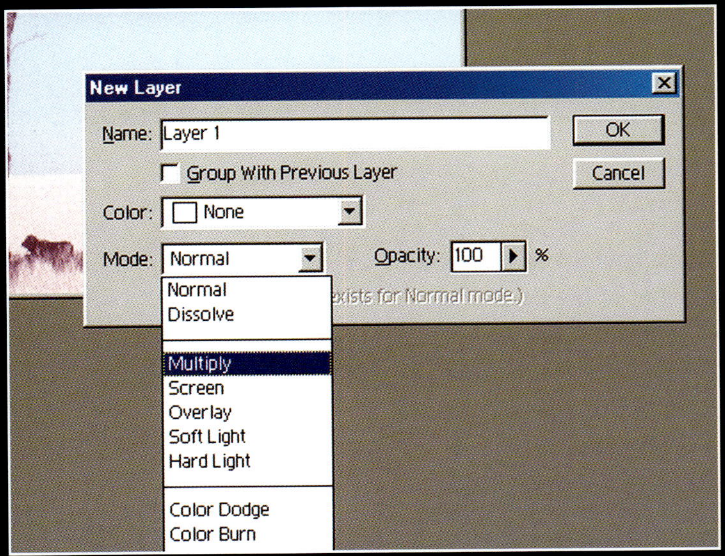

Fig 13.4

project 14

adding and removing figures

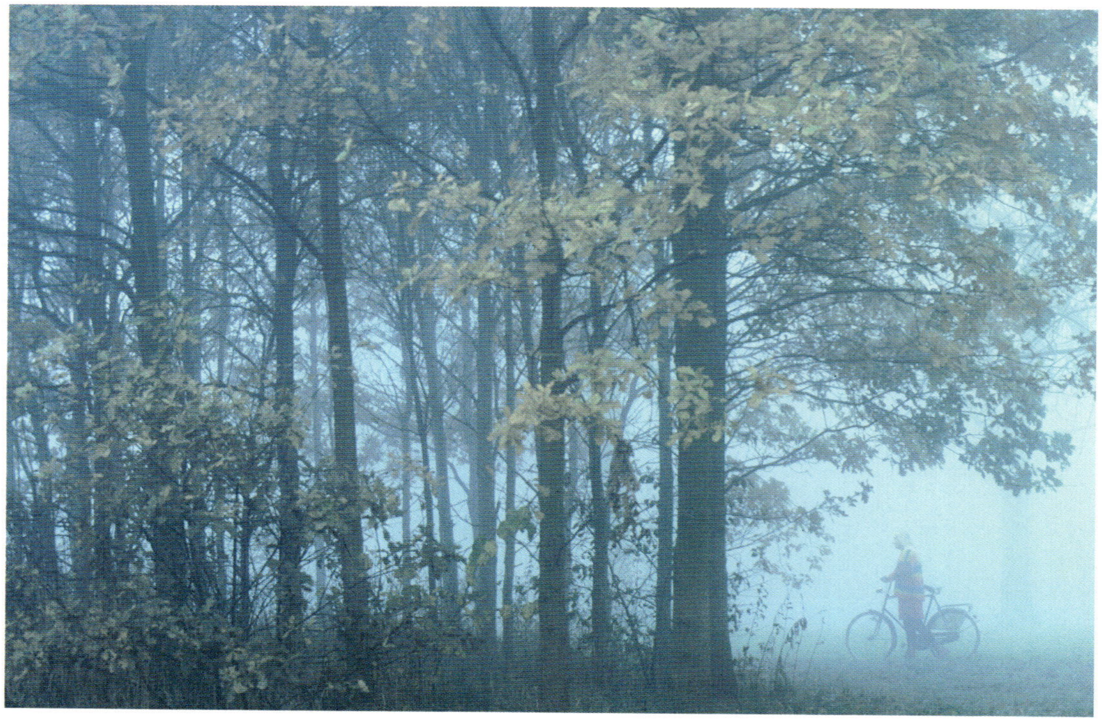

Fig 14.1 Never underestimate the power of a person in the landscape.

FLIP, CLONE STAMP

The projects in this book have used photographs that, generally, do not include people. Indeed, one or two of the images have used the computer to remove them. However, there are occasions when a landscape may benefit from the inclusion of a person. For example, you may wish to introduce someone to help give a sense of scale. Here, in *Forest Edge* (fig. 14.1), I asked a friend to help provide balance to the composition and fill in space.

Fig 14.2 Enhancing techniques learned here can be applied, just as easily, to your own photographs.

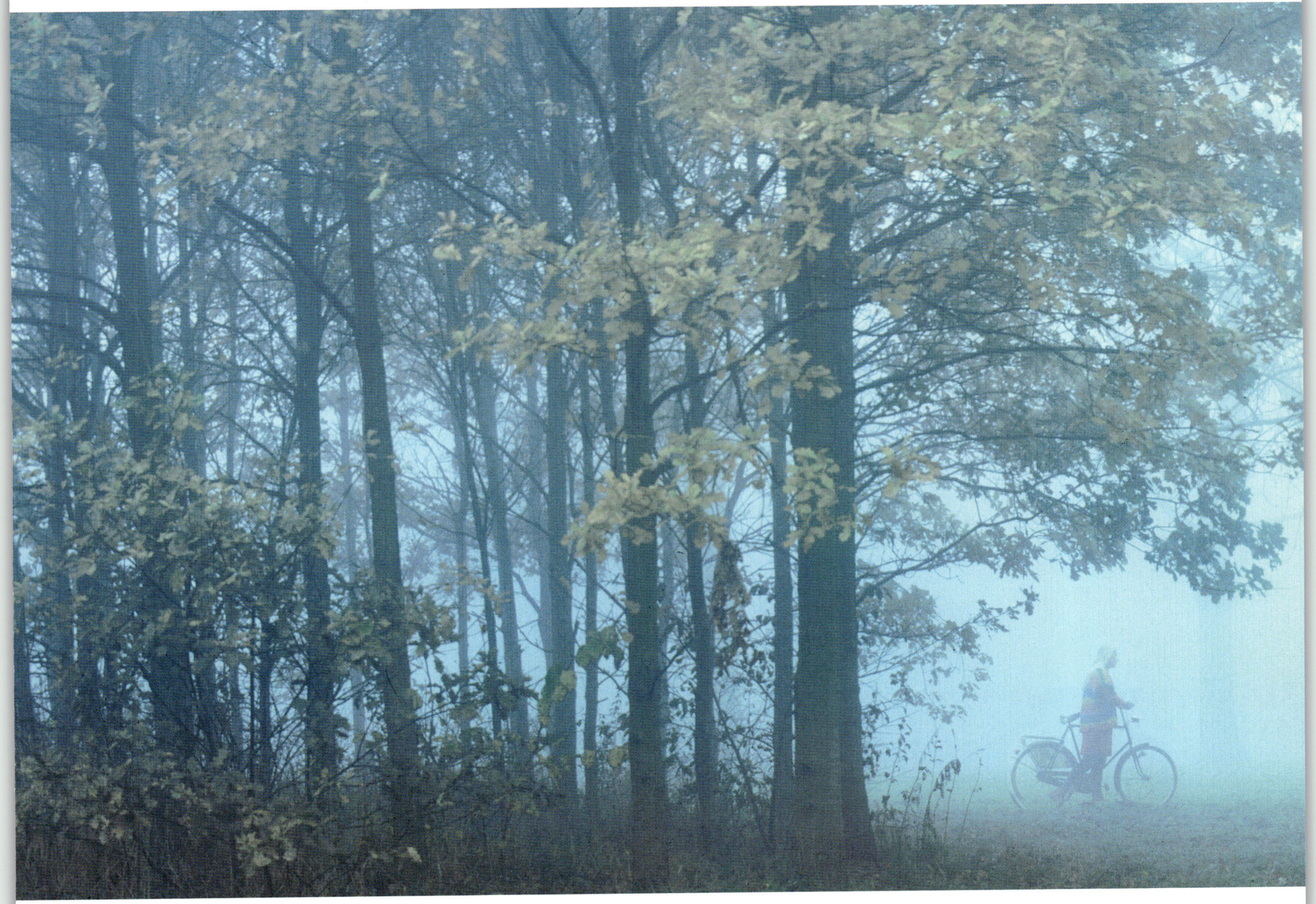

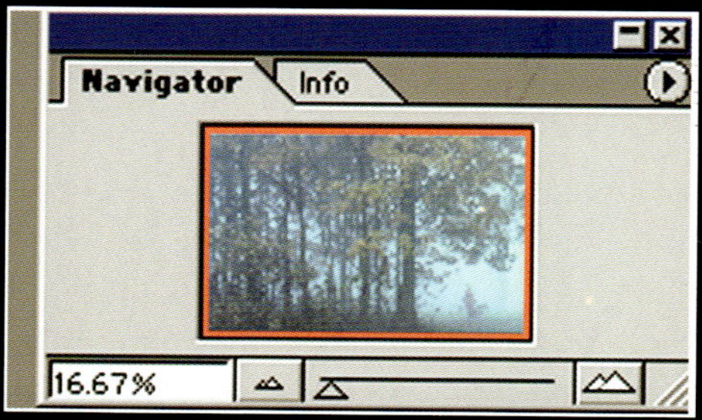

Fig 14.3

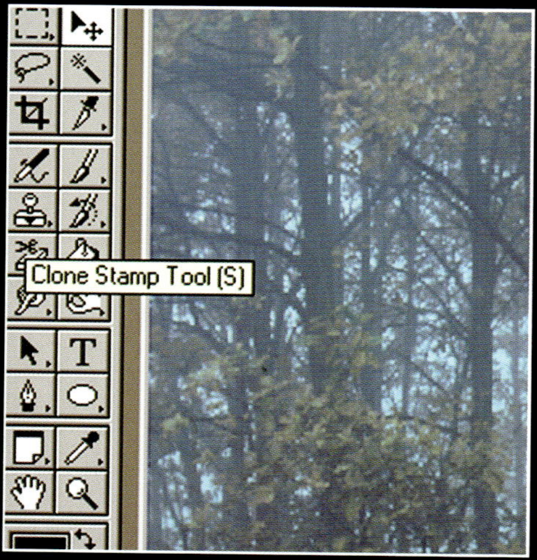

Fig 14.4

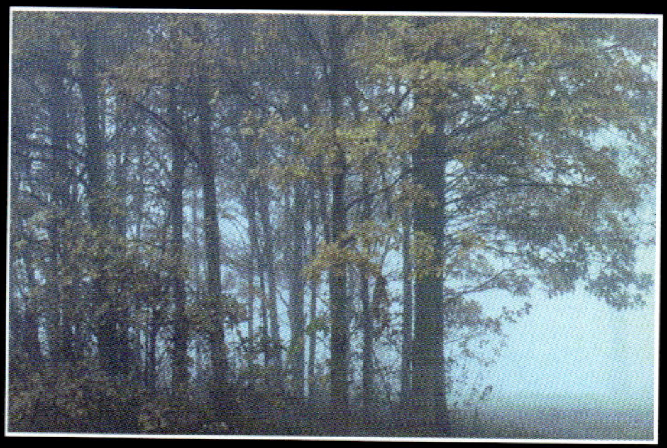

Fig 14.5

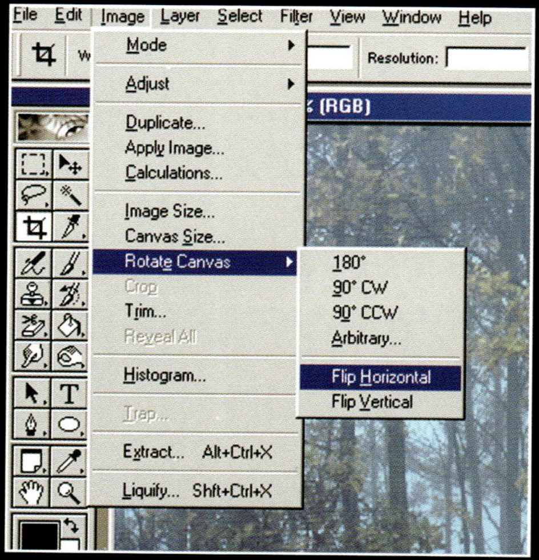

Fig 14.6

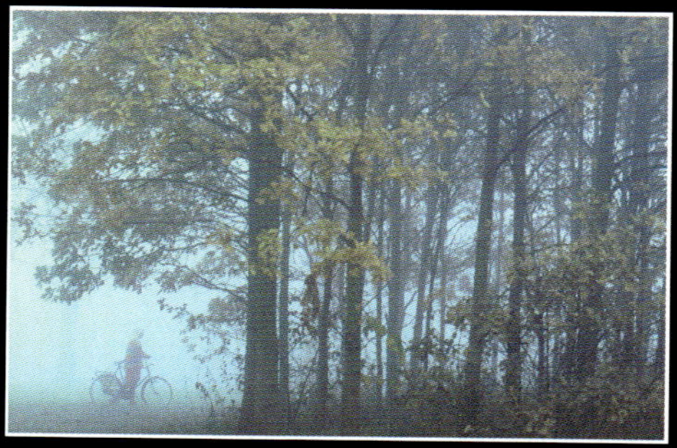

Fig 14.7

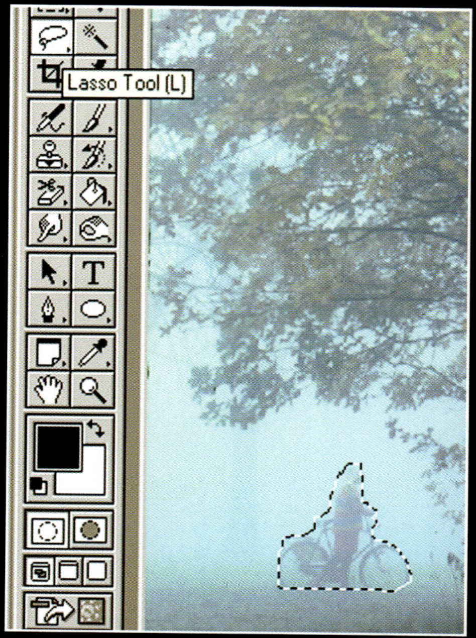

Fig 14.8

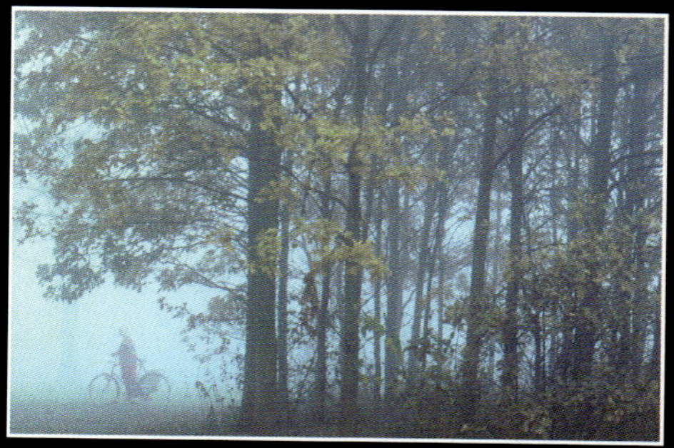

Fig 14.9

Although a person can improve a landscape, their impact can be such that it is important they appear on our terms. They must look natural, and be in a pose and position that is beneficial to the overall composition. You may be able to position them yourself, but where this is not possible the computer allows us to make any changes that we feel are necessary. We can also compare a landscape with or without the human form and decide which looks best.

First, we shall remove the figure to show just how much the human element, no matter how small it might appear, can influence a landscape. To add further interest and scope for compositional variation, we will then look at how to flip an image and how to flip part of an image within the whole.

Before we remove the cyclist, we use the NAVIGATOR (fig. 14.3) to zoom in on the area we want to work on. We drag the slider to the right to enlarge the image so that it more than fills the screen. Then, to locate the relevant area of the image, we use the mouse to move the small red rectangle contained in the navigator window.

To remove the cyclist we use the CLONE STAMP tool (fig. 14.4). We choose a PAINTBRUSH with soft edges and place it next to, but not touching, the head of the cyclist. We hold down the ALT key and click the mouse button, which creates a sample area for the paintbrush to use. Now we move our brush over the head and click the mouse until it disappears under the misty blue of its surroundings. In the same way, we remove the rest of the cyclist by selecting colours close to the parts we want to conceal. Soon, the cyclist is no more (fig. 14.5).

The technique used to flip an image is very simple. The computer does all the hard work for us, once we tell it what to do. Thus, IMAGE/ROTATE CANVAS/FLIP HORIZONTAL (fig. 14.6) gives us the right result (fig. 14.7).

To flip the figure with the bicycle and leave the rest, we make a duplicate layer. With the LASSO tool (fig. 14.8) from the toolbar we draw around the cyclist to make our selection and use EDIT/CUT to remove it. We can flip this removed part, but first we have to use the CLONE tool on the background to make sure that when we paste and then rotate it, there's nothing left to see of the original cyclist. Otherwise we will create a two-headed monster on a futuristic bike.

With the painting done, we use EDIT/PASTE and then EDIT/TRANSFORM/FLIP HORIZONTAL to point the bike in the opposite direction. With the MOVE tool we put everything in place (fig. 14.2). Of course, this result can also be flipped, if we use LAYER/FLATTEN IMAGE and IMAGE/ROTATE CANVAS/FLIP HORIZONTAL again (fig. 14.9).

project 15

correcting perspective

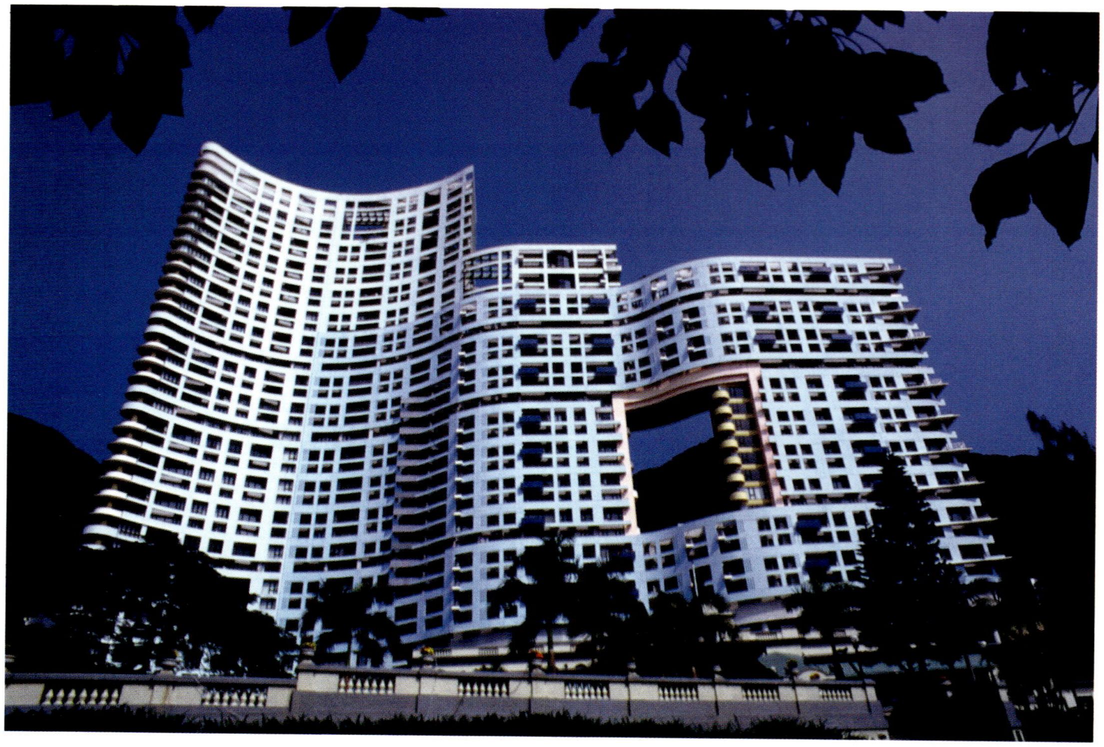

Fig 15.1 *Hotel* goes the way of most tall buildings when photographed from the base.

TRANSFORM/PERSPECTIVE

Previous projects in this book have mentioned the importance of understanding 'camera vision'. There are few instances where the difference between what the eye sees and what the camera sees becomes more apparent than when photographing tall subjects. My first-ever photograph of this type was a colourful cityscape incorporating an elegant row of trees backed by an equally elegant row of tall buildings. When the results came back from the photo lab I was dismayed to find that, in my photograph, every building, without exception, appeared to be falling backwards. Initially I struggled to overcome this

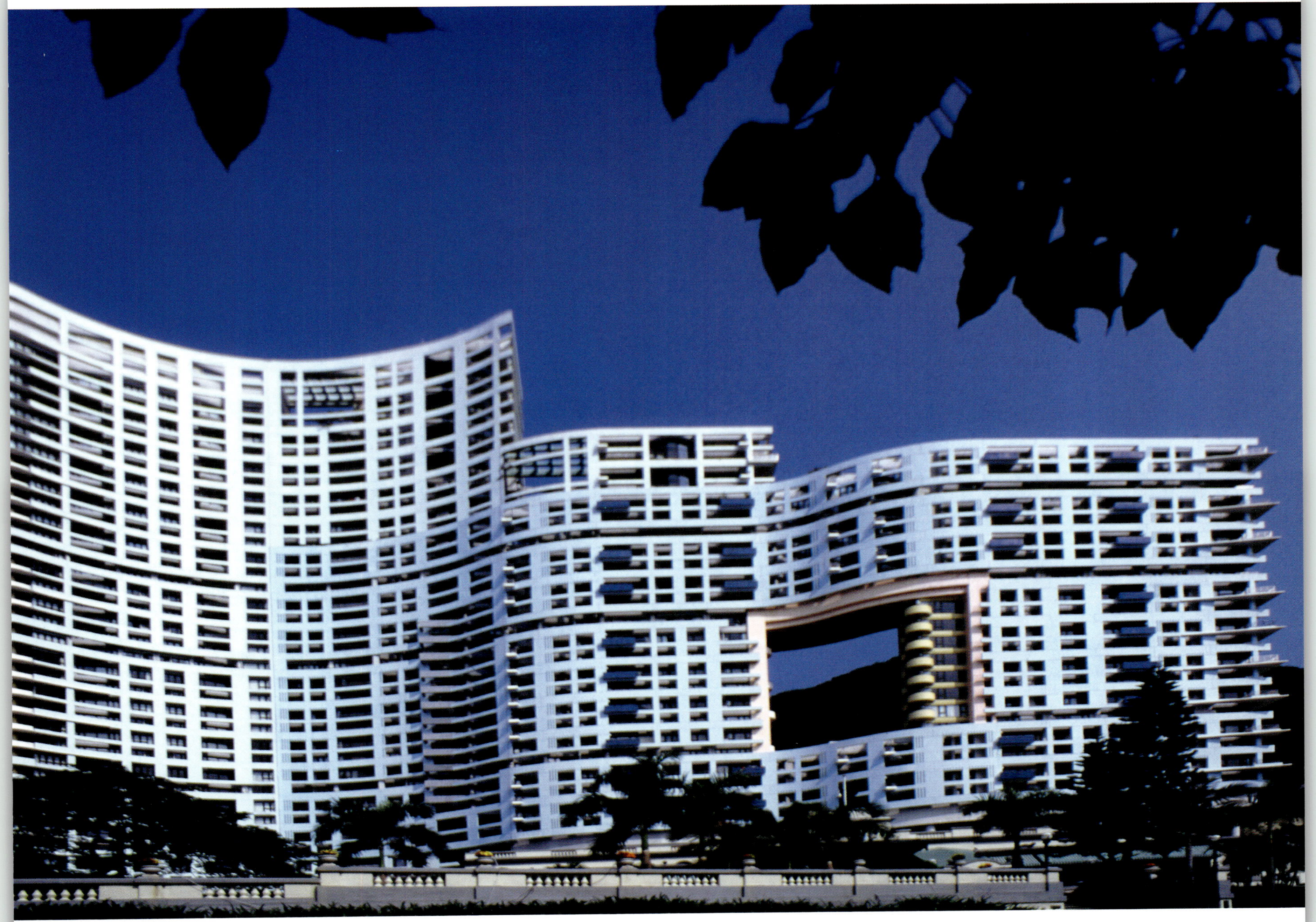

Fig 15.2 A long-standing problem is quickly erased when the TRANSFORM/PERSPECTIVE technique is introduced.

problem by using a long lens from a great distance, finding a higher level from which to shoot, or obscuring part of the building behind something else. It is possible to use a special lens to correct the perspective, but I have always felt that its cost would outweigh its use, and, ultimately, I found that I could turn this 'fault' into a feature.

Hotel (fig. 15.1) at Repulse Bay on Hong Kong Island not only dominates the landscape, it is the landscape – its photographic potential is almost as impressive as the cost of a room. While my changed thinking means I am perfectly happy with the altered perspective of the original photograph, it is ideal for illustrating how easily the computer can correct this problem that has taxed photographers for so long.

The following techniques may sound a little confusing when reading about them for the first time, but time spent practising and experimenting will make things clearer.

This is another situation where, first, we need to make a background layer to protect the original image. We do this, as usual, by clicking the right mouse button [CONTROL + mouse button] on the background layer bar (or by dragging the relevant bar in the layers window to the appropriate icon). We decrease the image size by using the NAVIGATOR window (fig. 15.3). The image window maintains its size, and this creates more space in which to work.

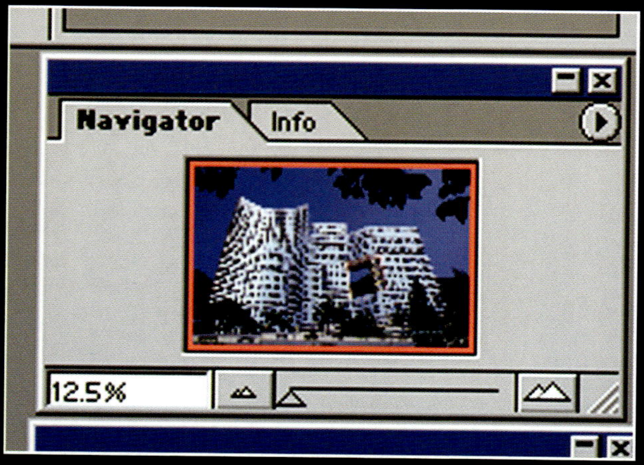

Fig 15.3

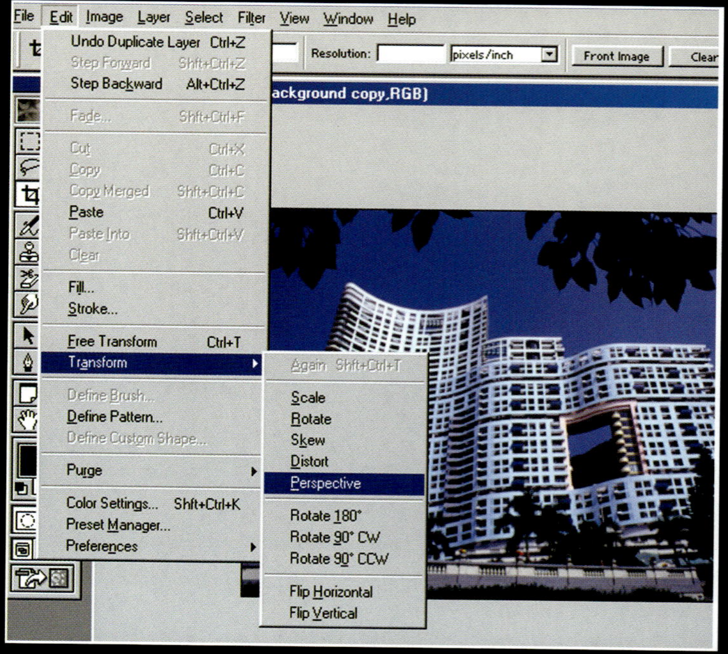

Fig 15.4

To alter perspective we use EDIT/TRANSFORM/PERSPECTIVE (fig. 15.4). After we click on this, the image is surrounded with a frame, which has tiny squares at key points. We place the cursor on the square at top left of the image. Holding down the left mouse button we drag this to the left. As we do so, the top-right corner moves to the right. We continue as far to the left as is required to straighten the left side of the hotel.

At this stage, the right-hand side still appears to be leaning to the left. To correct this, we continue to pull the left side of the hotel, overcorrecting the perspective until both sides have a slight tilt to the left. Now we press the ENTER key on the keyboard, or click on the MOVE tool and then APPLY in the window that comes into view (fig. 15.5). We then return to EDIT/TRANSFORM/PERSPECTIVE to correct the right side of the hotel. This time, we hold the square in the middle of the top line and move it a little to the right, just enough to straighten the right side. The left side also moves a little, but hopefully only enough to bring the whole building into line.

So that we can be certain that the sides of a building are straight, we use the computer to superimpose a temporary grid over our image. This option can be turned on and off by clicking VIEW/SHOW/GRID (fig. 15.6). Once we have checked that all of our adjustments are correct, we are left with a much more upright hotel (fig. 15.2).

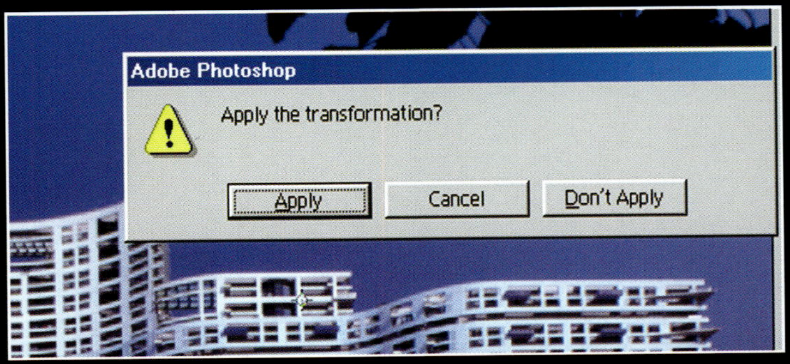

Fig 15.5

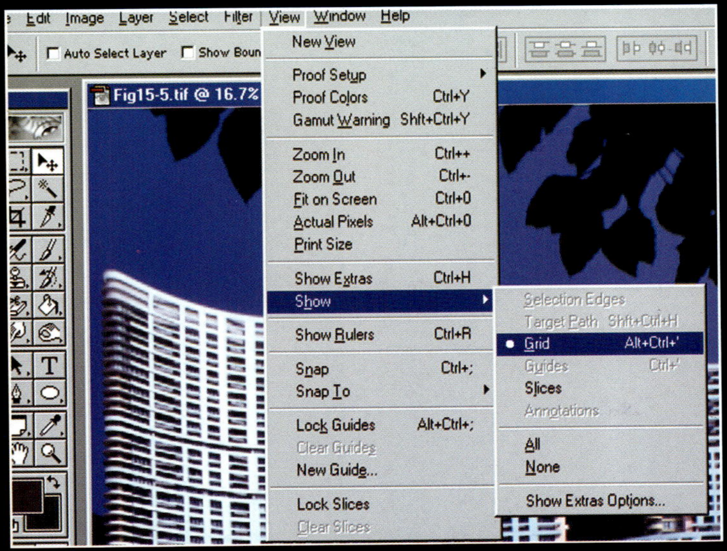

Fig 15.6

project 16

copying and adding detail

CUT, PASTE

Faced with a situation in which a view that I want to photograph is spoiled by elements beyond my control, I can do one of two things. I can walk on by, change my direction and my thinking, and photograph something else. Alternatively, I can try to make the most of the view. If I choose the second option, I will probably be, at best, disappointed with the result.

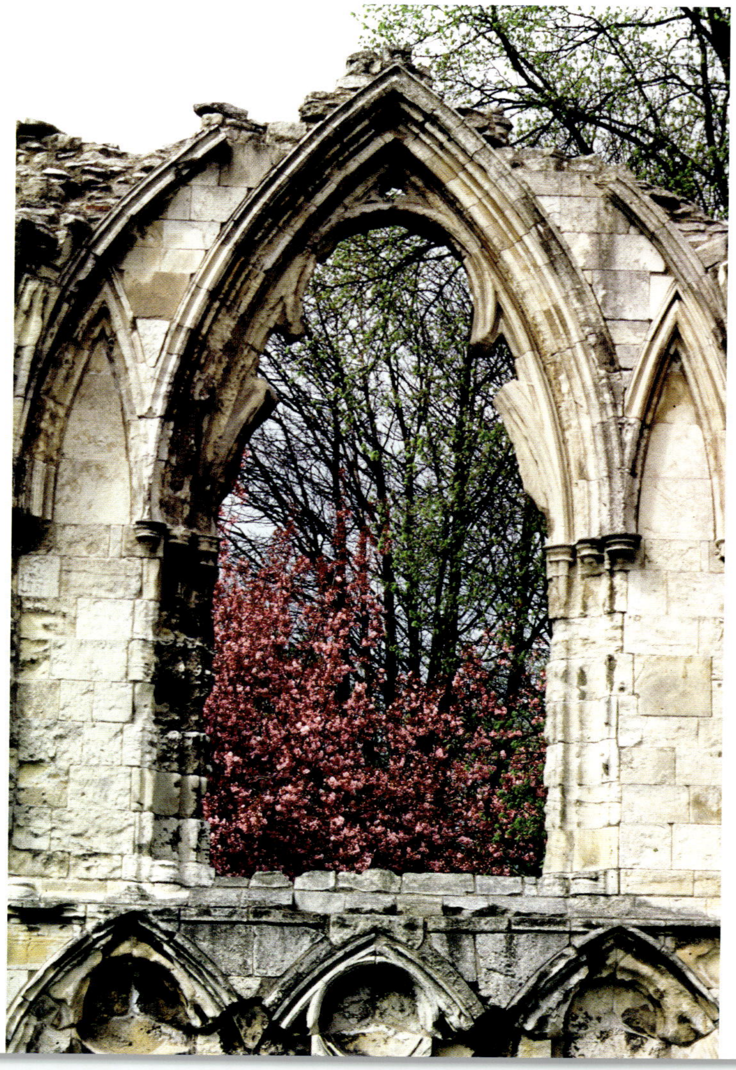

Fig 16.1 Due to a bland sky, *Ruined View* was exactly that.

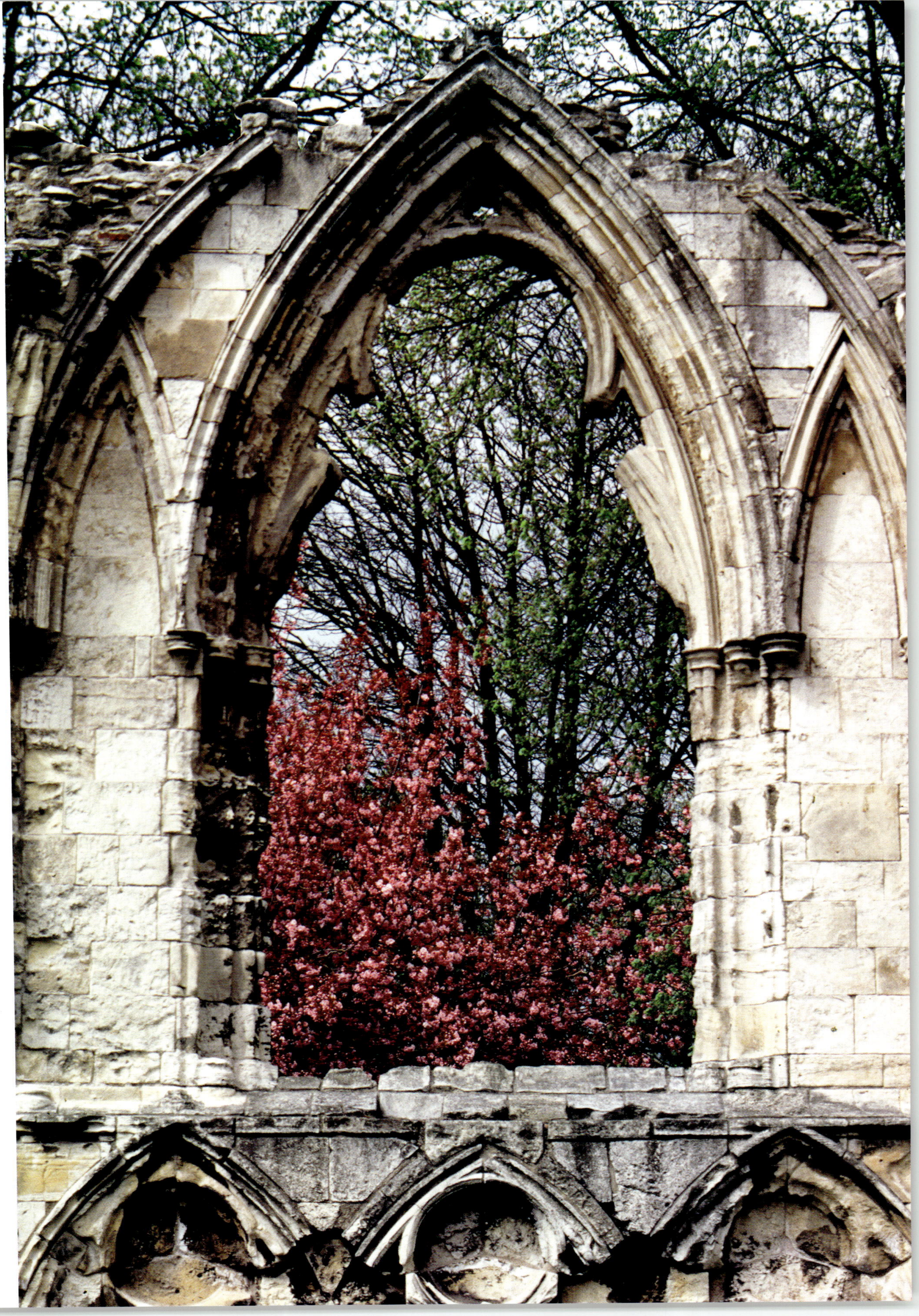

Fig 16.2 Clouds, or the lack of them, need never again prevent the taking of a photograph.

To make matters worse, I find as a rule that if I am initially disappointed with a photograph, I do not have a change of heart six months or even six years later. (Unlike good wine, a bad photograph rarely seems to improve with age.) Of course, a third option is to wait around for the view to improve, but that isn't always realistic or desirable.

In *Ruined View* (fig. 16.1) I faced the twofold problem of unwanted crowds and a bland sky. To help overcome the former, a small stepladder would have been useful. That is not as extreme as it might sound. I did carry one around in the back of my car for a couple of years and it more than paid for the inconvenience. I did not have it with me on this occasion, but thinking about it prompted me to look for suitable higher ground – in this case a low brick wall – from which I could shoot over the people.

The bland sky was not so easy to overcome. Over the years I have failed to photograph many outdoor scenes simply because the sky was not 'right'. On other occasions I have made my photograph and, while waiting for the processed result, hoped that the offending sky would change. (To date, this has never happened!) If I did take a photograph, it more often than not ended up in the rubbish bin. Due to the large patch of bland sky in the top left-hand corner of the frame, this was the direction in which *Ruined View* was heading, until the computer intervened.

In this case, there is no point in using the computer to re-paint the offending area to look like a bit of blue sky; the rest of the sky, as seen through the trees, is as colourless as our problem patch. However, experience has taught us that image enhancing provides a number of solutions for any given problem. The alternative used here is to 'plant' a tree on the left side of the photograph.

This is much easier than it might sound. First, we make a copy of the background in the layers window from which to work. We then use the LASSO tool to select the tree from the top right-hand corner of the photograph (fig. 16.3). We now turn to the EDIT/CUT command followed immediately by the EDIT/PASTE one. A section of tree with sky from the photograph appears as 'Layer 1' in the layers window. With EDIT/TRANSFORM/FLIP HORIZONTAL we point our new section of tree in the right direction. We activate the MOVE tool (fig. 16.4), move the branches to the bottom of the image, and leave them there until needed.

Next, we activate the background-copy layer, use the lasso tool to select a piece from the top left-hand side of the ruin (fig. 16.5) and again use the EDIT/CUT command. To put the branches in the right place at the top of our image, we activate Layer 1, select the MOVE tool, and position them correctly.

Unfortunately, our copied area does not cover the whole patch of sky. This is easy to rectify if we go to EDIT/TRANSFORM/SCALE. A series of little squares appears around the selection (fig. 16.6), and we drag the square in the middle of the right side to the right so it overlaps the tree on the other side and totally covers the 'bald' patch. So that we do not distort the image while enlarging it, we keep the SHIFT key pressed while dragging the square to the right.

The enlargement process creates a slight overlap with the ruins, but this is easily solved using the selection that we have cut from this area previously. We use EDIT/PASTE again to put this piece of the ruin back into the picture. In the layers menu a 'Layer 2' bar appears (fig. 16.7), and we drag this upwards so that it is above Layer 1. We move the section of the ruin to fit in with the rest of the image and cover the overlap of the tree. Finally, we use LAYER/FLATTEN IMAGE to complete our image with no 'bald' spot in sight (fig. 16.2).

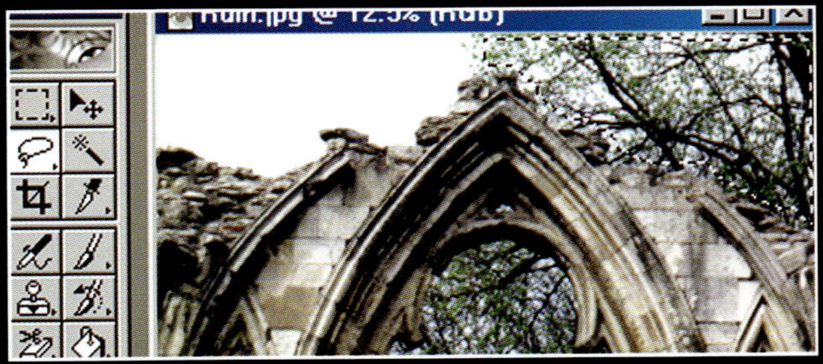

Fig 16.3

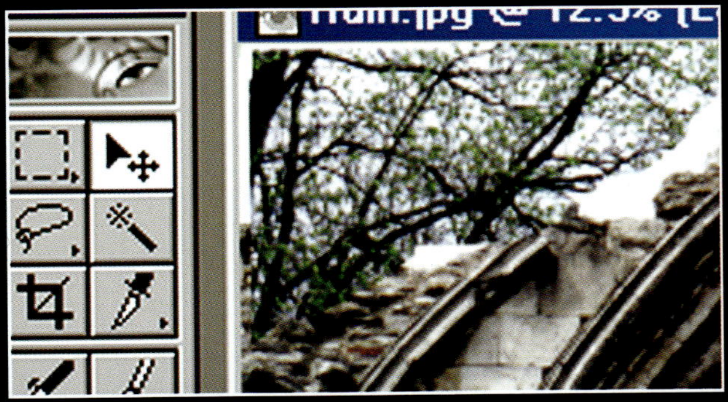

Fig 16.4

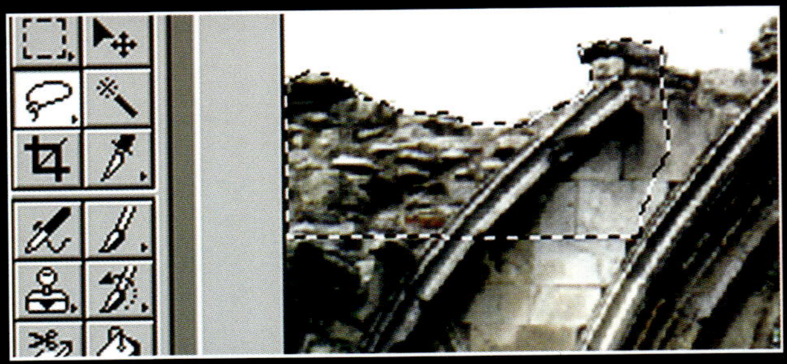

Fig 16.5

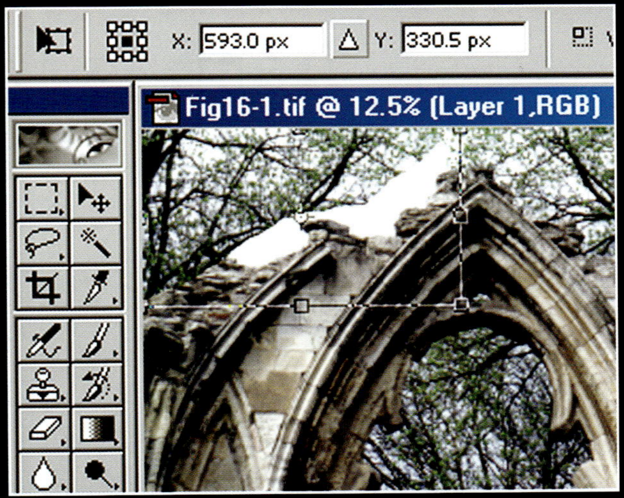

Fig 16.6

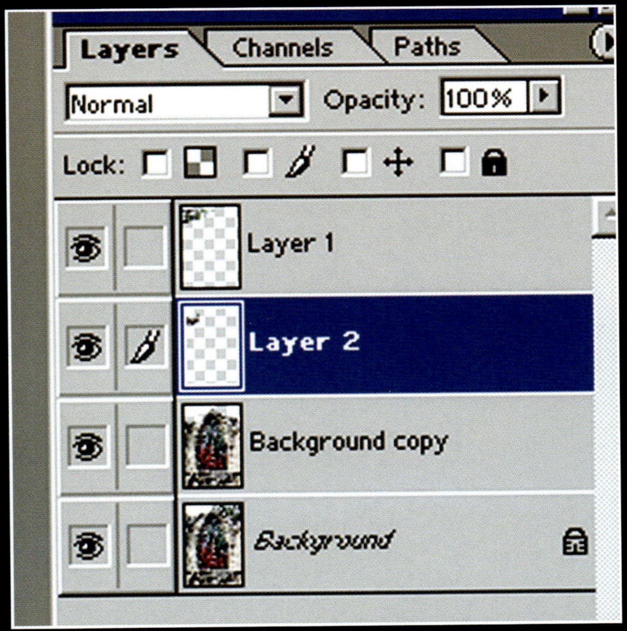

Fig 16.7

project 17

framing the subject

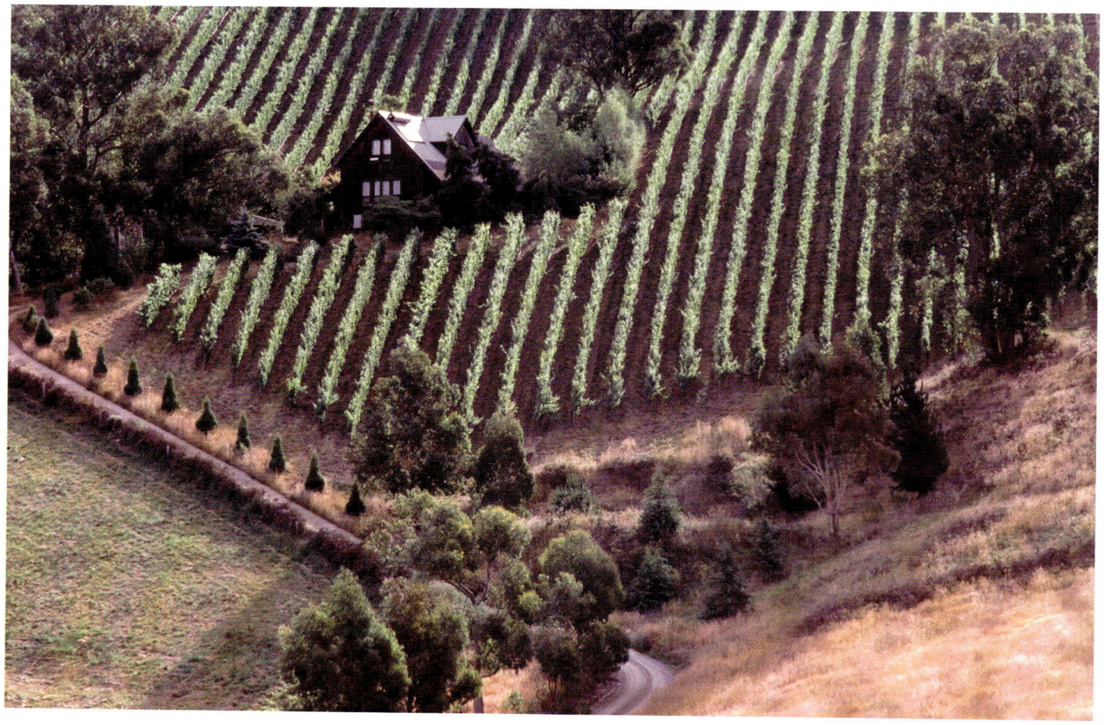

Fig 17.1 *House on the Hill* fails to focus on my intended subject.

CROP, ADJUST/HUE/SATURATION

At an early stage in my photography I joined a local camera club. On the evenings before the club's monthly competition night, another member and I would meet to discuss our proposed entries and, based on the constructive criticisms of the other, we would each try to strengthen our selections. One month's competition subject was 'Trees'. I was undecided on whether or not to enter a particular slide. It contained strong colour, dramatic lighting and a bold main subject. The problem lay to the left of the image, where, in the shadows, the insignificant detail of a winding country road could be seen. Did it distract? Would the competition judge notice?

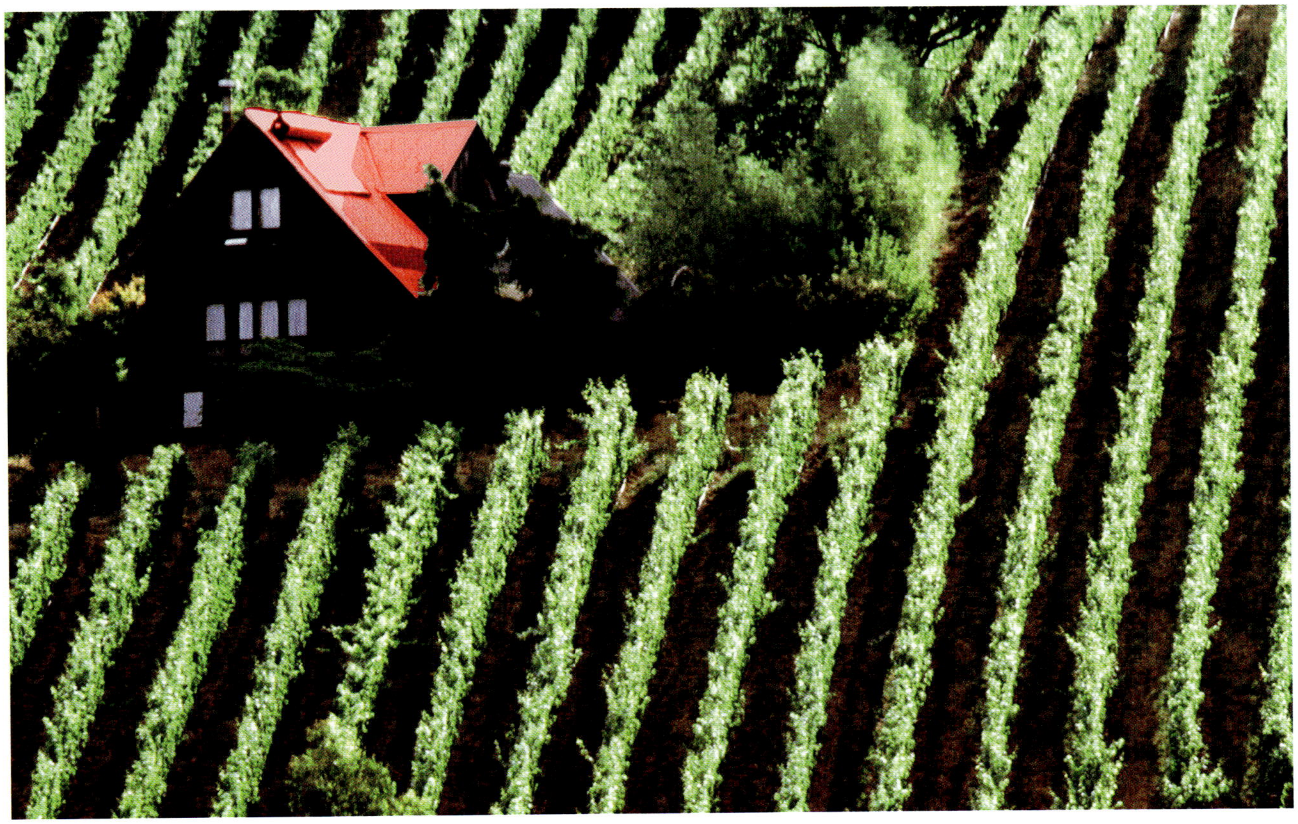

Fig 17.2 Details do make a difference. A digital-enhancement technique may only effect a minor detail in an image, but sufficiently so to make a major contribution towards perfecting the look.

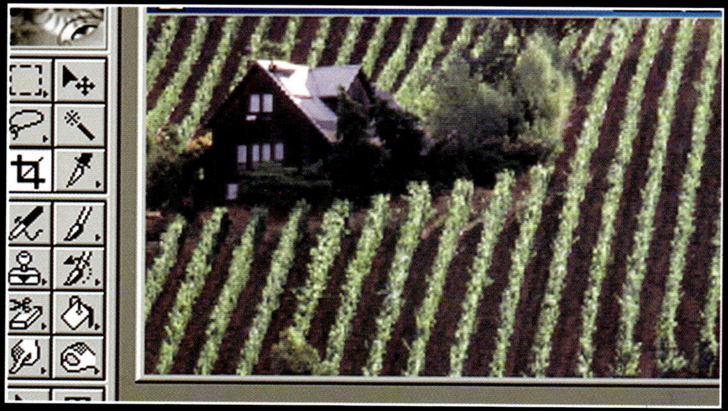

Fig 17.3

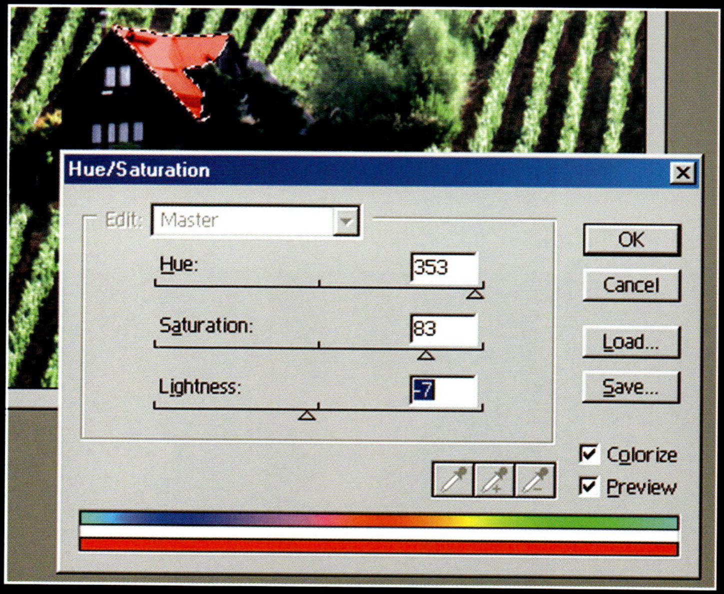

Fig 17.5

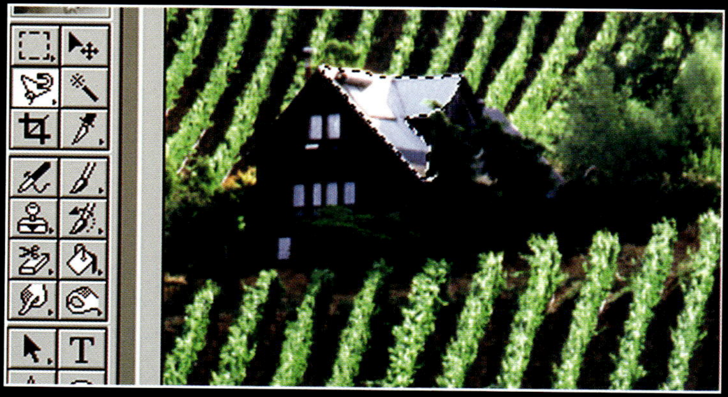

Fig 17.4

If it was shown at a camera club, I know that *House on the Hill* (fig. 17.1) would make a commenting judge's eyes light up as he gave the well-intended but predictable comment that I should have moved further to my left to take the shot. In this instance, however, if I had moved anywhere at all I would have fallen off my perch and got nothing but bruises. My cause would have been helped further if I could have used a longer lens, but no matter how much equipment we carry, situations always arise where we wish we had just one more piece.

When I first saw this house I imagined it on its picture-book hillside surrounded by neat, uninterrupted rows of fruit trees in idyllic isolation. I also saw 'salon photograph' written all over it. However, we cannot always create the photographs we wish – even in our own back garden where we have greater control than elsewhere – and the inclusion or omission of a particular detail can influence the final outcome of an image dramatically. As the photograph stands it does not focus on the scene that I wanted to convey, but it includes it. Therefore, it holds the potential to approximate the image I would like to have taken given the opportunity in the first place.

The projects in this book deal with photographs that are 95% perfect and need that little extra before the photographer is completely satisfied. The aim is not to change a photograph beyond recognition or to create something entirely new. In *House on the Hill*, however, there is a minor departure from the norm. Here, we pursue the 'idyllic' theme and give the roof a facelift, courtesy of a new coat of paint. Green is the colour that dominates this image and painting the roof red introduces its complementary colour. (We know that these two colours offer a perfect contrast, because of their opposite positioning on the colour wheel.)

This is one of those cases where we have to use the layer menu. First, we need to make a copy of the area we wish to retain from the scene. We activate the CROP tool (fig. 17.3) and make the precise selection of our choice (for an explanation of how to use this technique, see Project 4, page 28). At this stage, we can also use IMAGE/ADJUST/LEVELS to enhance the picture.

Before moving on, we make a copy of the background using LAYER/DUPLICATE LAYER. To make a selection of the part of the roof we would like to re-paint, we use either LASSO or MAGNETIC LASSO (fig. 17.4) with SELECT/FEATHER set to a value of 1. We activate IMAGE/ADJUST/HUE/SATURATION and click on COLORIZE (fig. 17.5), by moving the sliders about we try to produce the colour that contrasts most with the surrounding greenery. We could have used another option, such as the PAINT BUCKET tool, to change the colour of the roof. However, using ADJUST/HUE/SATURATION allows us to retain the roof's original details, as we can see in the enhanced image (fig. 17.2).

project 18

strengthening the composition

RECTANGULAR MARQUEE

To me, the search for the perfect landscape is also a search for perfect light. This can be a matter of luck, of being in the right place at the right time. However, this is only part of the story. Sometimes we may be lucky with our landscape photography,

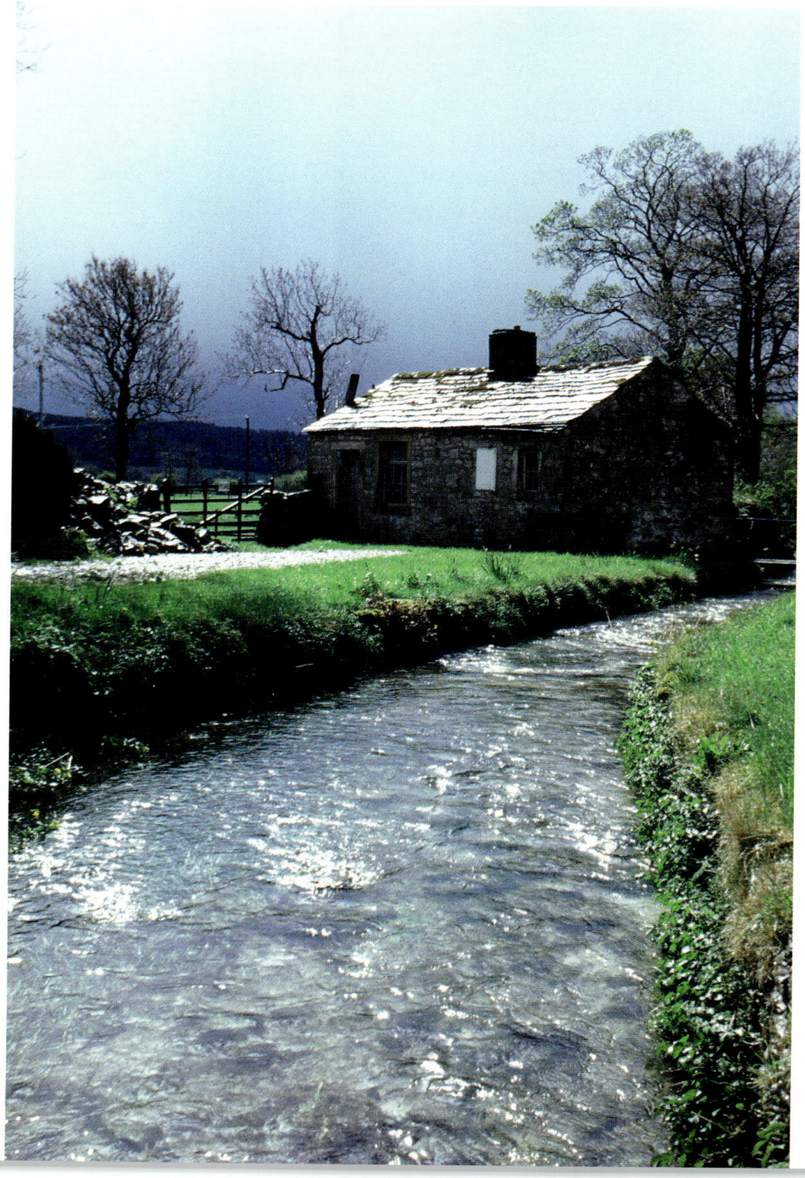

Fig 18.1 An English cottage, when caught in the right light, becomes a rich subject for both camera and computer.

Fig 18.2 Without light there would be no photographs, but good composition cannot be ignored.

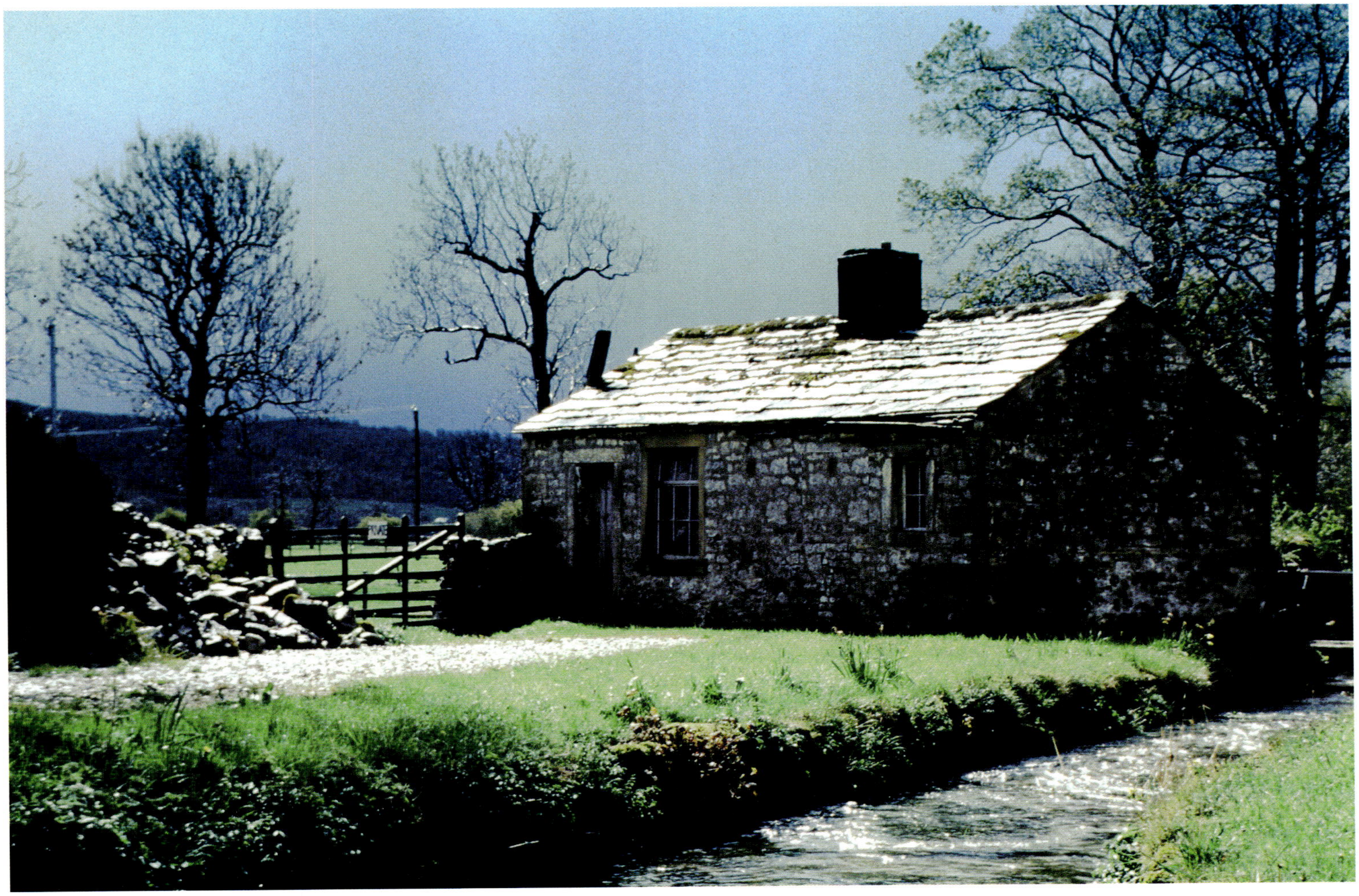

but I would like to think we make our own luck by practising the art of seeing and, in particular, seeing light. Also, although without light there would be no photographs, a good photograph requires good composition. If I wish to make a statement with words, how I arrange or compose them has much to do with the effectiveness of my statement. Similarly, how I arrange the elements within my photograph has a direct bearing upon how others will interpret it.

Different parts of the world present different problems regarding light. Years ago I spent ten months in Darwin, in the far north of Australia. I arrived in 'The Dry' and departed in 'The Wet'. During the dry season I did not see a drop of rain for eight months, and the only variation in the continually clear skies was the build up of smoke, caused by bush fires, towards the end of the season. The weather was predictable and, along with it, the light.

Contrast this with the UK, where it is possible to experience all four seasons in a single day. I happened to be hiking there when a sudden burst of sunlight quite literally stopped me in my tracks. The contrast was made all the greater by the dark, wintry weather of the previous hour. From the spot where I stood I looked around for something to photograph and snapped in the direction of *English Cottage* (fig. 18.1). The light, so fleeting, made everything around me appear magical, but I did not have the luxury of time to weigh up options, choose different lenses, or consider various viewpoints. If I was to capture the light before it disappeared I had no alternative but to shoot instantly and worry about the content and composition later.

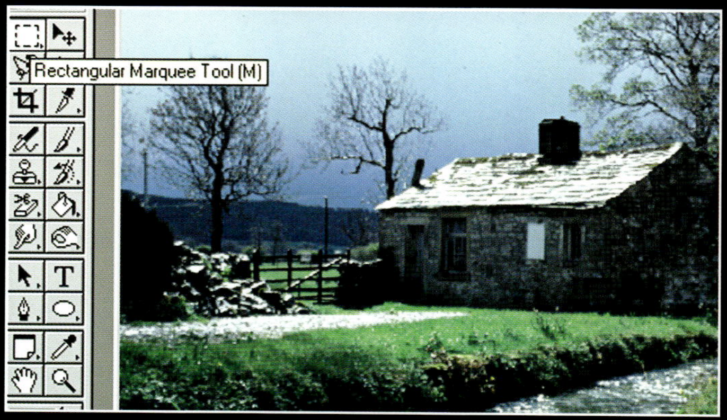

Fig 18.3

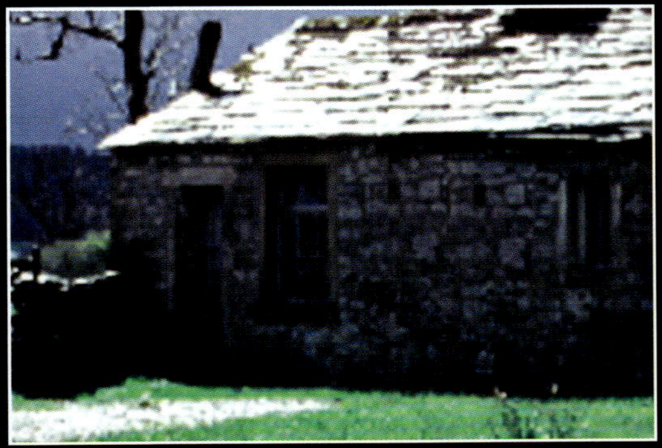

Fig 18.4

This is not a photograph I shot with the computer's salvaging act in mind. I do not see the computer as a safety net to catch all failing photographs. However, there are occasions when a photographer, aware of the computer's potential, can look forward to some future help.

We start by cropping the picture to find our preferred composition (for details on how to use the CROP tool, see Project 4, page 28). As soon as we have done this, we find that the white board to the left of the window on the front of the cottage has assumed an unwanted prominence and decide to remove it. Our image-editing software offers us a number of techniques to achieve this. For example, we could use the CLONE STAMP tool. However, because the board is a fairly regular shape, we have chosen a different method here.

We make a copy of the background layer, and use the RECTANGULAR MARQUEE tool (fig. 18.3) from the toolbar to make a selection of the wall next to the window. Next, we click EDIT/CUT followed by EDIT/PASTE, and then use the MOVE tool to place the pasted part over the white noticeboard (fig. 18.4).

With LAYER/FLATTEN IMAGE, we make the image one layer. To enhance the picture further, we go to IMAGE/ADJUST/CURVES (see Project 2, page 20) and experiment until we achieve the result that pleases us the most (fig. 18.2).

project 19

manipulating opacity

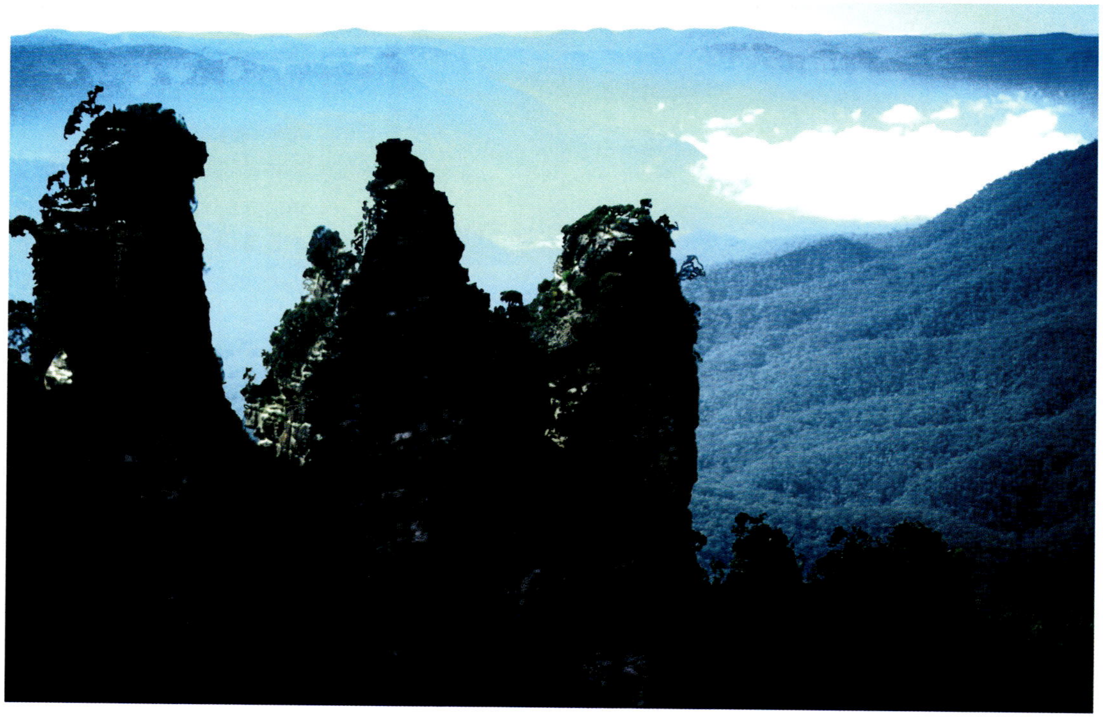

Fig 19.1 Reality never did match expectation in *Mist in the Valley*.

LAYERS, PAINTBRUSH

I once read that one of the main differences between a painter and a photographer is that a painter starts with nothing (an empty canvas) and adds to it, whereas a photographer starts with everything and must subtract. And yet, how easy it is to 'take' too much into a photograph.

Fig 19.2 With a little practice, PAINTBRUSH helps restore the situation.

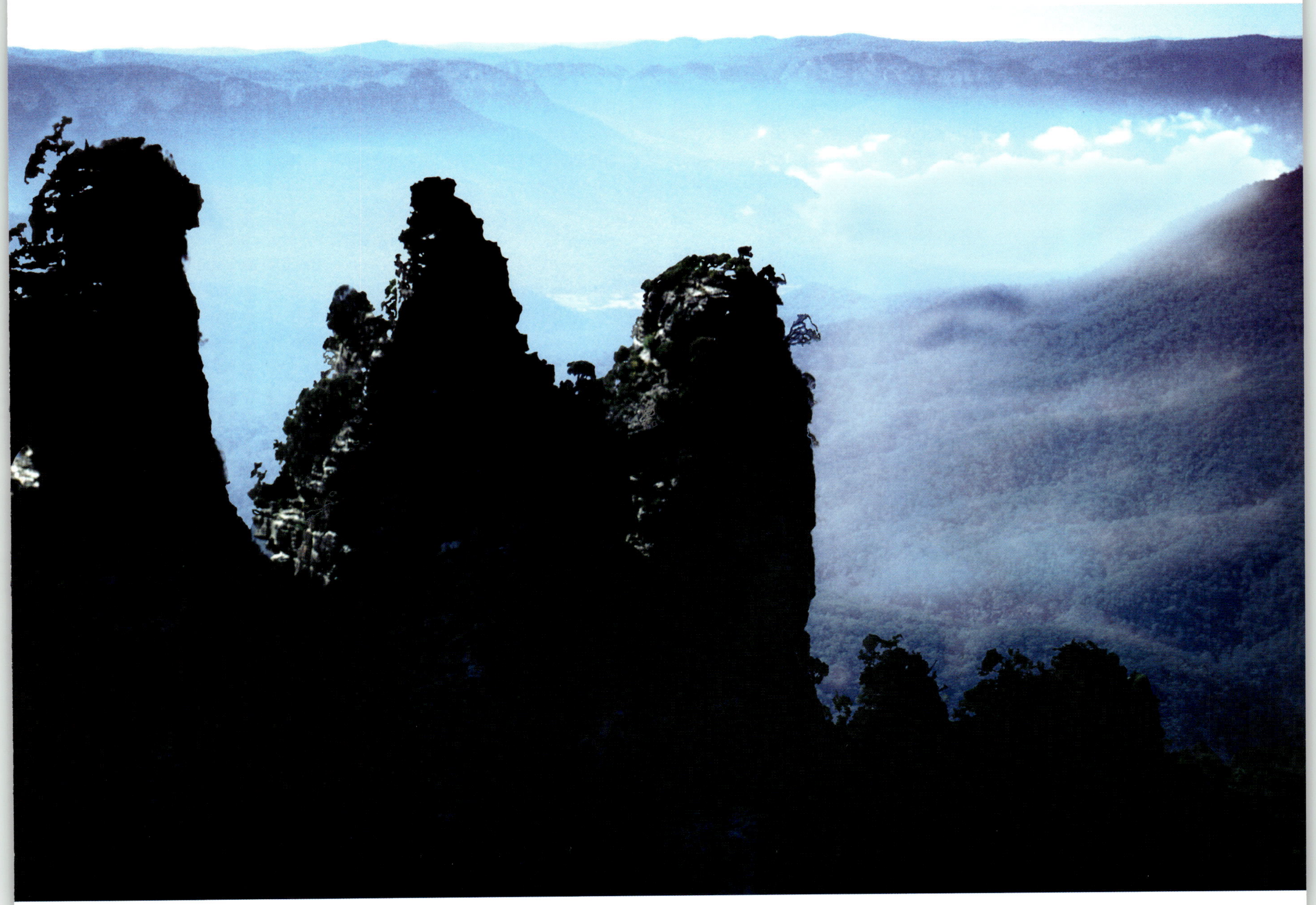

When I was a young boy at boarding school, I read Jerome K. Jerome's *Three Men in a Boat*. As well as being one of the funniest books I have ever read, it taught me one lesson that I have never forgotten: when going on a journey, don't take with you what you can do with, only take with you what you cannot do without. If we apply this principle to our photographs, and try to leave out everything that does not matter, our compositions can become much stronger as a result. I have applied it to practically every successful photograph I have ever made.

Under normal visiting conditions, I found the natural landscape setting of *Mist in the Valley* (fig. 19.1) to be both dramatic and disappointing. It was dramatic because of its unusual formation, and disappointing because it presented so many of the usual problems associated with photographing from a lookout point, as discussed earlier (see Project 6, page 36). Then I came across this view in a painting in which a most alluring mist filled the valley. Whether the mist was real or imagined, I was drawn to the photographic possibilities that it presented.

Many landscape photographs rely on timing; not just the timing of a change in shutter speed, but also the time required for a change in season. Thus, having ascertained the time of year when valley mists were most likely to occur, I made a number of visits to this location. Unfortunately, on all but one of those occasions, my photographs remained mist free. The exception is the photograph you see here, and even that falls far short of the memory I had of the mist in the painting.

For the solution, we can turn to the computer. However, if there is a danger in taking too much into a photograph, we must also remember that the danger is multiplied when we consider the limitless possibilities of enhancing an image on the computer.

If we were to choose the cut-and-paste technique, the resulting image would look very artificial. A better option is to use the PAINTBRUSH. This is so versatile that it will accomplish exactly what we want. First, we use LAYER/NEW/LAYER (fig. 19.3) to create a layer on top of our image on which to paint. If we do not like the result, we can simply remove the layer and start again. With the EYEDROPPER tool, we select an appropriate colour from the misty patch (fig. 19.4). Now we have to decide on a brush.

When we click on the PAINTBRUSH, we see a brush menu (fig. 19.5) at the top of our screen in the top bar. The options available include the size and type of brush, and also the MODE (which allows us to choose a brush with sharp or smooth edges) and the OPACITY (which alters the thickness of the paint applied). We begin with a larger brush that has very smooth edges, which we use to paint roughly where we want the mist to appear. To complete the task, we need to work on the edges of the misty area to give them a natural, misty appearance. This can be achieved with a smaller brush that also has smooth edges, but using reduced OPACITY to give a more translucent coat of paint (fig. 19.2).

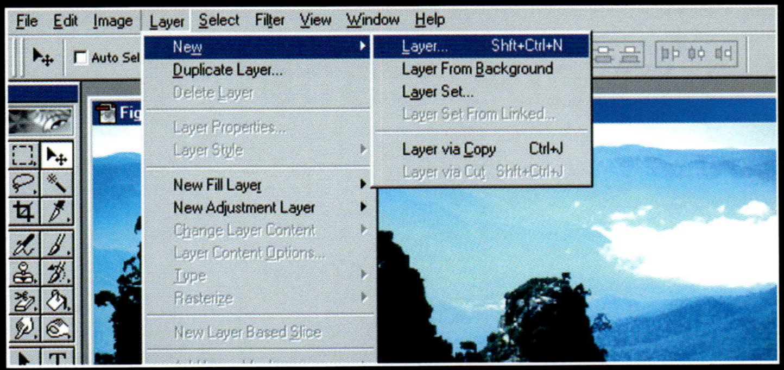

Fig 19.3

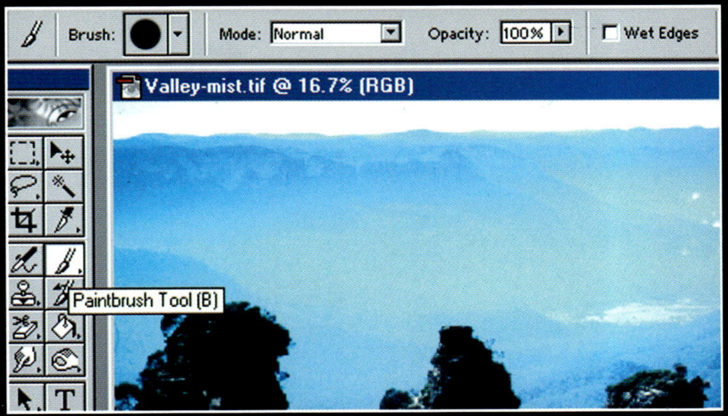

Fig 19.5

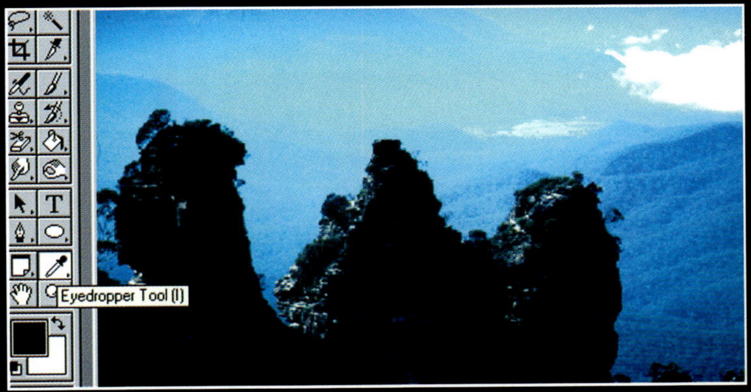

Fig 19.4

project 20

rearranging compositional elements

BACKGROUND ERASER, PASTE

I like to think of the search for the perfect landscape as a journey towards an ideal, something to aim for in our landscapes, without which we would be poorer as both photographers and individuals. Conversely, with it, our

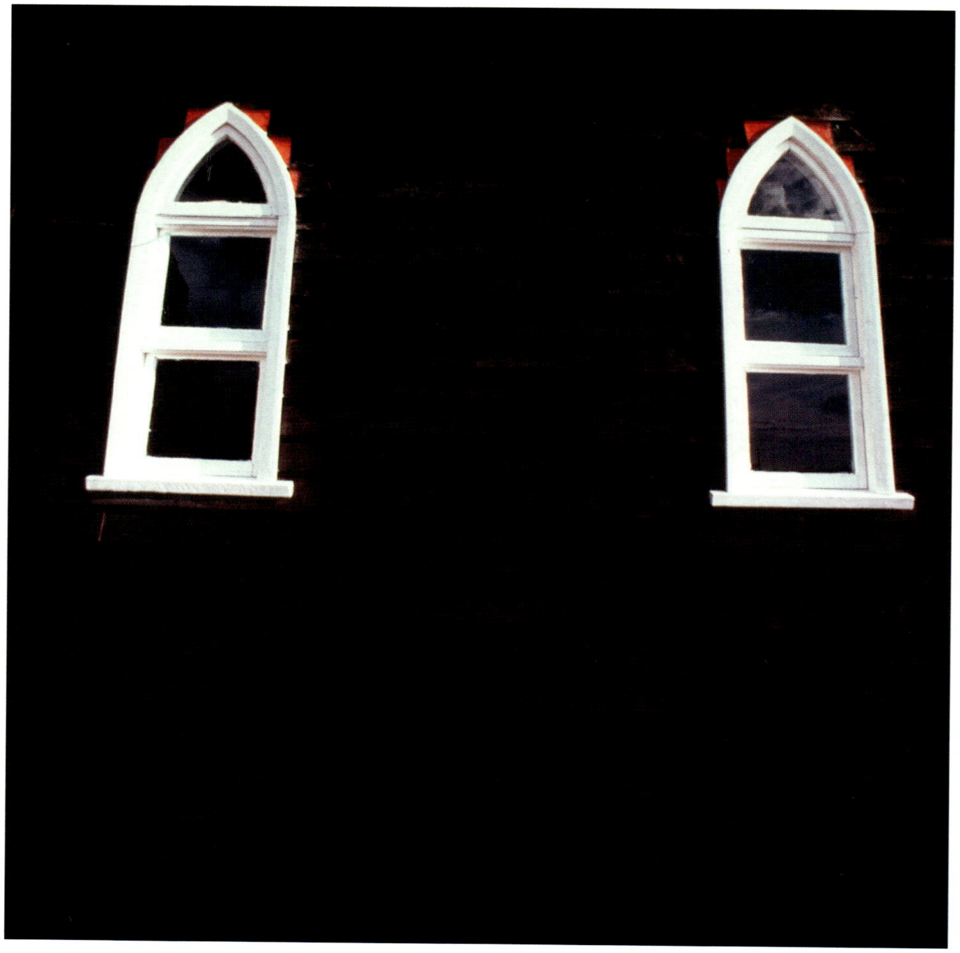

Fig 20.1 Two subjects, separated in reality by an uncompromising fence, were photographed separately with the computer in mind.

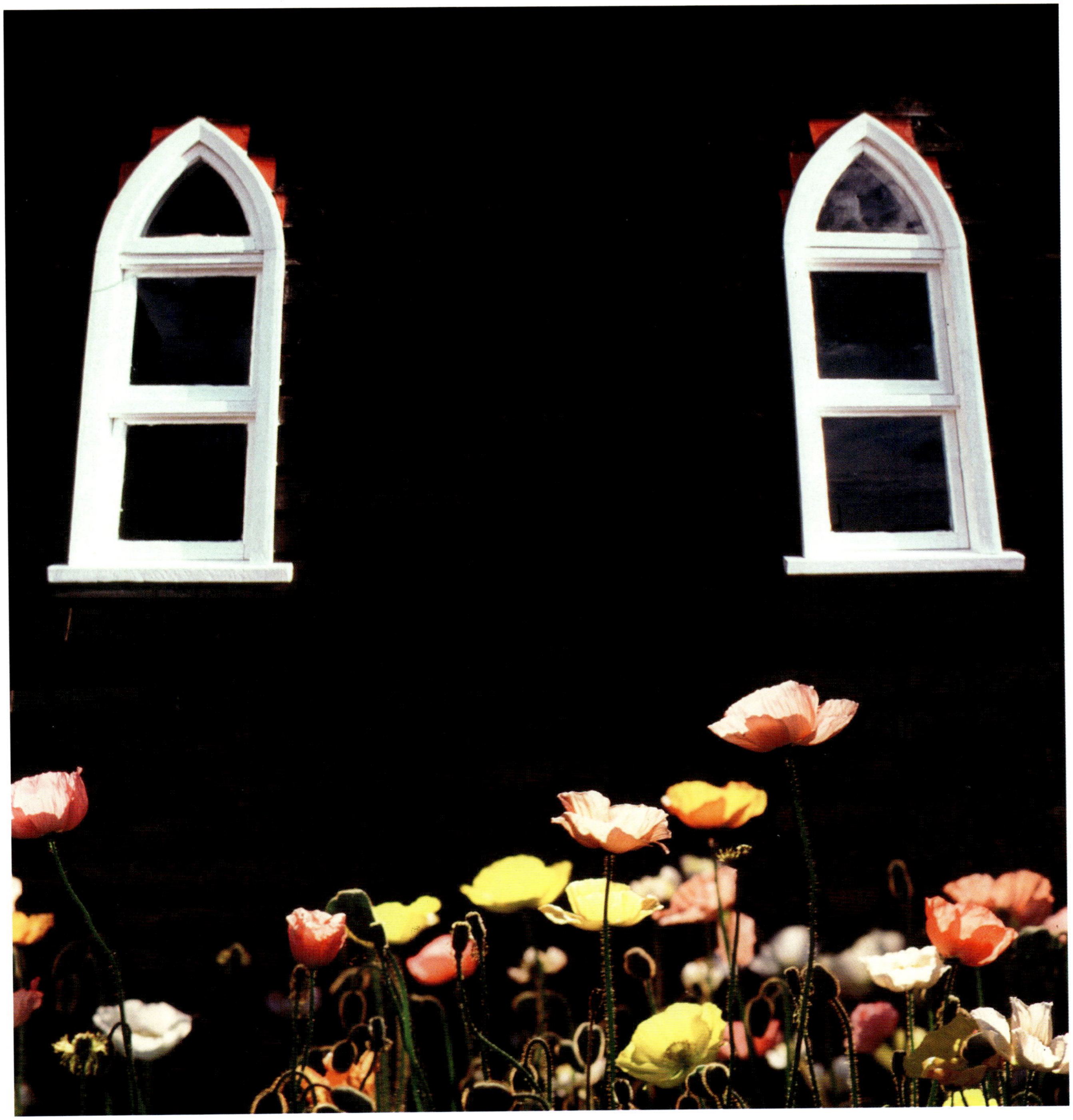

Fig 20.2 The image is completed when the ERASER and PASTE techniques are applied.

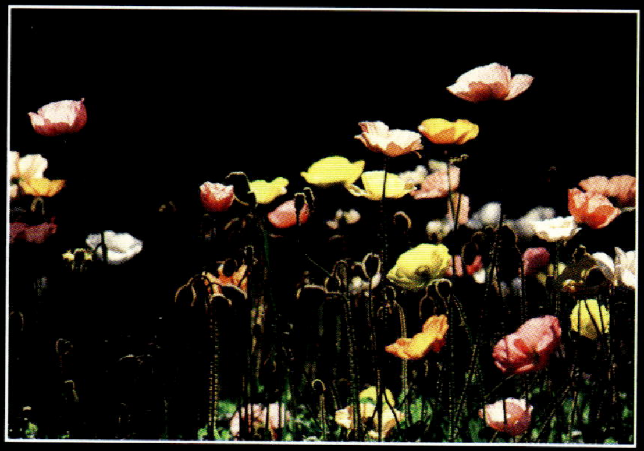
Fig 20.3

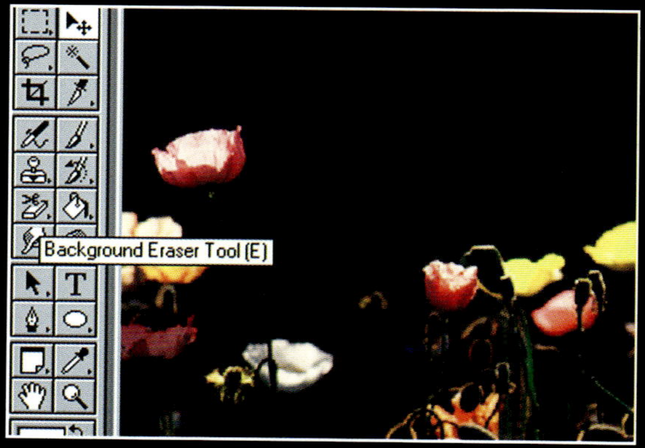

Fig 20.4

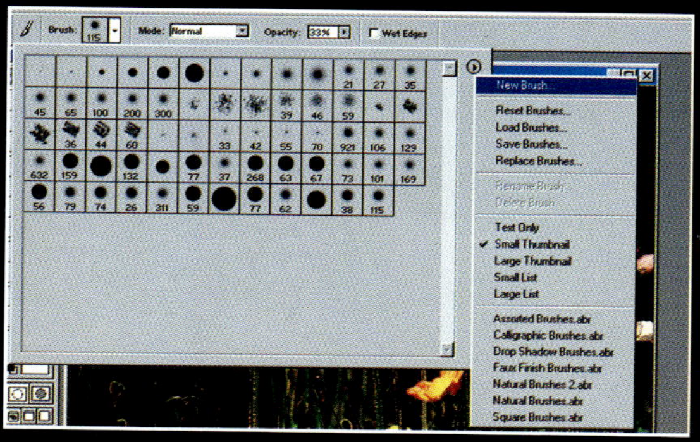

Fig 20.5

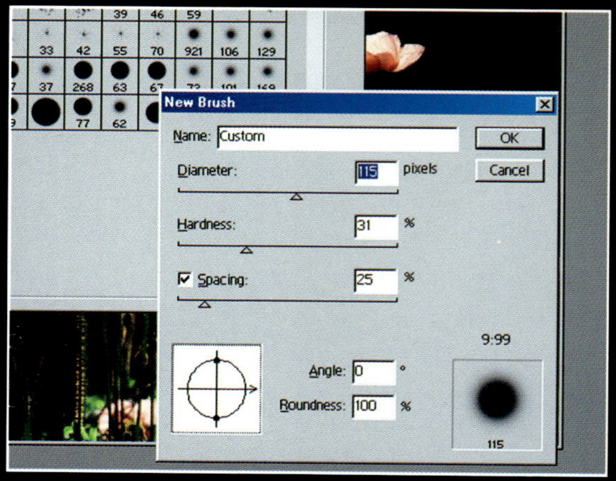

Fig 20.6

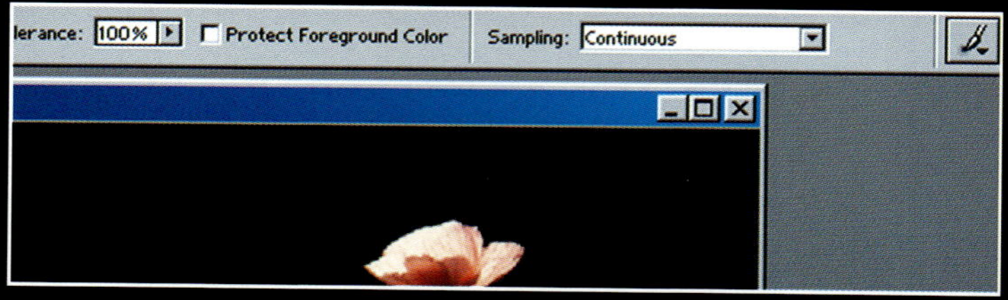

Fig 20.7

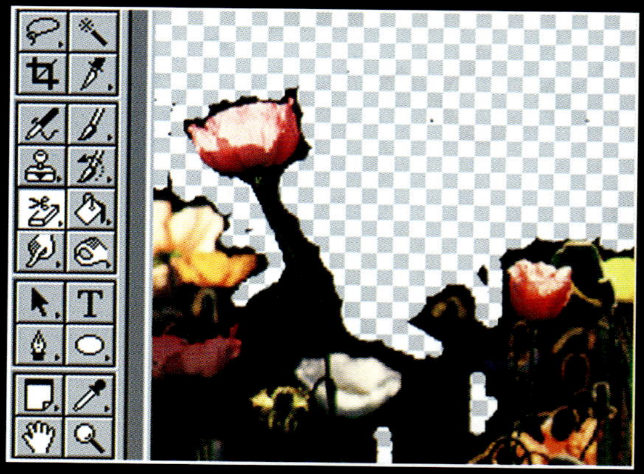
Fig 20.8

landscape photographs will reach new heights as we extend ourselves. In the past, we may have struggled for self-expression in our photographs due to lack of technique, limited choice of equipment, timing or the weather. Today, the computer, through simple enhancing techniques, can help solve many of these problems.

Unusually for the photographs in this book, *Chapel with Flowers* (fig 20.1) was taken specifically with the possibilities of digital enhancement in mind. To realize why, it is necessary to understand the situation as I encountered it. The scene that I found, and wanted to capture, included two distinct elements: the flowers and the chapel. The flowers represented much of the colour and excitement of spring, for which the chapel wall was a perfect foil and most suitable background.

Unfortunately, I also found an unavoidable and out-of-character fence erected between the two. By photographing the required elements separately, then using the computer to combine them, I could complete the scene in the way that I would have photographed it had it been possible to do so in the first place.

Our first step could have been to address the perspective problem (see Project 15, page 74) of the chapel windows. Leaving them as they are accentuates the thrust of the flowers towards the viewer and encourages that feeling of 'being there' in the final image.

To create a new foreground for our original photograph, we load the image of the flowers (fig 20.3). We want to remove most of its background in order to retain as much of the chapel's plank structure as possible. We activate the BACKGROUND ERASER tool (fig. 20.4) from the toolbar to do this.

We click on the little black triangle beside the brush selector on the options bar. A window appears, which also has a small black triangle on the right-hand side. We click on this, and then choose NEW BRUSH (fig. 20.5). We use the slider to define the DIAMETER and set the HARDNESS to 100% (fig. 20.6). A large brush can be used to remove most of the easily accessable areas of the background and a small one for the trickier bits.

The BACKGROUND ERASER tool also has a SAMPLING function, which is located on the right-hand side of the options bar (fig. 20.7). Selecting the ONCE option allows us to remove all the pixels of a single colour, whereas CONTINUOUS, as its name suggests, samples colours continuously. Since our background is mainly one colour, we select ONCE and then erase it until we are left with just the flowers (fig. 20.8).

By using the MOVE tool we can drag the flowers into the window containing our chapel image. We use EDIT/TRANSFORM/SCALE (see Project 16, page 78) to resize the flowers and make them fit into the foreground. Finally, LAYER/FLATTEN IMAGE reduces our completed image (fig 20.2) to a single layer.

project
21

creating a panoramic shot

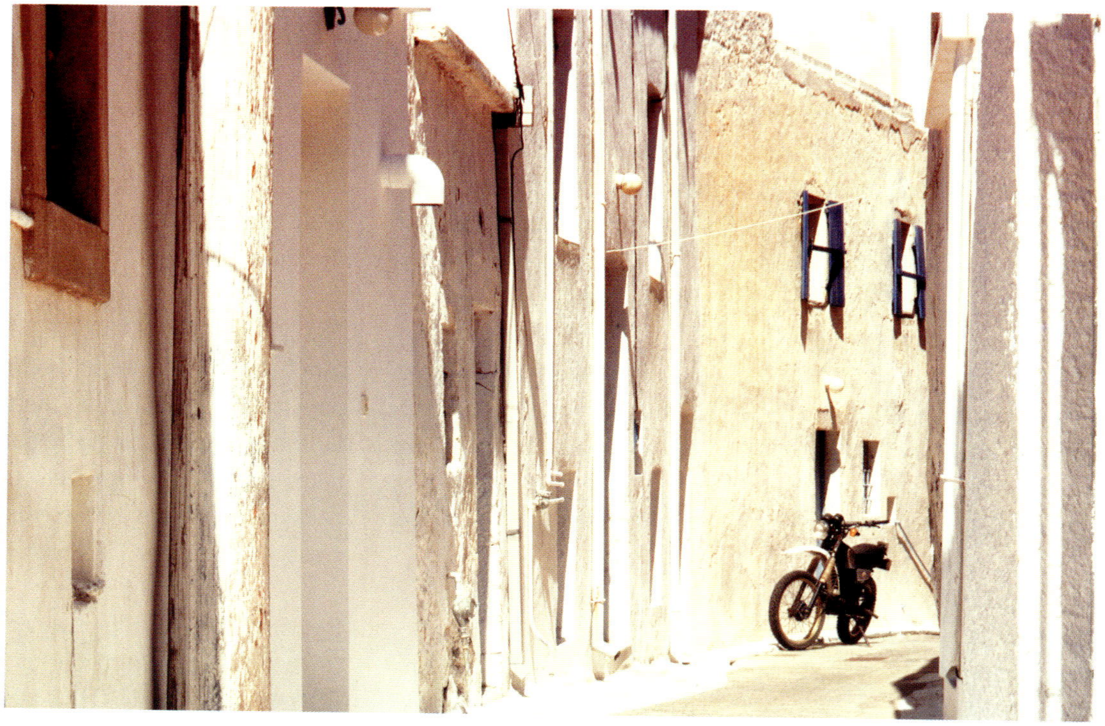

Fig 21.1 A narrow back street provides an improbable subject for a wider view.

CANVAS SIZE, TRANSFORM/SCALE

When we think of 'the wider view' in the context of landscape photography, wide-open spaces, panoramic cameras and a sense of freedom possibly come to mind. If pushed for details, we might start to think of specific items of equipment and particular views, perhaps from the top of a tall building or looking down into a valley. But 'the wider view' has other implications for a landscape photographer. What about how you lived last month and what you had for today's breakfast?

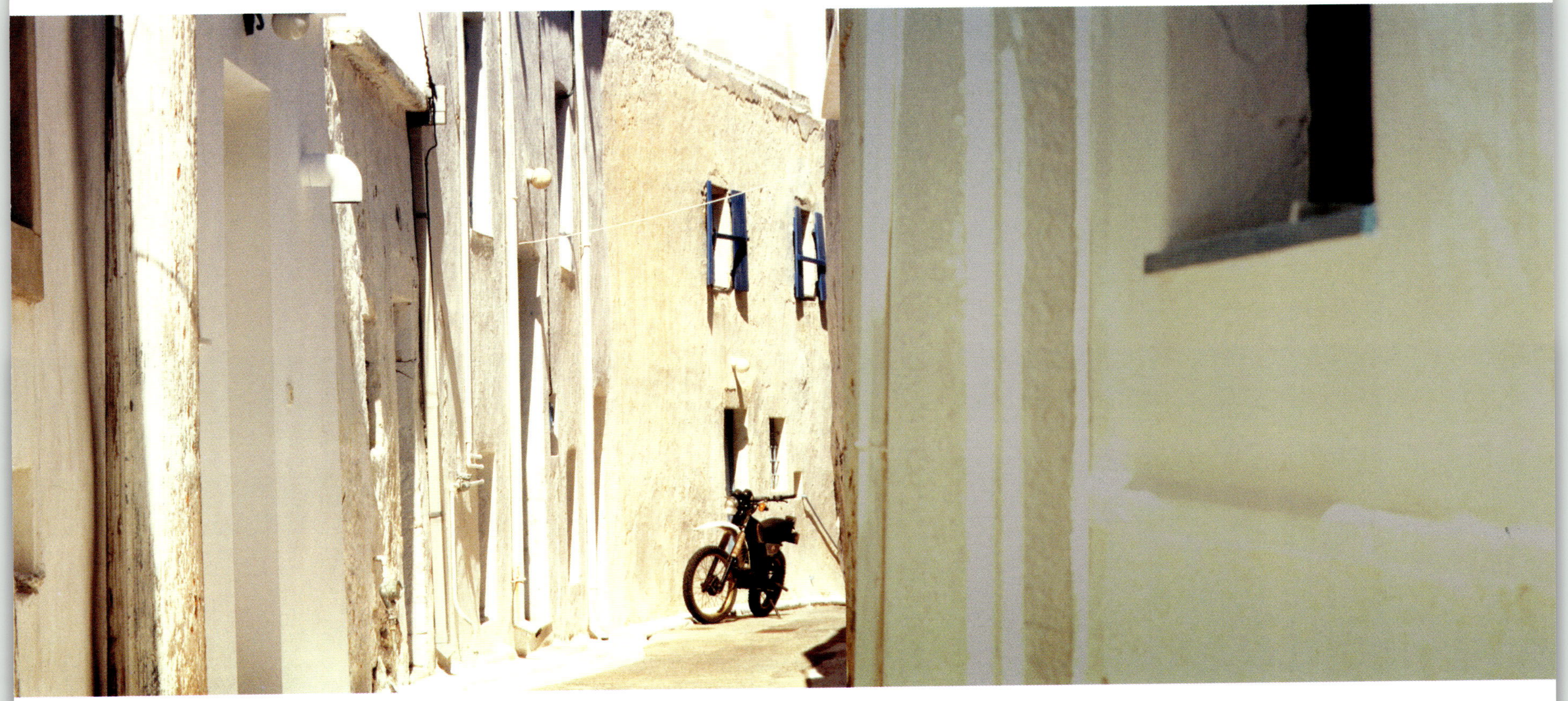

Fig 21.2 A motorbike creates a focal point and reduces the novelty value common to many panorama pictures, as the computer effortlessly widens the view.

You may be wondering what on earth what you did last month has got to do with it. If your last month was spent sitting at an office desk, the chances are that the previous 12 months were spent in much the same way. Imagine that you are about to go on holiday in search of landscapes of wide-open spaces; the chances are that you will spend much of your time walking. Even if you plan to take panoramic photographs from the rooftops of tall buildings and the last part of your journey before each shoot is in an elevator, the earlier part will probably be on foot. I remember spending a week in New York doing just that, and it took me three months to get fit for the experience.

Likewise, it is important to make the most of your breakfast. A cup of coffee won't be sufficient for a day of landscape photography, especially if your plan is to start early and finish late to make the most of the light, or if you have to carry camera bags and tripods over unfamiliar terrain.

Something else to consider is that panoramic photography is not simply about mountain ranges and cityscape horizons. Photographed on the island of Kythera, *Greek Island Backstreet* (fig. 21.1) is all that the title suggests: narrow, non-threatening, photogenic, and with the wrap-around feel ideal for a wider format. Many panoramic pictures survive on novelty value and often lack a focal point. Here, the motorbike provides the focal point in both the original photograph and the enhanced image.

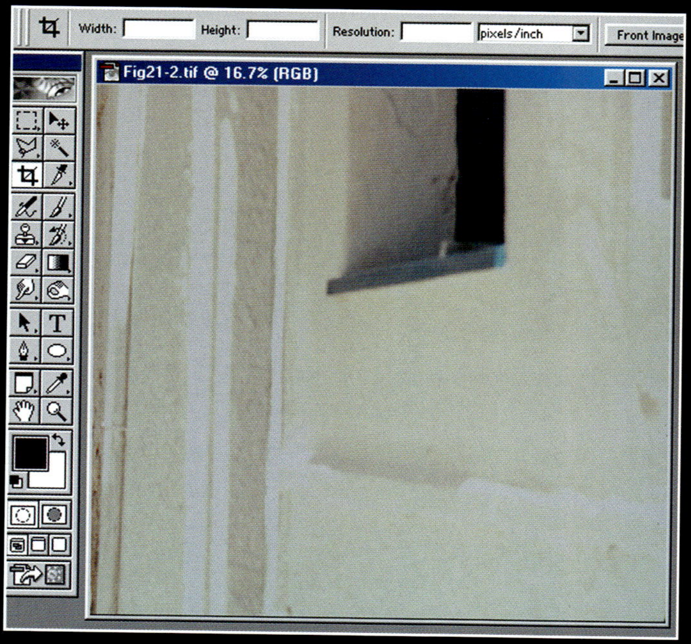

Fig 21.3

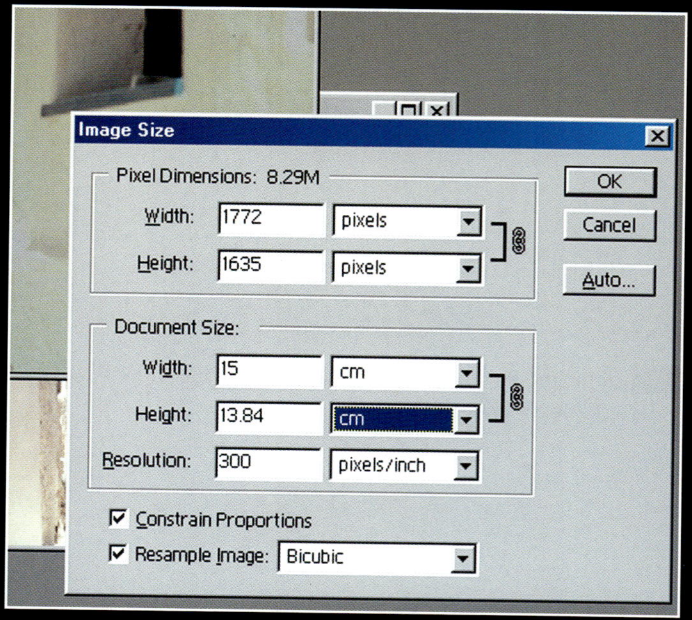

Fig 21.4

We load our original picture, followed immediately by a second one (fig 21.3), which is going to be added to the right-hand side of the first. Clicking on IMAGE/IMAGE SIZE allows us to check its measurements (fig. 21.4). It is the width we need to take into account, because that is the measurement we must add to the canvas size of the first image. This will enable us to attach our second picture to the first.

We activate the first loaded picture and go to IMAGE/CANVAS SIZE. On the screen appears a window in which we can add to the width, in this case 15cm (fig. 21.5). We click on the square that is on the left of the middle line, and notice that all the arrows now point to the right to show that this where the area will be added (fig. 21.6). To add this to the image, we click OK.

Our first picture reappears on the screen, but with an empty area to its right. We activate the second picture, select the MOVE tool, then click on the picture and drag it across to this empty area. It may overlap a little, but we can use EDIT/TRANSFORM/SCALE to make it fit (holding down the SHIFT key while making the changes to keep the same proportions). The height is not, generally, so important. Often, one picture (i.e. the shortest) will dictate this, so we use the CROP tool to cut the other picture to this height.

The end result (fig. 21.2) shows the wider view and illustrates the need to think on a broader plane if the full joy of landscape photography is to be realized.

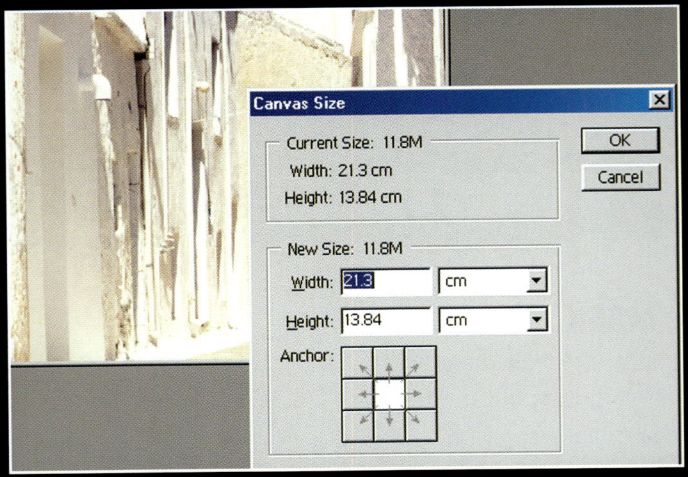

Fig 21.5

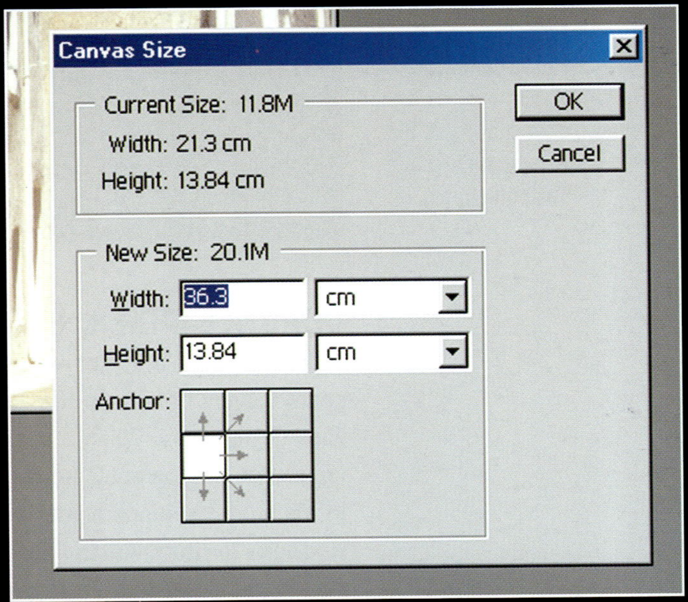

Fig 21.6

project 22

converting to monochrome

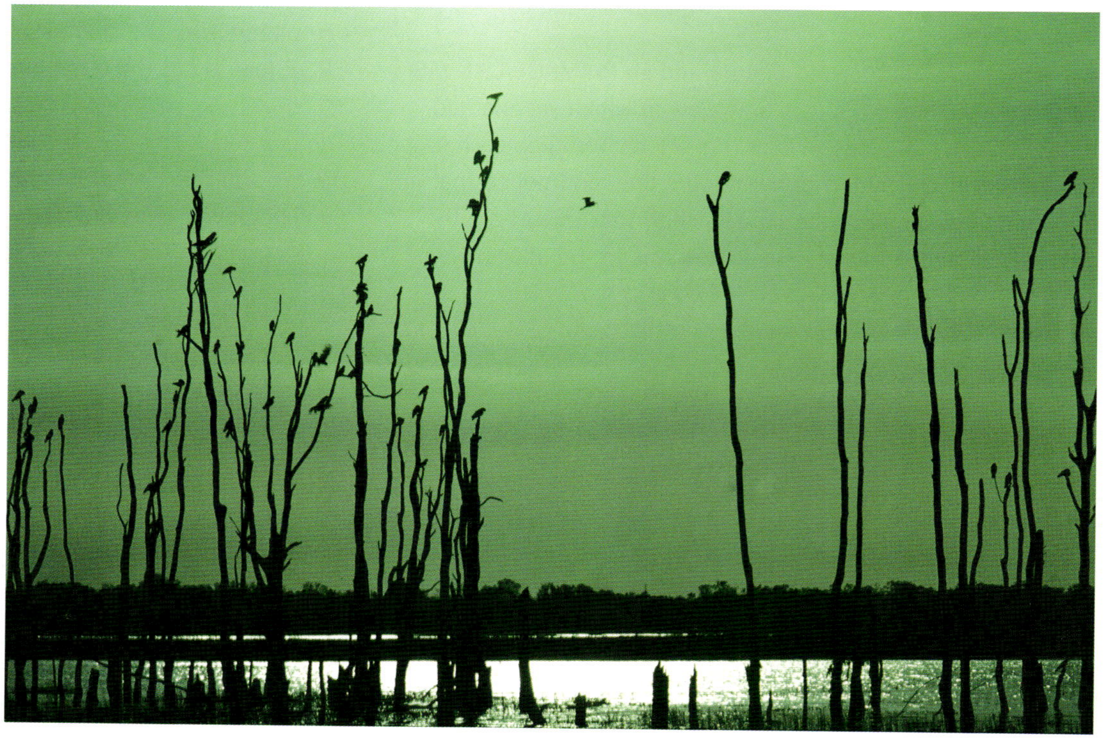

Fig 22.1 Colour can become too garish in a photograph, as the green cast of *Fogg Dam* illustrates.

CHANNEL MIXER, UNSHARP MASK

I like a surprise and, thanks to photography, I receive many. Of course, every processed film can present surprises, but it often goes beyond this. When a pilot I met heard that I enjoyed landscape photography, he invited me to take a flight with him in his light aeroplane across the 'Top End' in the north of the Northern Territory, Australia. I had spent most of my years working at street level in British cities like Leeds, Edinburgh and London, and this was a surprise opportunity to attempt a very different type of photography.

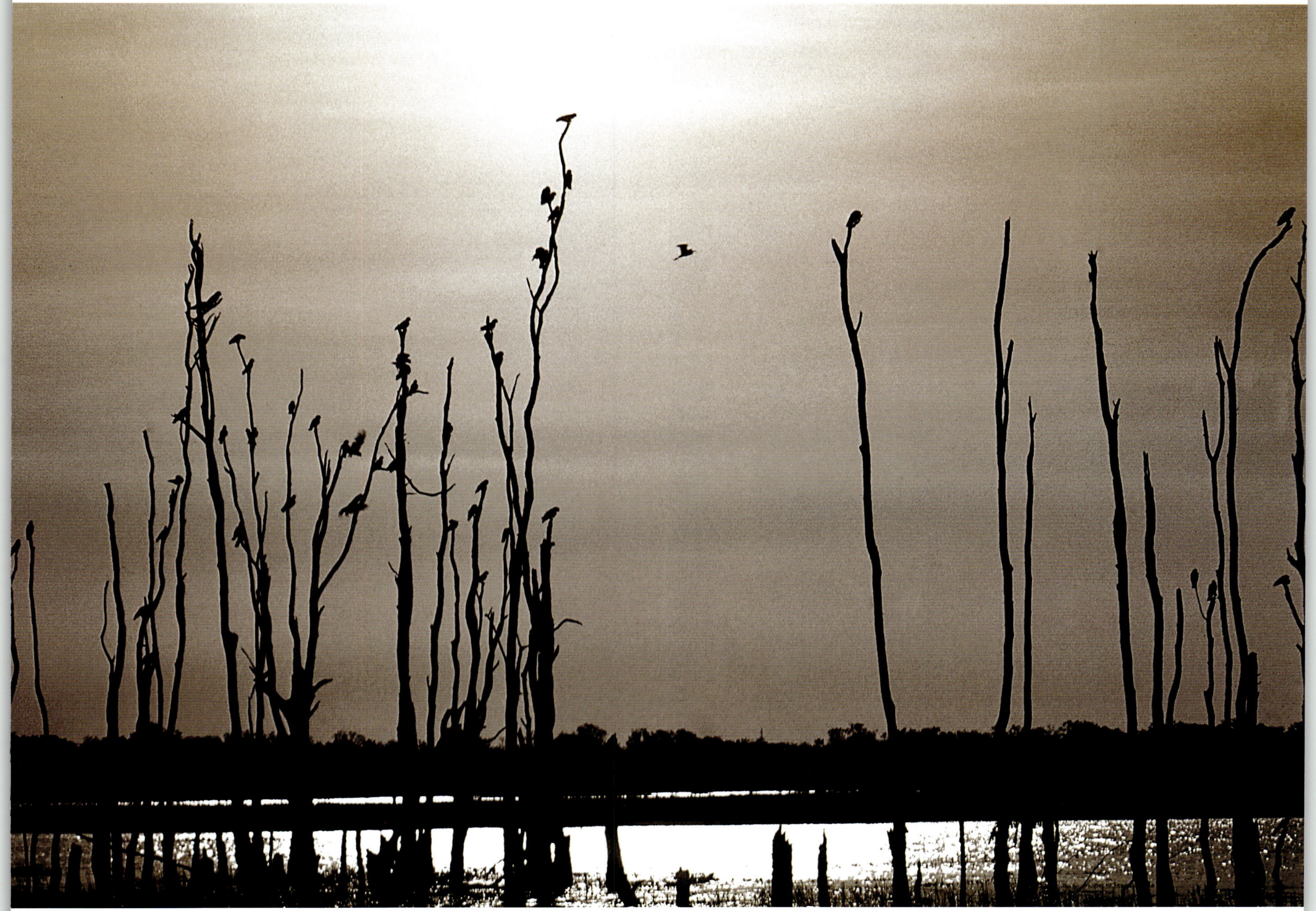

Fig 22.2 A GREYSCALE rendition gets rid of the unpleasant green colour cast.

Often flying no more than a few hundred metres above the inhospitable terrain, the bush took on a whole new meaning. If we had crashed I believe we would never have been found in such a dense, vast and remote wilderness.

The problem was, while thoroughly enjoying the journey, I was not taking any worthwhile photographs. However, a few weeks later I received another surprise when invited to travel over some of the same terrain in a four-wheel-drive vehicle. This allowed me to discover that what had seemed like monotonous and continuous bush from the air, held a fascinating variety of fauna and flora at ground level.

Egrets and jabiru, comical lizards and water buffaloes, colourful wild flowers and restful billabongs presented a feast of subjects for my camera. Fogg Dam, when photographed at sunset, gave some excellent results. But this shot (fig. 22.1), taken some hours earlier, revealed an unpleasant green cast. To remove this, we can use the computer to convert the image to black and white. At the same time, we can erase some of the atmospheric haze by using a sharpening option.

We load the photograph on to our screen and go to IMAGE/ADJUST/CHANNEL MIXER. A screen appears (fig. 22.3) and we click on the MONOCHROME option in the bottom left-hand corner. This turns our picture from colour to black and white. If we had selected IMAGE/MODE/GREYSCALE to do this, the computer would have chosen a predetermined combination of RGB values for us. By selecting CHANNEL MIXER, we are able to use the RED, GREEN and BLUE sliders to produce our desired shade of black and white, and the correct contrast. To add the finishing touches, we sharpen the picture. For this we go to FILTERS/SHARPEN/UNSHARP MASK (fig. 22.4). We

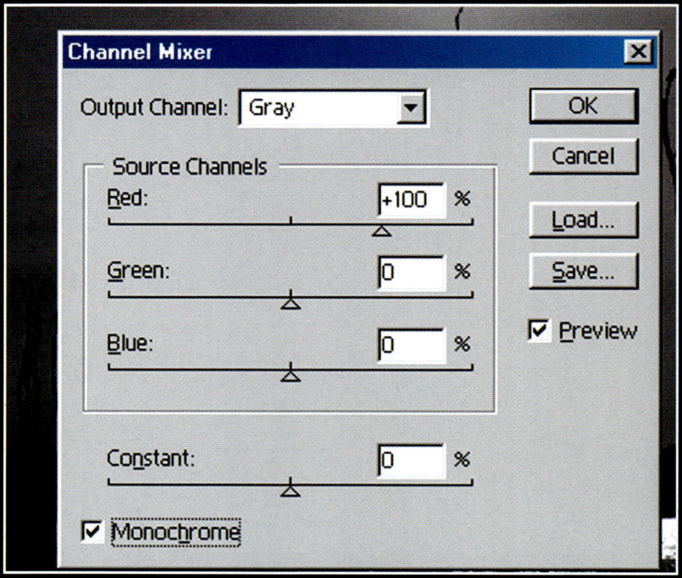

Fig 22.3

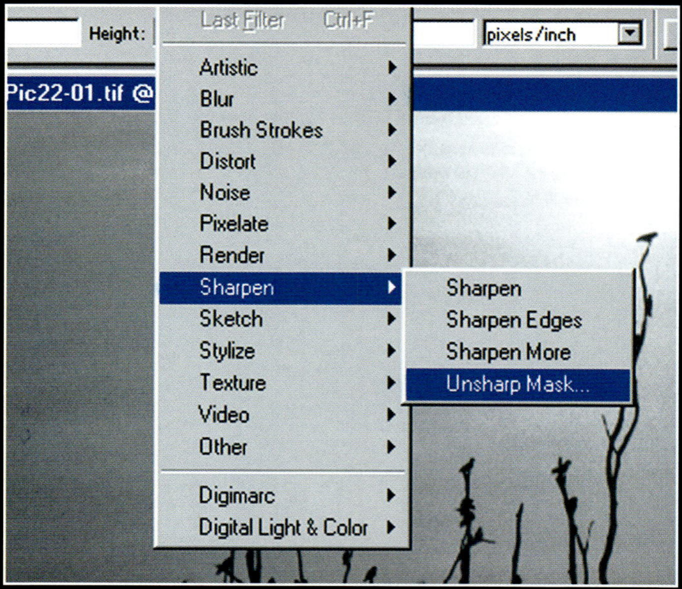

Fig 22.4

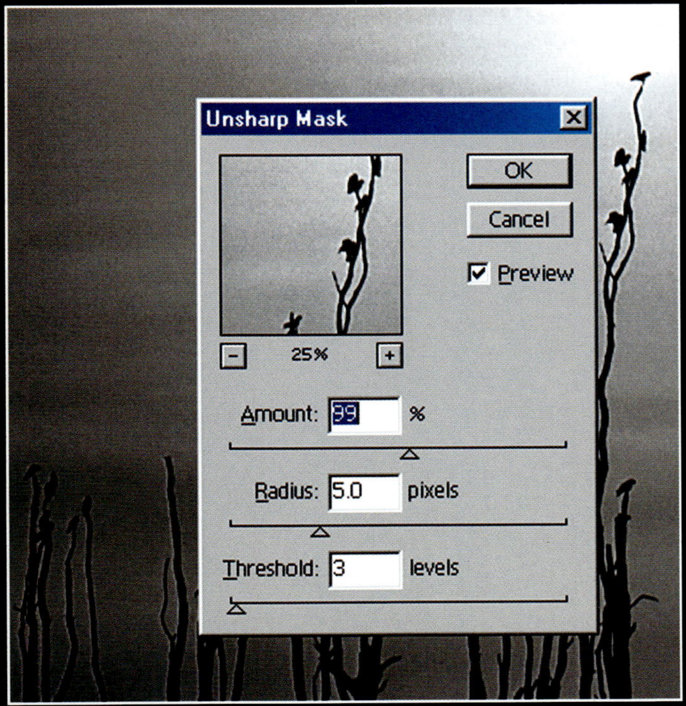

Fig 22.5

never resize a sharpened picture, so this technique is always used at the final stage of an operation.

The screen that appears contains three sliders (fig. 22.5). The values on the THRESHOLD slider go from 0 to 255. We use it to make sure that tones within certain values will not be changed. A threshold of 4, for example, will ignore all tones within a level value of 4 of each other. We keep the THRESHOLD slider close to the left edge (i.e. set at a low value), and then adjust the AMOUNT and RADIUS sliders. The AMOUNT slider changes the amount our image is sharpened, while the RADIUS slider influences the number of pixels surrounding the 'edge pixels' (i.e. the pixels that define the edges in our image) that are affected. If we raise the latter too high we see a dark or light halo appear along the edges in the image.

When sharpening an image it is best to ensure that both the percentage (i.e. the magnification of our view) of the picture we want to sharpen, and that of the UNSHARP screen, are more or less the same. For example, if one is set at 16.7%, make sure that the other is similar.

The computer offers a number of options for correcting problems with colours, and the difference made by converting an image to monochrome is easy to see (fig. 22.2).

project
23

sepia toning

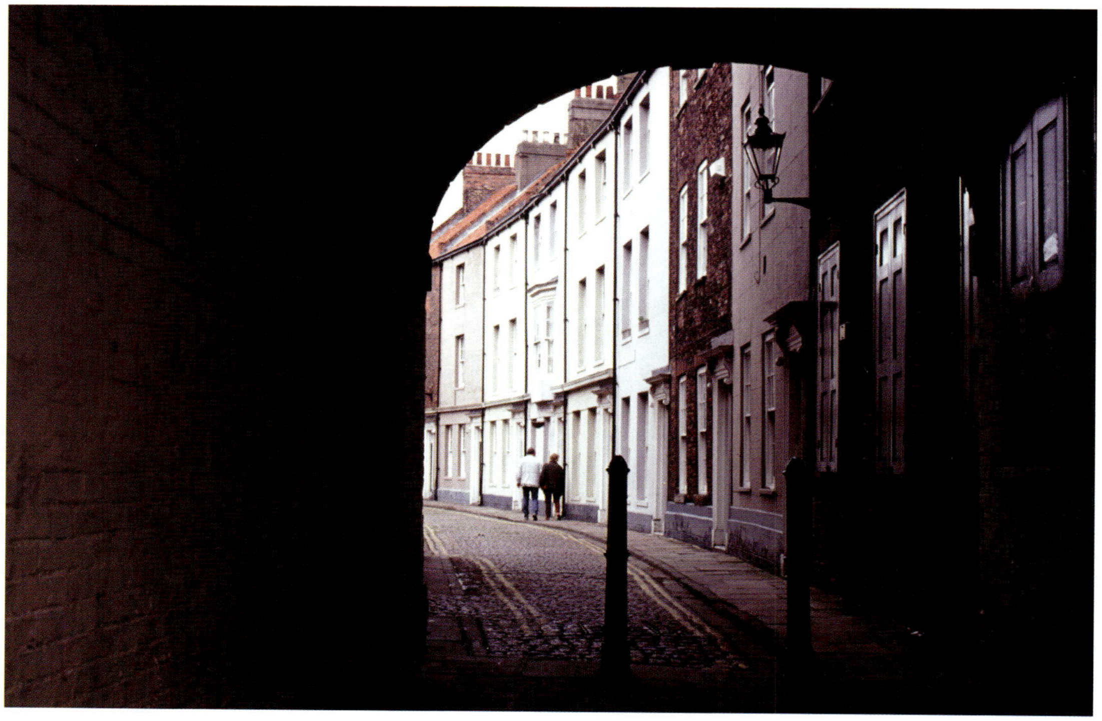

Fig 23.1 The sense of history this photograph evokes in me could be conveyed more forcefully.

CHANNEL MIXER, MONOCHROME

Little can match the joy of experiencing the swings and roundabouts of life, and having the opportunity to photograph them. Added to this is the pleasure of sharing such special moments with family and friends through photographs, and further sharing one's experiences with a wider audience through exhibitions, magazine portfolios and the pages of a book. Being paid for all of this becomes a bonus.

Fig 23.2 Sepia adds the touch of nostalgia I was looking for.

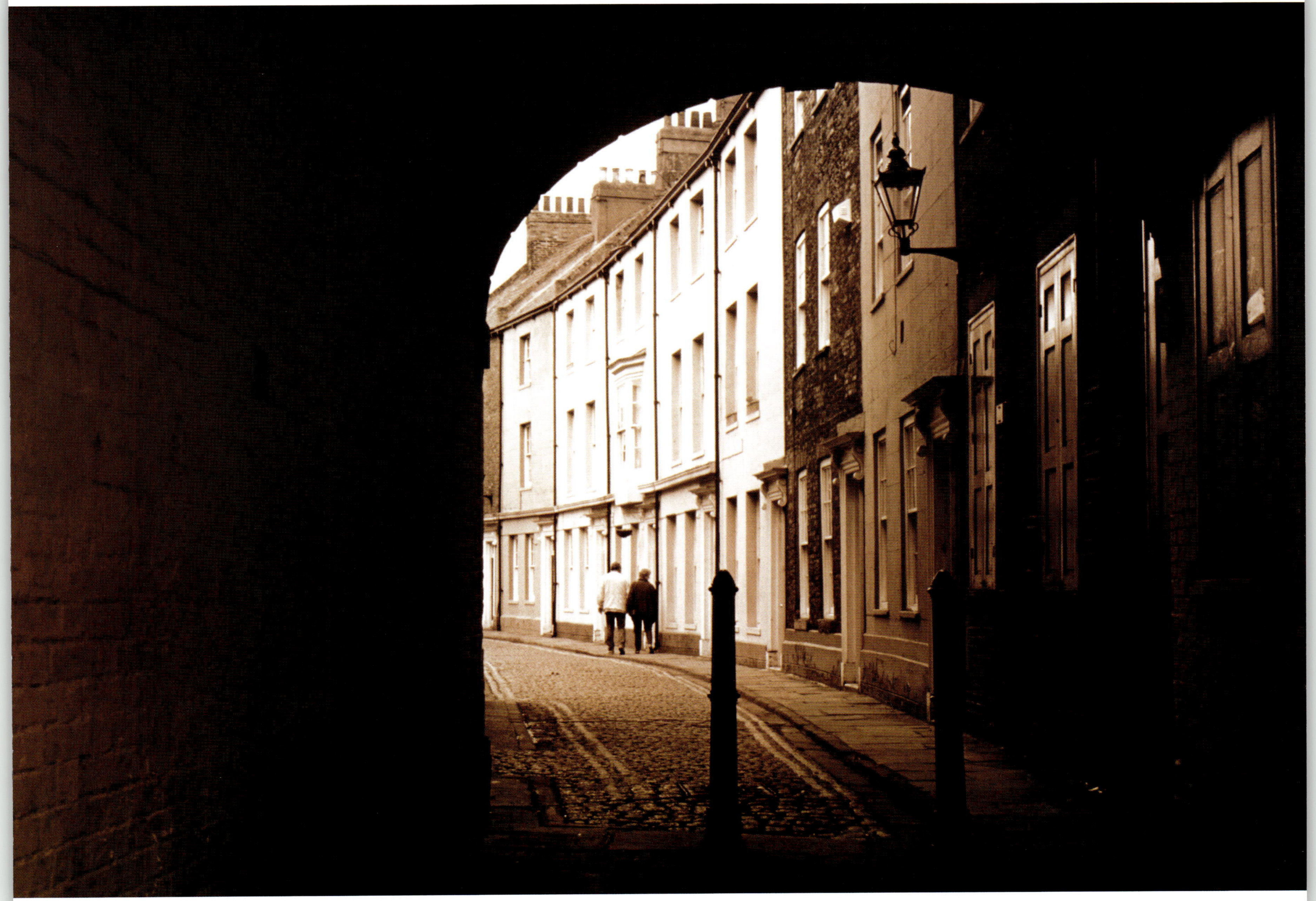

To an extent, every photograph is personal to the one who takes it, but there are some photographs that are more personal than others. *Down Memory Lane* (fig. 23.1) is one of mine. To the casual observer there is nothing unusual about this street; to me it is special because it reminds me of the street where I grew up. I left my native Yorkshire, in the north of England, as a teenager, and returned over a quarter of a century later in order to photograph it. This was an occasion when my camera gave me the perfect excuse to re-live childhood memories, as I documented the present and re-interpreted the past.

The computer can assist in further personalizing photographs, whether in restoring old photographs (in a fraction of the time and with none of the costs of the more traditional methods of restoration) or in enhancing a photograph to emphasize a point as shown here in *Down Memory Lane*. Changing this photograph to sepia highlights the thinking behind it both literally and symbolically.

As the original photograph is in colour, our first step is to change it into black and white using IMAGE/ADJUST/CHANNEL MIXER with the MONOCHROME option activated (see Project 22, page 102). By adjusting the three colour sliders we try to produce the best possible contrast to use as a starting point for our sepia colouring.

Next we turn to the selection of the correct colour cast for our image – the most critical stage of this exercise. We click on the square for foreground colour and the now familiar COLOUR PICKER screen appears (fig. 23.3). If we cannot find the right combination here, we click on CUSTOM (fig. 23.4) to increase the range of available colours. When we are satisfied we click OK. This colour becomes the new foreground colour.

We now use LAYER/NEW/LAYER and click on OK in the window that appears. An empty layer is added to the layers menu. We activate the PAINT BUCKET (fig. 23.5) from the toolbox and click on the picture of the arch. Everything now changes to our chosen colour because the OPACITY value of the layer currently reads '100%' (fig. 23.6). If we click on the little black triangle to the right of this a pop-up slider appears. When we move it to the left, the colour changes. We move it to the position that gives us the effect we have been looking for in combination with the monochrome print with which we started (fig. 23.2). If necessary, we use IMAGE/ADJUST/LEVELS (see Project 1, page 16) to enhance the end result of our work.

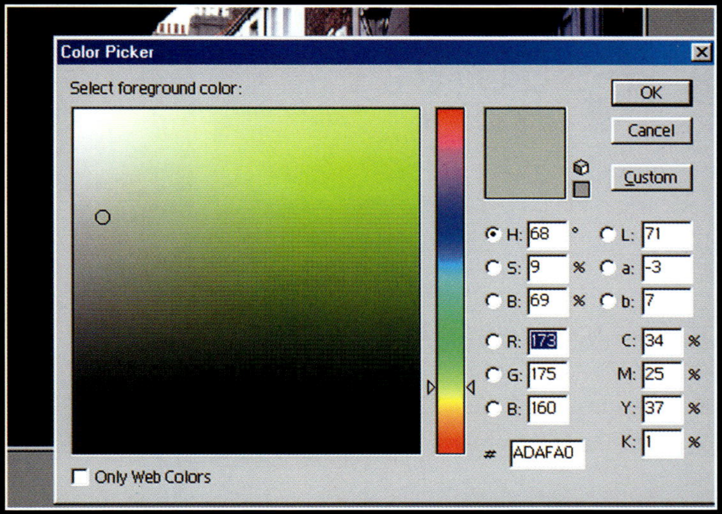

Fig 23.3

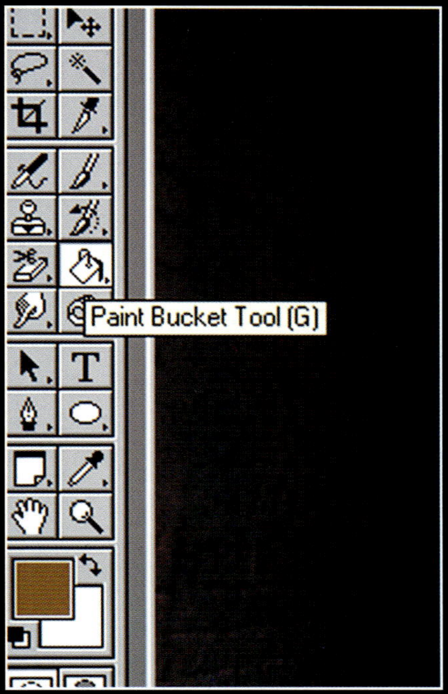

Fig 23.5

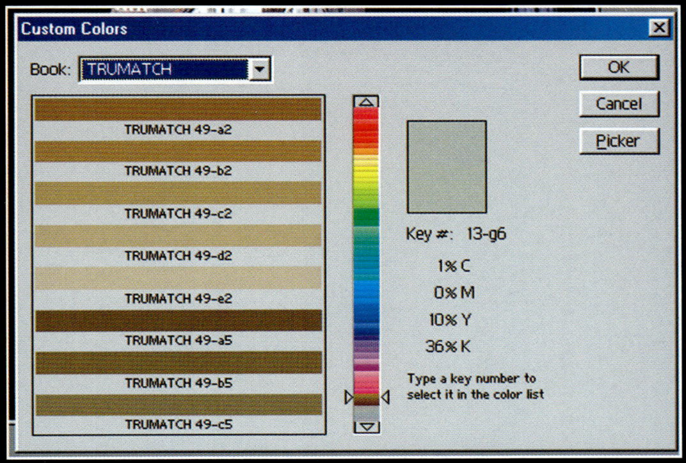

Fig 23.4

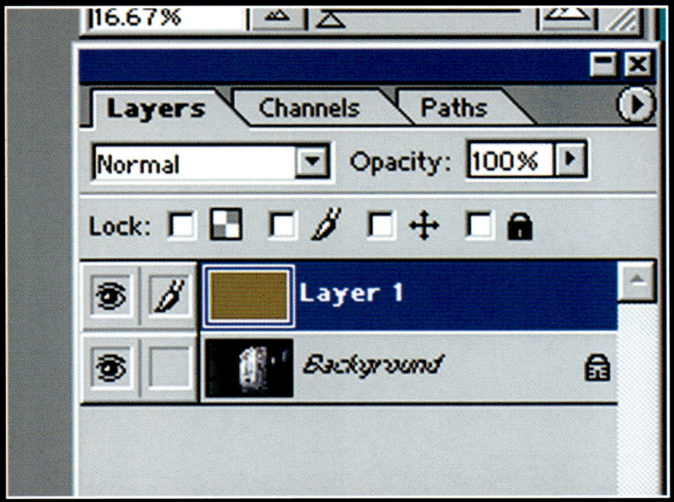

Fig 23.6

project
24

highlighting a subject

POLYGONAL LASSO

When photographing the world's most famous and celebrated locations, it is easy to get swept along by the crowd and concentrate on the clichés. If you are ever unsure of the obvious ones, you will find plenty of examples on the many

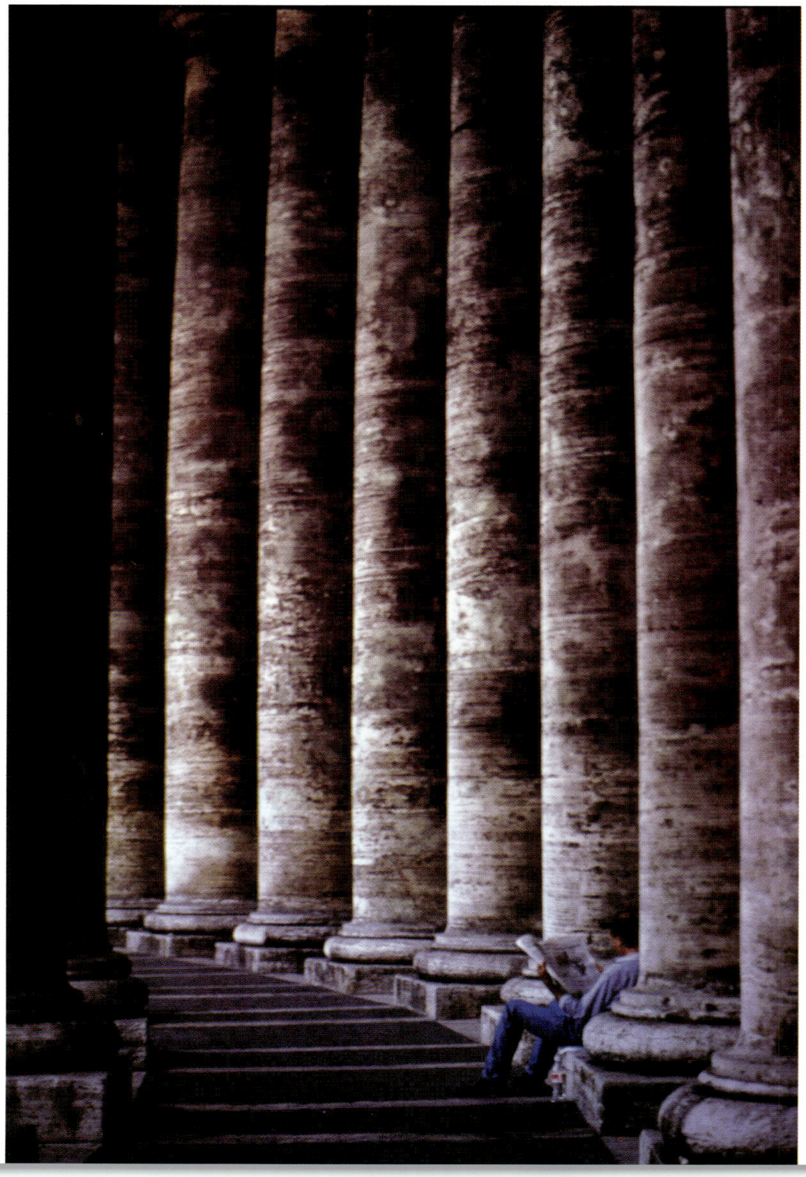

Fig 24.1 *Vatican Tourist* disappoints me as it fails to capture the contrast of the two distinct worlds I see before me.

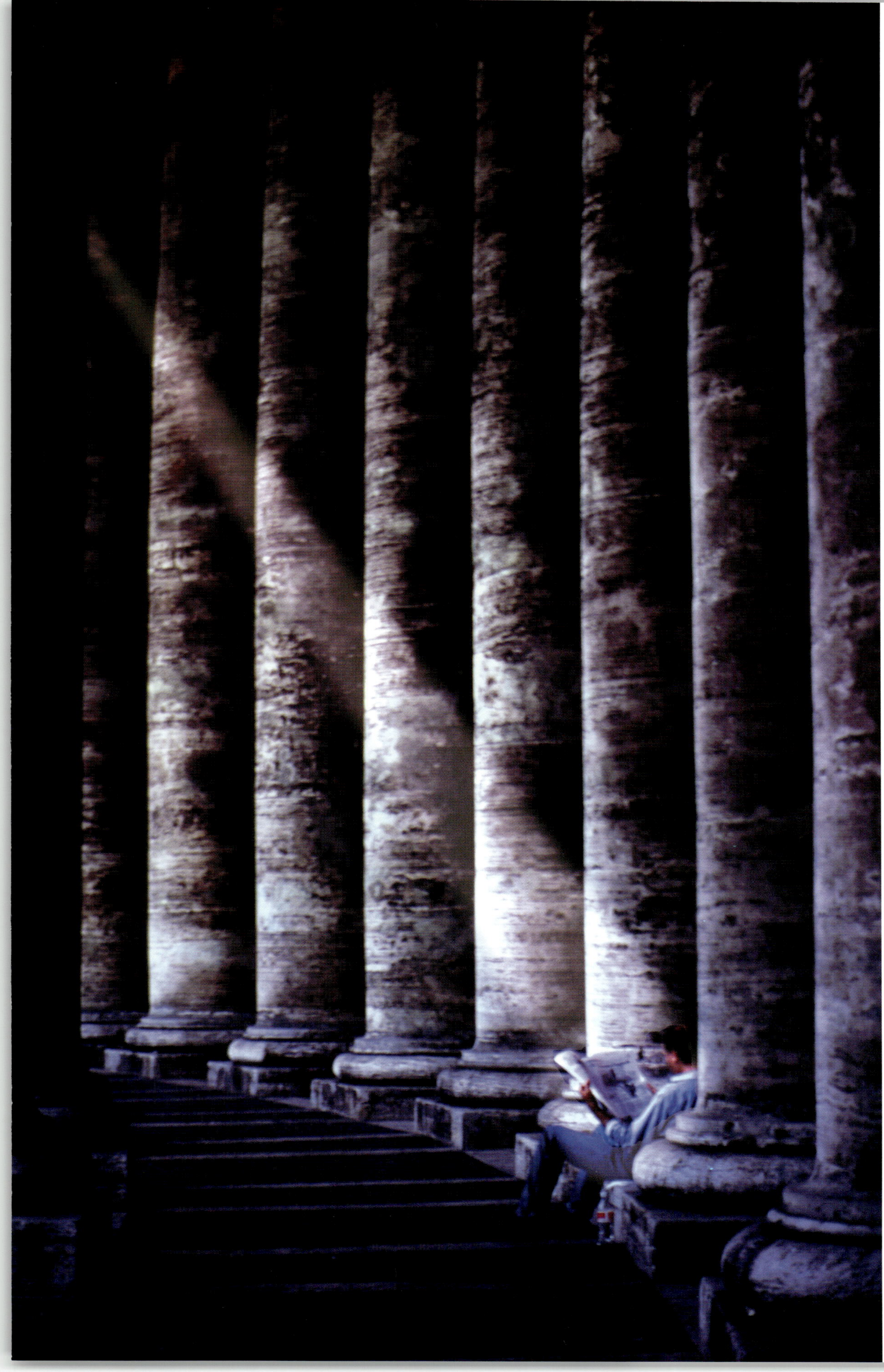

Fig 24.2 Simple enhancing techniques emphasize the contrast and turn around my disappointment.

postcards, calendars and other gaudy souvenirs that are available. I am not suggesting for one moment, while you are visiting such popular sites with your camera at the ready, you go scavenging down side streets searching for symbols of scarcity. Rather, that you add something of your own – perhaps even with a whimsical touch – to create a lively contrast with the aura of history.

This was my intention with *Vatican Tourist* (fig. 24.1). On the one hand, there is the ageless splendour of the Vatican's massed columns. Until a few minutes before, I had never seen them. And yet, their familiarity was such that I felt that I had known them for many years. Like enormous giants they surrounded me and filled my world. It is a world of religious history, politics and architecture. The world beyond still exists, but at this moment, as I release the shutter, this is my world, my landscape.

But I have another world in my sights, one that symbolizes my role as a tourist and also brings together two contrasting worlds in one photograph. The slumped figure of a tired tourist sits reading a newspaper. The shade brings relief from the heat of Rome, and a cool drink has been finished recently.

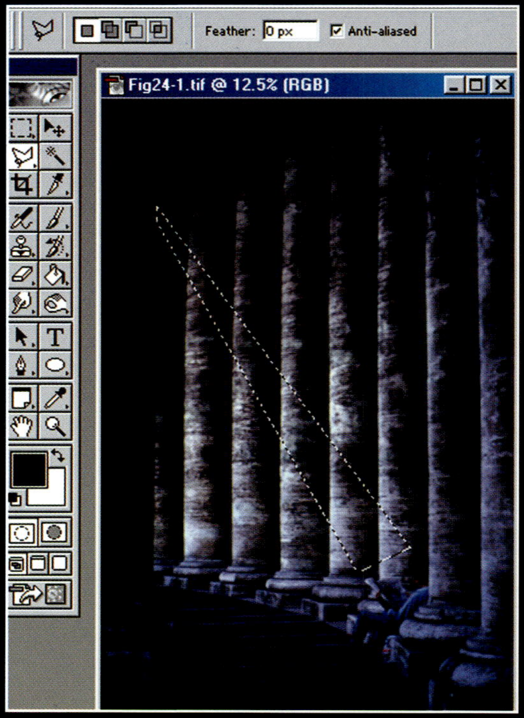

Fig 24.3

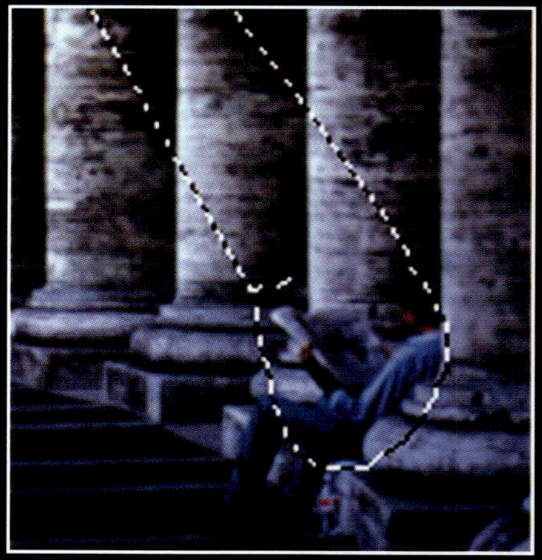

Fig 24.4

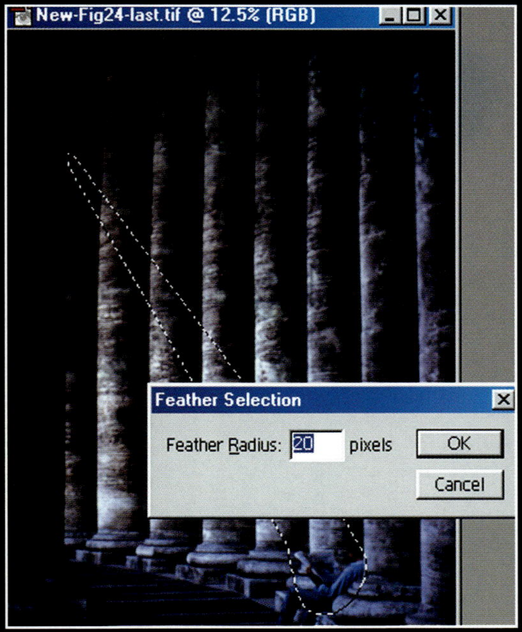

Fig 24.5

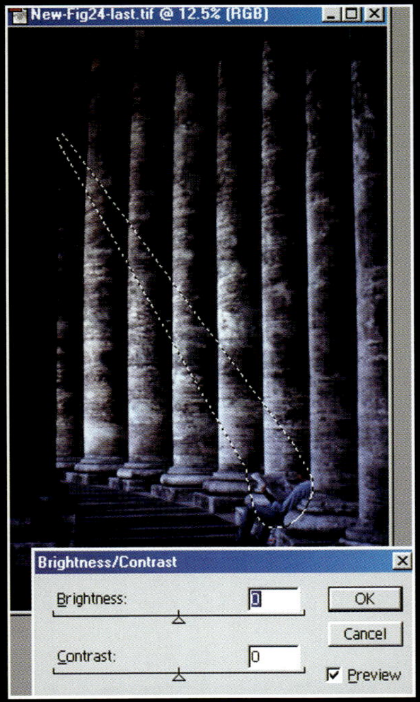

Fig 24.6

Unfortunately, when I received the processed image, the contrast was not as prominent as I had hoped. If every picture tells a story, the point of this story needs to be more clearly revealed. In the past, it would have been easy for me to drop this photograph into the wastepaper basket. I believe that if a photographer wants to be noticed, then there is room only for his or her best work to be on show. Today, however, I could weep over the images I have thrown away over the years, as many of them could now be corrected easily with a little help from the computer.

In this case, we enhance our image to highlight the contrast. We start with IMAGE/ADJUST/LEVELS (see Project 1, page 16), but since we want to put more emphasis on the person reading, we choose the POLYGONAL LASSO to create a beam of light leading in his direction (fig. 24.3). Now, again with the LASSO tool, and with the SHIFT key pressed down, we add a semi-circular part to our selection (fig. 24.4). With SELECT/FEATHER, we put in a FEATHER RADIUS of 20 to give it a natural look (fig. 24.5). Our final step is to use IMAGE/ADJUST/BRIGHTNESS-CONTRAST (fig. 24.6) to lighten our selection, place further contrast on the figure, and complete our image in a way that satisfies our interpretation (fig. 24.2).

project 25

adding frames

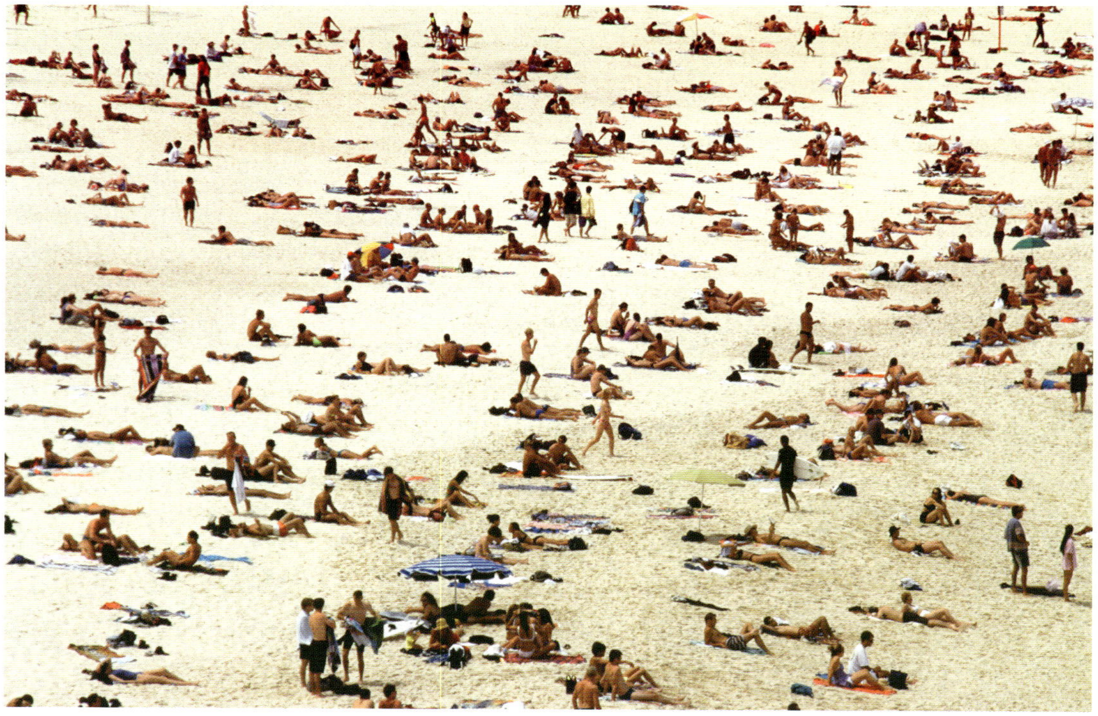

Fig 25.1 If computers are changing the way we think about a photograph, should we not give more thought to framing?

RECTANGULAR MARQUEE, RULERS

When we make a landscape photograph we often exclude what we would like to include if only it were possible, and we are all aware that a landscape photograph shows but a segment of the whole. I do not refer only to the amount of land included or excluded from a composition. There is not a landscape photographer who has not felt, at some time or other, utter frustration at having failed to portray a scene adequately.

Fig 25.2 A thoughtless frame need never again ruin a thoughtful photograph.

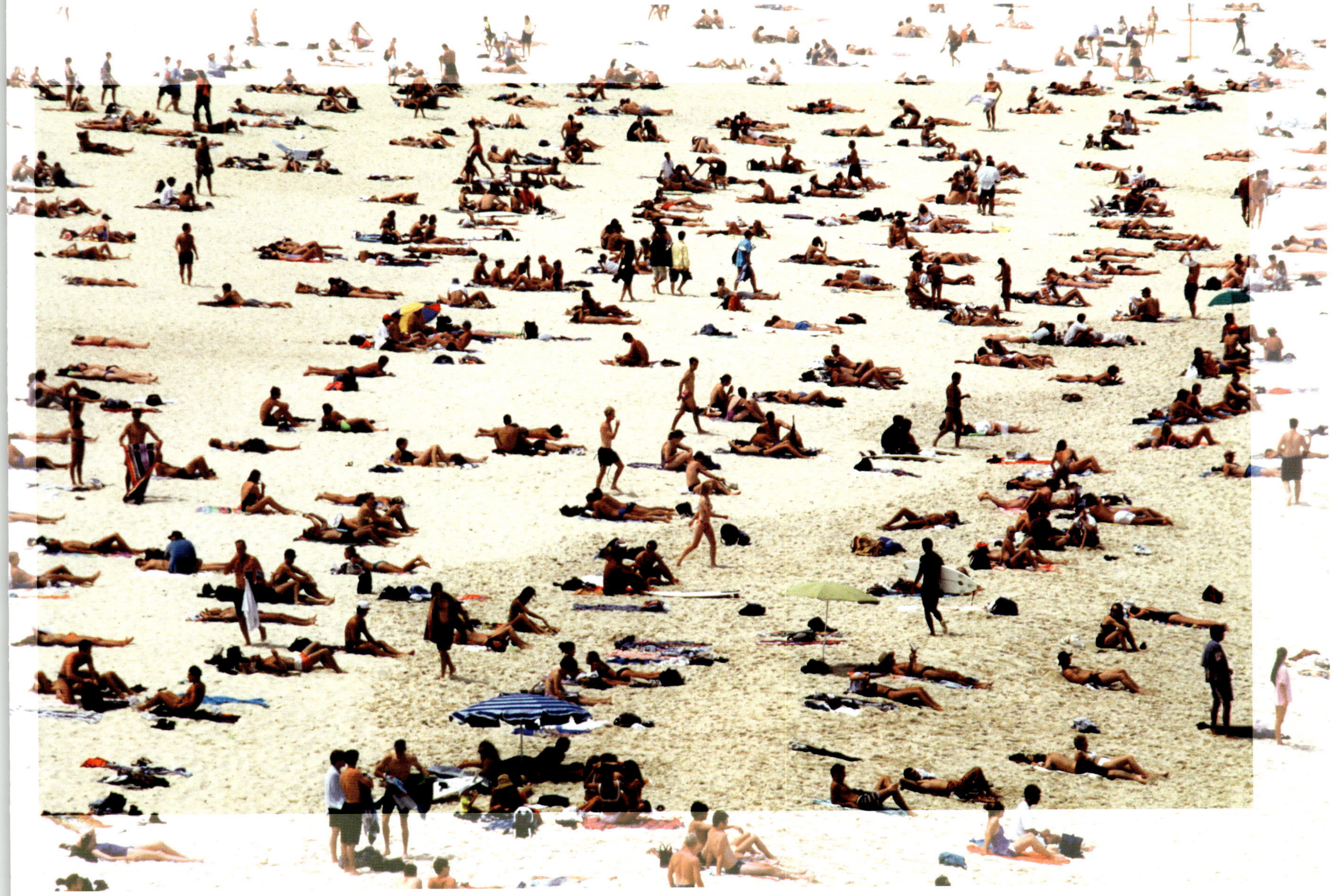

There are various pieces of equipment available to help photographers put back into many of their landscape photographs some of that lost in the transition from reality to film. For example, I remember clearly my excitement when first shown a little of the potential of using a polarizing filter. My acceptance of the value of a frame was not, however, as sudden. As a photographer shooting the bulk of my work on transparency film, framing was not an issue at first. Generally, I left to others the occasional mounting of prints for an exhibition or the arrangement of an album of prints for a client, preferring instead to get on with what I loved most: making photographs.

Photography is often described as a thinking person's hobby. It is especially so when applied to the landscape photographer. Then why do so many thoughtful landscape photographs end up so thoughtlessly framed? There may have been an argument of sorts in the past, when the choice of frames was more limited. Perhaps, once the photograph was taken, some photographers believed their work or role to be complete and that, to them, the frame was not important?

With the introduction of the computer into my world of photography and the increase in options that it has brought, framing has become an integral part of my photographic presentation. I now embrace its potential with as much enthusiasm as I once did the polarizing filter. Adding a filter to a lens and adding a frame to a print are realms apart, but if I can replace something of what is lost in a final print then I am all for it.

Bondi Beach (fig. 25.1) records the height of Sydney's summer season – the sun, sand and surf. Of course, a single photograph does little to capture the experience and a traditional frame only emphasizes the cut-off point. However, with thoughtful use of the computer we can allow the inspiration of the day to flow on beyond the frame.

We start with IMAGE/ADJUST/LEVELS to enhance the image's contrast. Next, we make a copy of the image using either the LAYER/DUPLICATE LAYER pull-down menu (fig. 25.3) or go to the layers window on the right of the screen (fig. 25.4). A second bar appears containing a copy of the background. We now make the new layer active by clicking on the relevant bar in the layers window (when active, the bar's colour changes to blue).

Our next step is to select the area of our image that we wish to keep, and then fade the surrounding area to create a soft, hazy border or frame. We use the RECTANGULAR MARQUEE tool to select the area we wish to retain. To help us make our selection in the right position we use VIEW/SHOW RULERS (fig. 25.5). This creates some guidelines from which to work. Once we are happy with our selection and the frame that it leaves, we use CUT from the EDIT pull-down menu.

To change the appearance of the border, we go to IMAGE/ADJUST/BRIGHTNESS-CONTRAST and move the sliders until we obtain the desired effect. Finally, after removing the rulers, we use LAYERS/FLATTEN IMAGE to complete the desired effect (fig. 25.2).

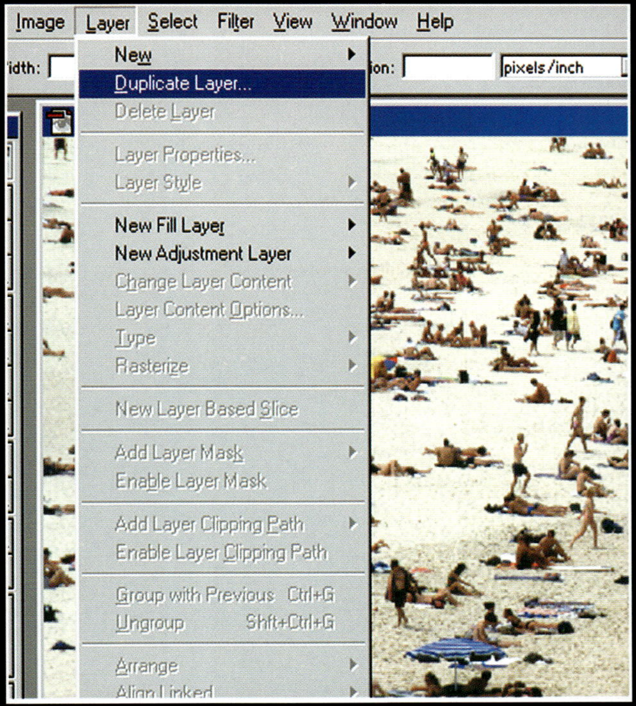

Fig 25.3

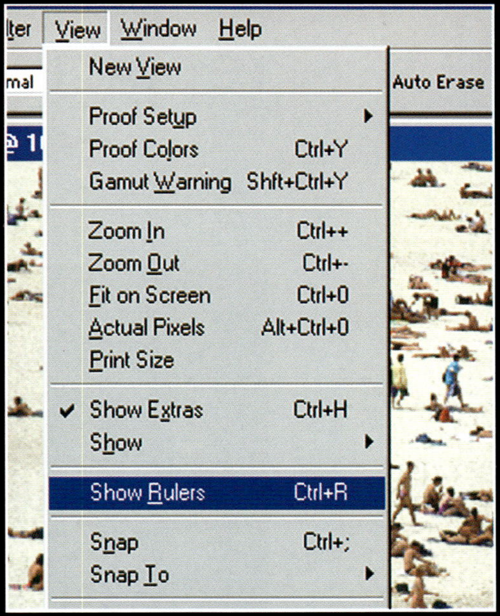

Fig 25.5

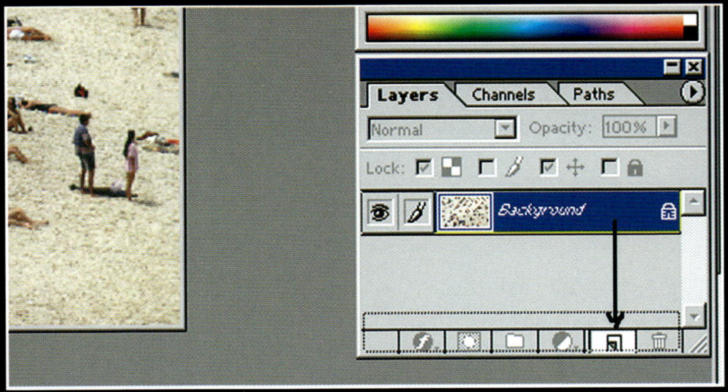

Fig 25.4

project 26

repairing damage

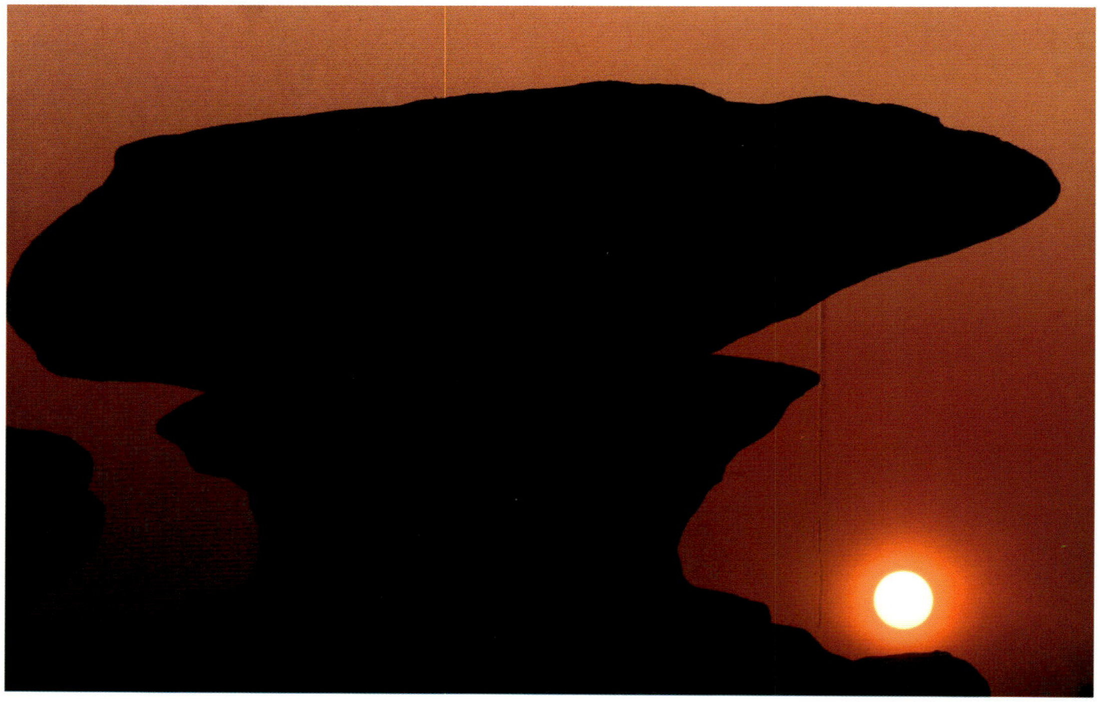

Fig 26.1 In the case of *Brimham Rocks*, bad luck has led to a damaged transparency and a marred image.

CLONE STAMP

Whenever I run a photographic workshop, I always ask the participants to fill in a questionnaire after each field trip. The results of a photography trip can be disappointing for a number of reasons, but I never cease to be surprised at the answers given by my students to the question: 'What was the low point of your trip?' Some people complain that they forgot their film, others that they tried to carry too much equipment or wore inappropriate footwear. What makes this even more surprising is that most of my students are mature photographers, some with years of semi-professional experience.

Fig 26.2 All evidence of the scratch is removed using the CLONE tool.

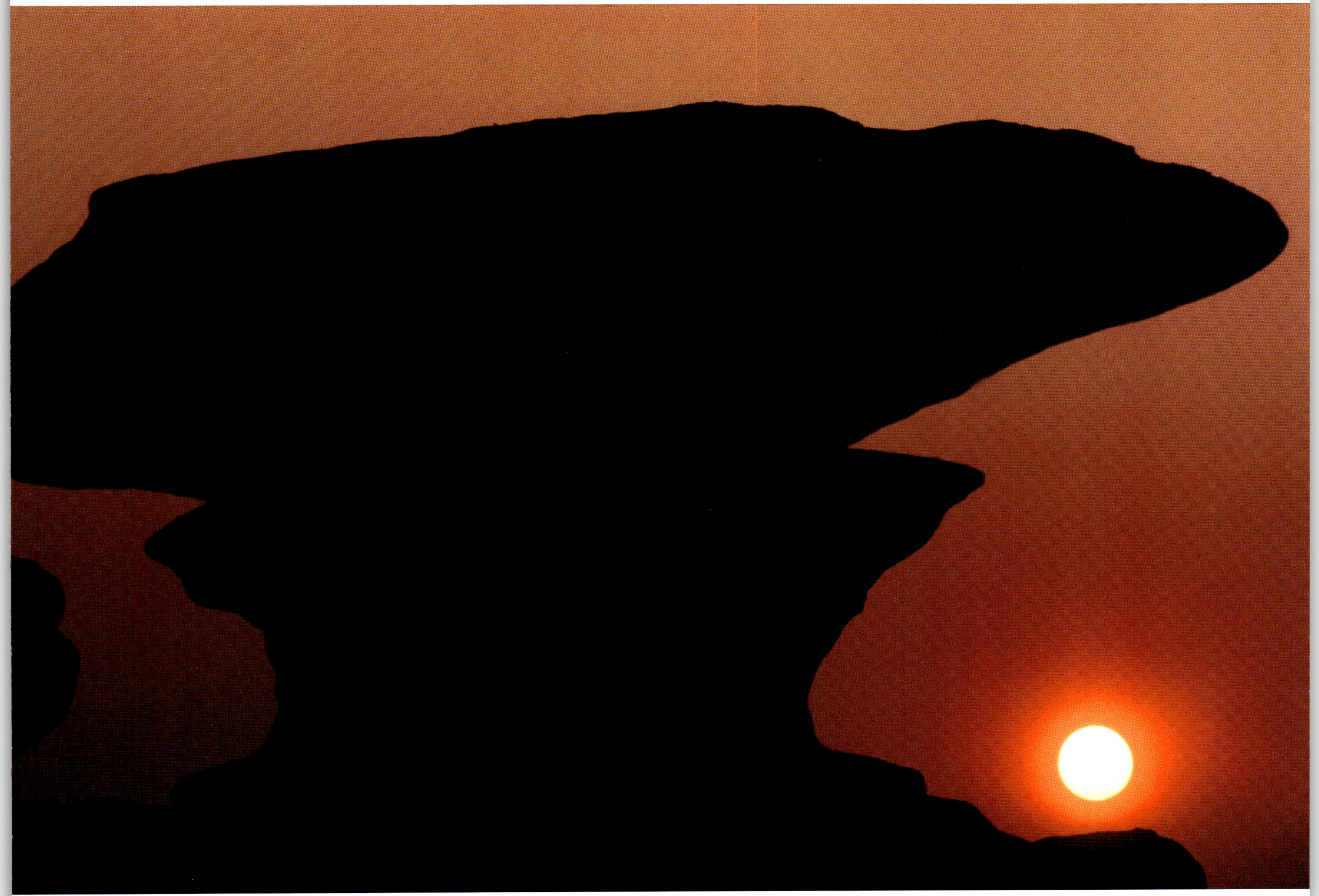

As I recall, Murphy's Law states that if something can go wrong it will, and at the worst possible time. Bearing in mind the potential for unseen problems, as landscape photographers we should do all we can to make sure that we do not shoot ourselves in the foot.

Another problem comes from lack of understanding. I am embarrassed to admit that, in the early days of my life as a photographer, I had great problems when photographing sunsets. No matter how glorious the sunset, the result was always the same: a bright yellow ball surrounded by a black mass.

Two contradictory viewpoints stand out when I think of photographing a sunset today. The first argument is that you can rarely miss when photographing one. Thus, underexposure simply makes a photograph look darker (and therefore taken later in the evening), and an overexposed shot appears to have been taken earlier. An alternative viewpoint likens photographing a sunset to stalking big game: you can plan all you want but there are no guarantees.

This brings me to *Brimham Rocks* (fig. 26.1). Despite having to stumble over rocks and trying to anticipate where to place my tripod to catch the sun in just the right spot at the right time, I had not made any simple mistakes. Nor had I failed to understand the exposure required for creating the desired effect. My satisfaction was short-lived, however, when I saw the result. It would appear that no matter how carefully we handle our transparencies and negatives, accidents do happen. It only takes a very small scratch to ruin an original piece of work, but this is another area where the computer can help to repair the damage.

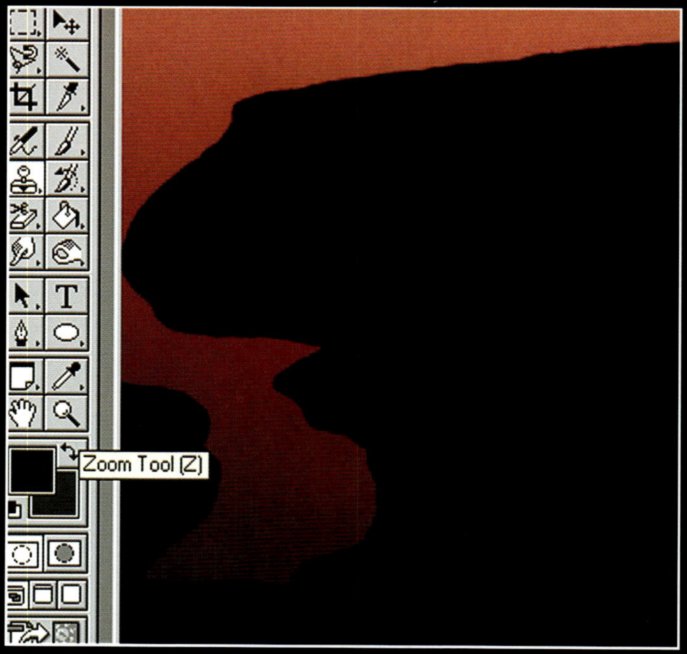

Fig 26.3

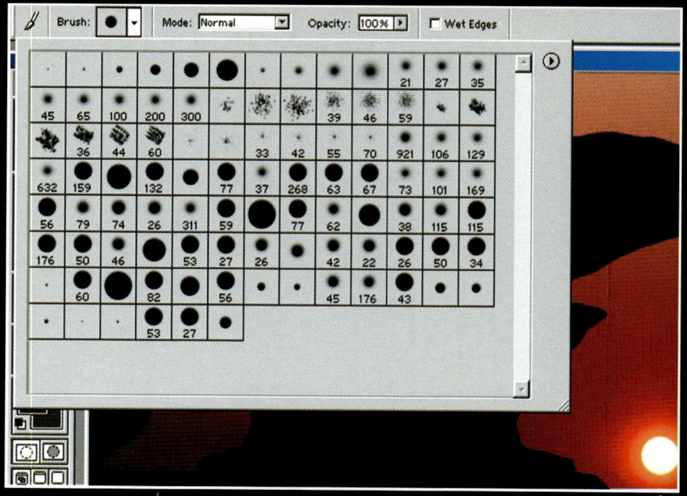

Fig 26.4

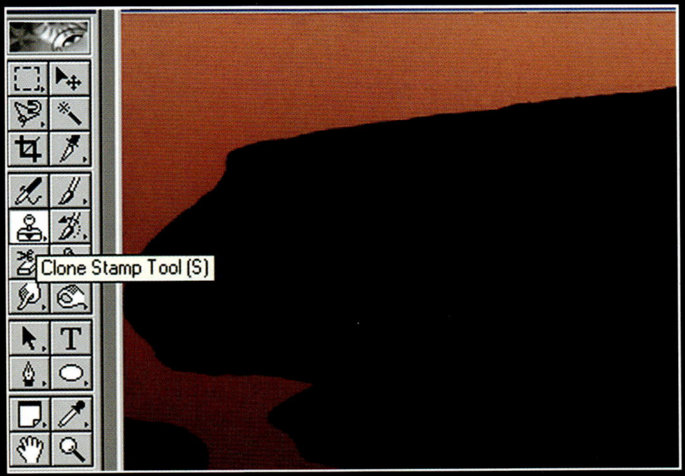

Fig 26.5

On the computer, a scratch like this can be repaired in one of two ways. We can use either the CLONE STAMP tool or the EYEDROPPER tool with a BRUSH. But, first, we must use the ZOOM tool (fig. 26.3) to enlarge the section we want to work on and decide precisely which areas needs to be repaired.

If the damaged part of a photograph has little colour variation it is easier to use the EYEDROPPER and BRUSH combination to carry out repairs. We click the EYEDROPPER, which samples colours from an image, as close to the scratch as possible. With the correct colour defined we choose a BRUSH from the brush toolbar (fig. 26.4) and paint over the damaged area. If the result is not satisfactory, we move to EDIT/UNDO and try again.

In a situation where almost every pixel appears to have a different colour the CLONE STAMP tool, which continuously copies pixels from the area next to the damaged parts, must be used (fig. 26.5). When many colours are involved care must be taken to choose a small brush size. As in Project 14 (see page 70), we activate the tool then move our mouse pointer to a spot next to the damage and click the left button while keeping the ALT key held down. By moving our mouse pointer over the damaged area repeatedly, the chosen part is copied and the damaged area slowly disappears. This may seem difficult at first, but it is soon mastered with practice.

In the case of *Brimham Rocks* we used the EYEDROPPER and BRUSH to repair the damage in the black areas (of the rock) and the CLONE STAMP tool for the remainder (fig. 26.2). Scratches caused by specks of dust and rough handling, as well as annoying and unwanted elements, like telegraph wires, can be removed just as easily.

project 27

improving brightness selectively

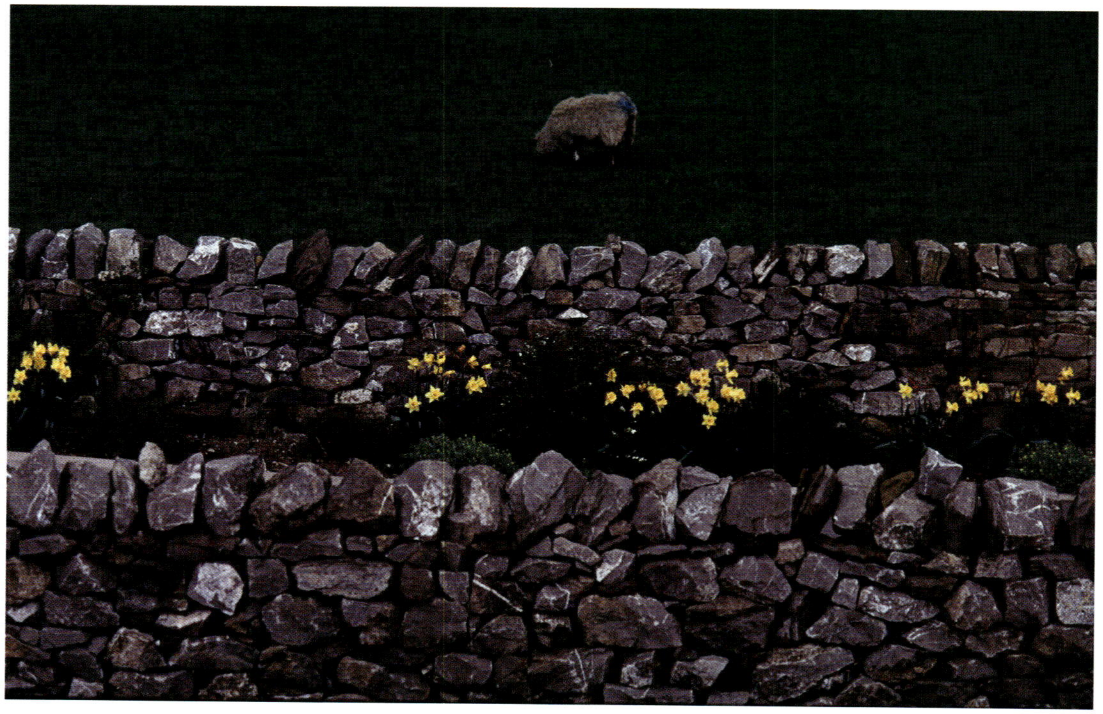

Fig 27.1 A lack of brightness curbs my intended symbolism.

LASSO

As outdoor photographers, there will always be obstacles standing in our way, but if we hope to work to the best of our abilities we have to overcome those obstacles. In this respect, what seem like stumbling blocks can in fact become stepping stones. *Dry-stone Walls* (fig. 27.1) not only serves to illustrate an enhancing technique, it shows a literal barrier (i.e. a wall) and how a barrier can be used as a storytelling landscape photograph in its own right.

Fig 27.2 The computer helps to add a touch of light to our enhanced photograph.

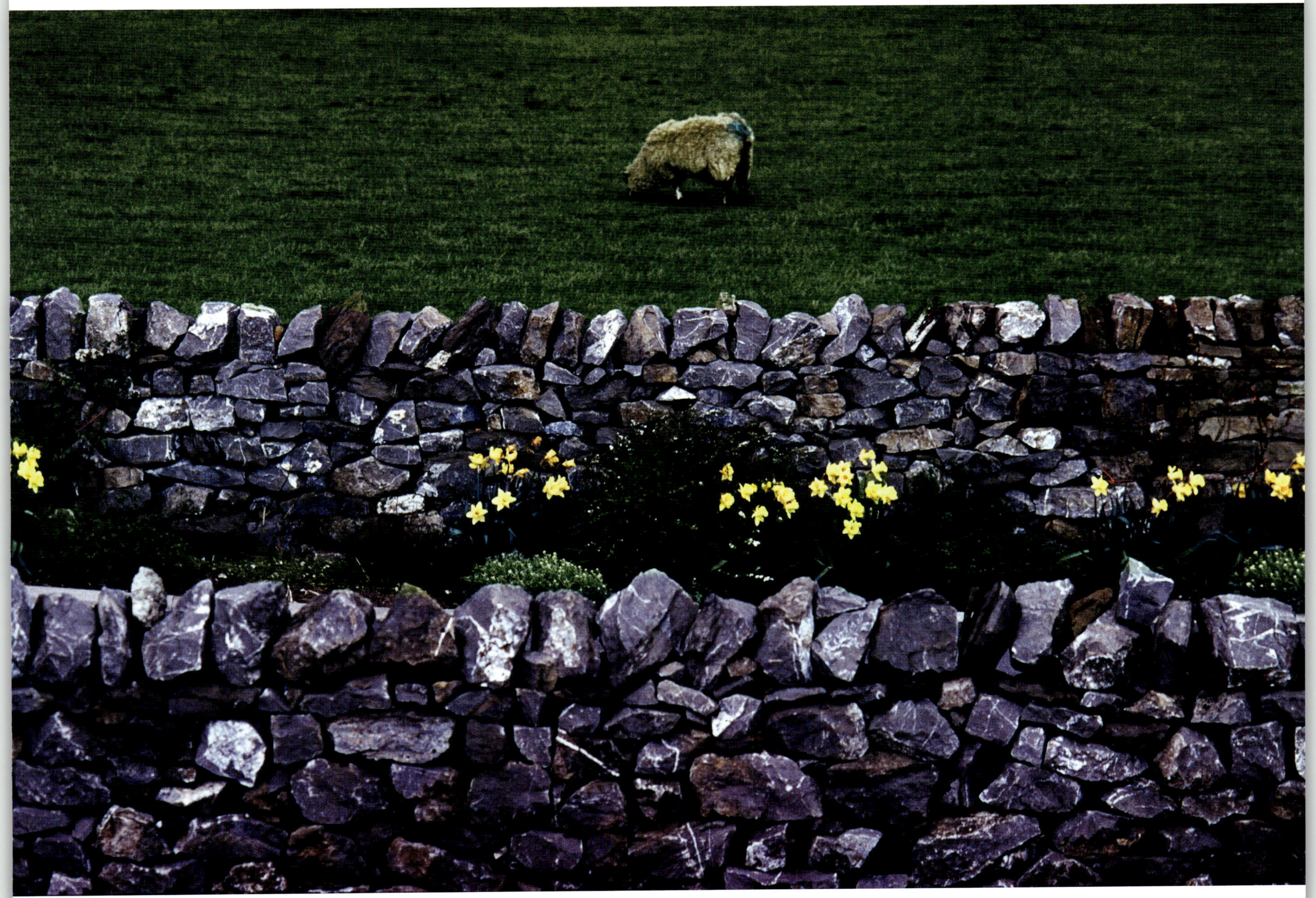

This composition is rich in symbolism, and I consider it to be perfect. Not in the Western style, with its preoccupation for perspective, but following the stacking-of-the-elements Eastern tradition. On top of the stack stands a sheep. Its central position in the photograph is symbolic of its central role in the surrounding landscape. The dry-stone wall highlights the barrier to the landscape, and yet, amid this, the colourful daffodils thrive.

For me, this photograph also represents success over a very literal barrier. Security is at an all time high. Signs block out the scenery and keep out landscape photographers, who, whether in town or country, face an ever-increasing dilemma as a consequence of those who have gone before them. On this occasion, despite my careful planning, one such keep-out sign – newly erected to ward off trespassers – blocked my path. By finding the property owner and gaining his permission and encouragement, I was able to photograph more than I had hoped.

However, the greyness of the day posed one final obstacle, and it is left to the computer to shed some light on the subject.

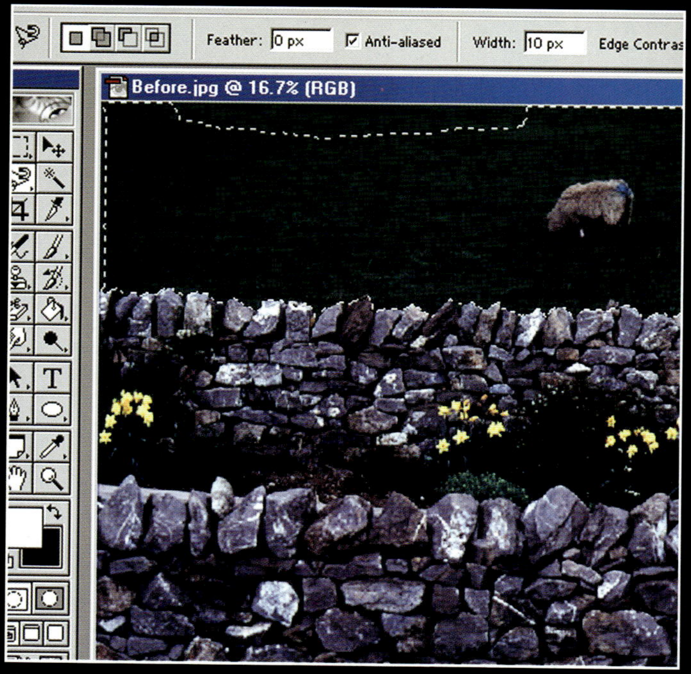

Fig 27.3

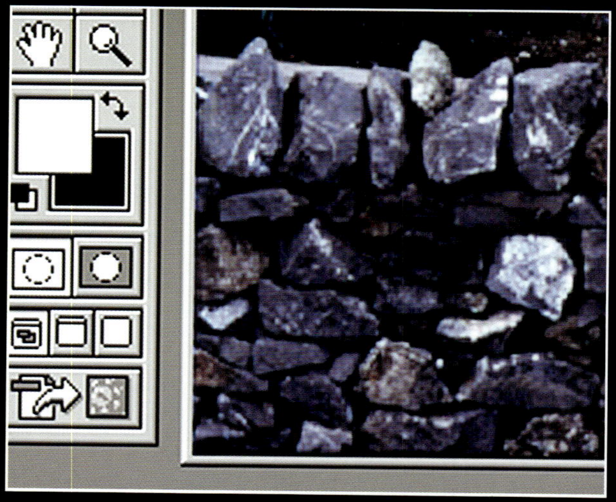

Fig 27.4

We could use IMAGE/ADJUST/LEVELS to increase the colour of the overall picture, but to work on specific parts of the picture, we use the MAGNETIC LASSO tool. In this case, we draw around the green grass (fig. 27.3). Any small parts missed around the edge of our selection can be fixed by clicking on QUICK MASK MODE, the button for which is located in the toolbox under the area of the background and foreground colours (fig. 27.4). Everything outside our selection now turns to red (fig. 27.5). To add to or deduct from our selection we choose white or black respectively as our foreground colour, and paint over the area we wish to change using a BRUSH of appropriate size.

We activate our completed selection by clicking on STANDARD MODE (its icon is located on the left of the QUICK MASK MODE icon). We can now change the colours in our selected area as we wish using IMAGE/ADJUST/COLOUR BALANCE (see Project 11, page 58).

The garden area between the two walls can also be brightened using the LASSO tool. We make a rough selection (fig. 27.6) and change the colour using IMAGE/ADJUST/COLOUR BALANCE to produce our final image (fig. 27.2).

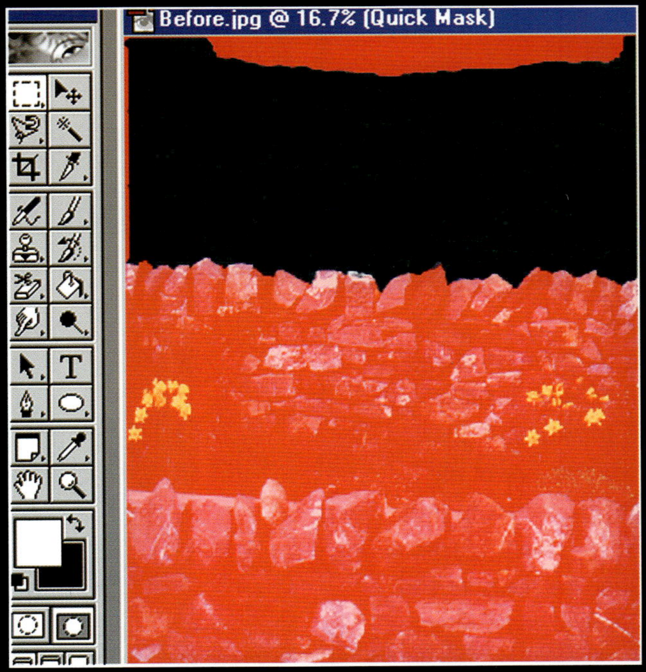

Fig 27.5

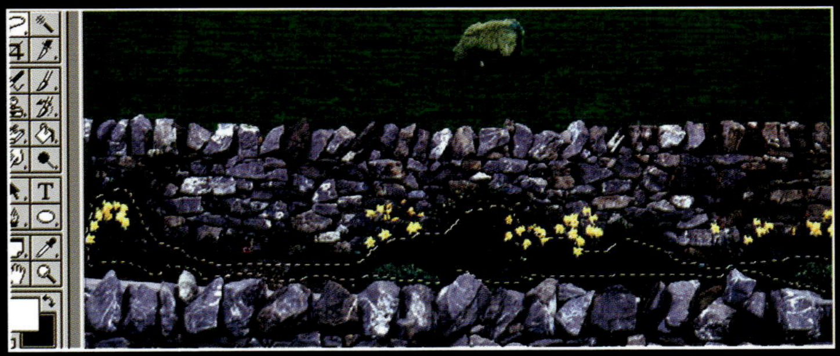

Fig 27.6

project 28

balancing zones

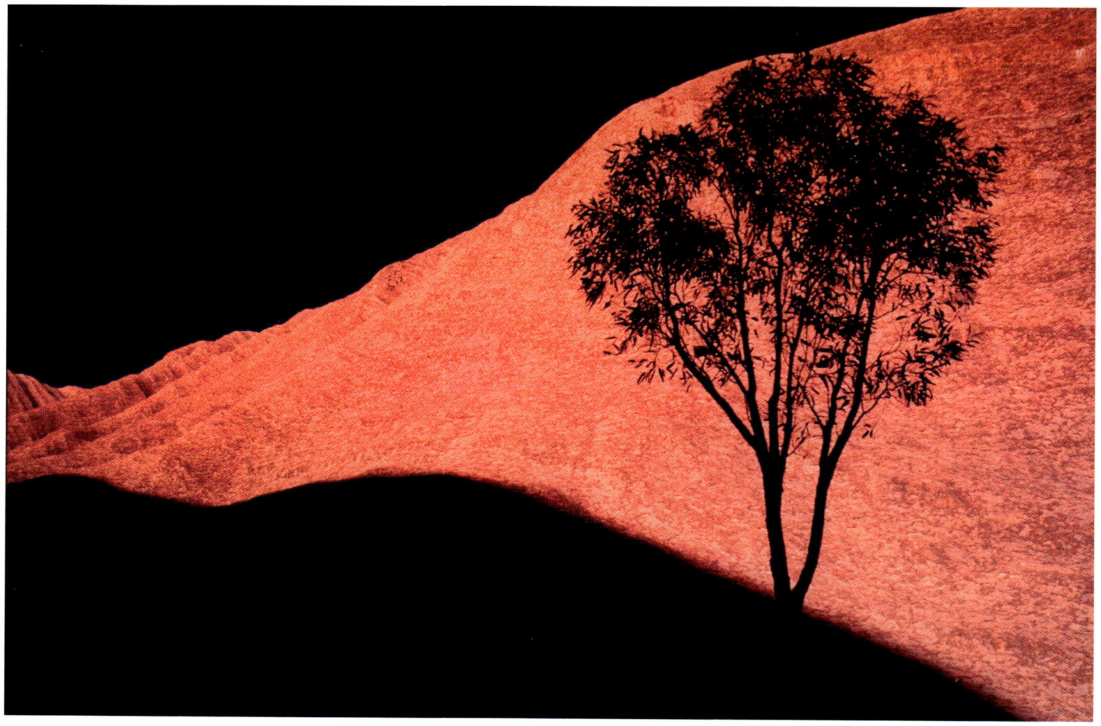

Fig 28.1 The over use of a polarizing filter has made this image a little over the top and in need of correction.

MAGNETIC LASSO, QUICK MASK

When checking through what I consider to be my most-valued photographs it becomes noticeable that very few of them relied on anything other than a camera, lens and tripod. With a few exceptions, there was little evidence to show that any of my 'special effects' equipment, which most photographers turn to at some point, has proved, in the long term, to be either special or effective. This is not to deny their use, nor the pleasure and experience I gained from them over time. Indeed some filters

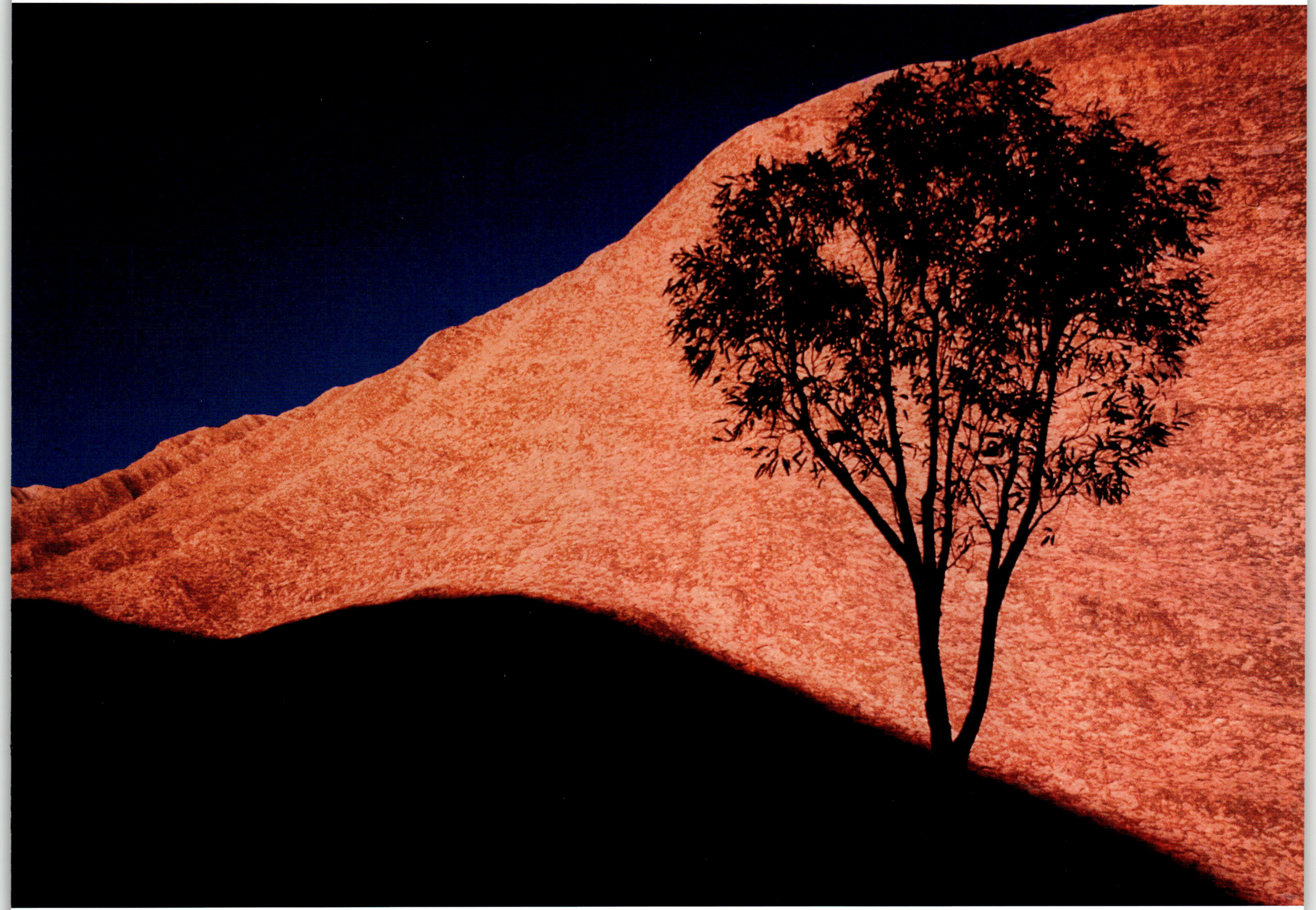

Fig 28.2 An easy mistake made with the camera is corrected with almost equal ease using the computer.

have proved to be exceptions. A tobacco gradient can occasionally enhance a dull sky, a mist filter can emphasize an early morning or late afternoon mood, and I have a polarizing filter and lens hood to fit each lens I carry.

Rock Face (fig. 28.1) was shot at that photographically dynamic time of day, and a strong sun hovered above the horizon providing a dramatic setting. It was the kind of idyllic moment that makes me indebted to photography. However, to share the magical moment with others and capture as much of the reality before me as possible, fast work was needed. Any number of camera accessories might have helped to convey the scene, but a setting sun does not wait for a photographer to sort through a gadget bag. Turning to mine, I took out my polarizing filter.

My experience that day may well have been perfect, but the resulting photograph, to match the occasion, needs a nudge in the right direction. Captivated by the simple lines and strong colour, I over-polarized the azure sky. It was a mistake as easy to make in the field as it is to correct with the computer.

To improve this image we have to change three different areas: the sky, the hill and the tree, and the dark foreground. By selecting one element at a time, we can adjust them separately. We start by selecting the sky using the MAGNETIC LASSO tool (fig. 28.3). We use the QUICK MASK MODE to refine the precise selection, and when complete use SELECT/FEATHER to apply 1 pixel feathering. Finally, with the option IMAGE/ADJUST/COLOUR BALANCE we change the colour to one with more blue (fig. 28.4).

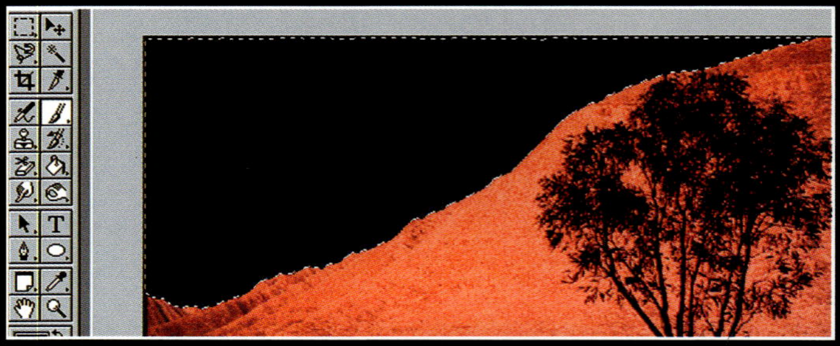

Fig 28.3

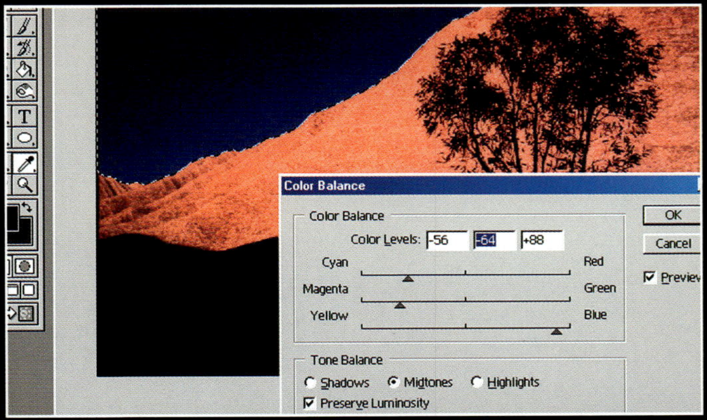

Fig 28.4

Our second selection is made in the same way, and we change it with IMAGE/ADJUST/BRIGHTNESS-CONTRAST (see Project 3, page 24). We make our third selection, again using MAGNETIC LASSO, and this time we adjust the area with IMAGE/ADJUST/LEVELS (see Project 1, page 16). The completed image achieves a perfect balance between these three areas (fig. 28.2).

Here we have used three different methods of adjusting tone and colour, rather than just one. Although there are certain similarities in these techniques, one should look at a picture, decide what is required and then use the right tools to accomplish the job. Each of the three selections required a slightly different adjustment (where the first one needs more blue, the second needs more contrast and the last more saturation), and the computer provided the right option for each one.

project 29

sharpening the focus

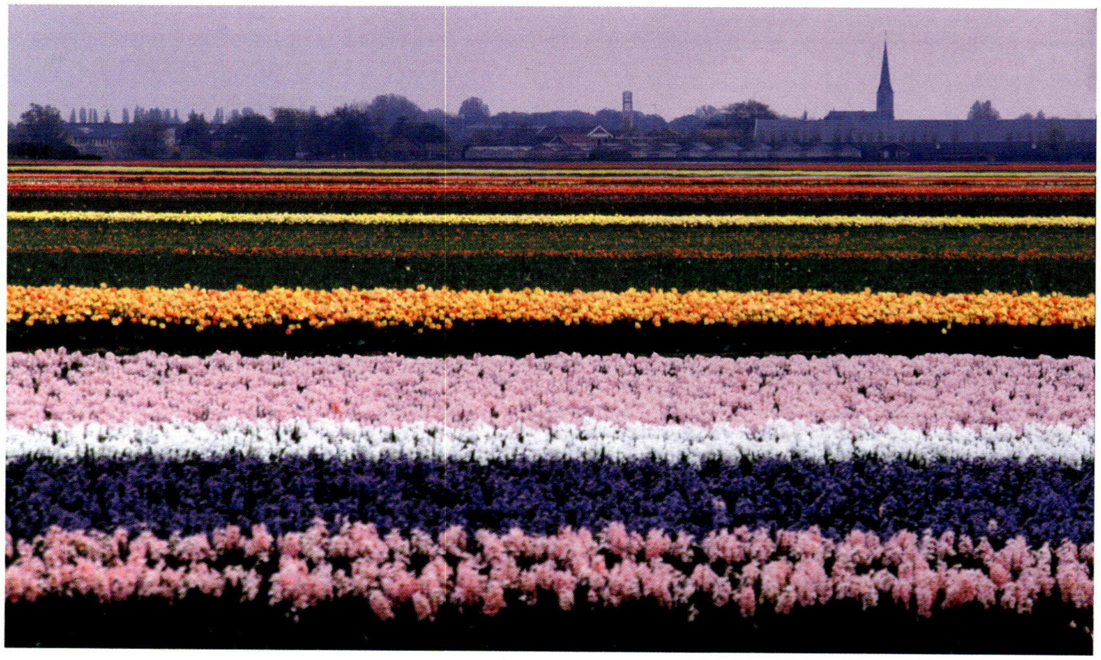

Fig 29.1 The bulb fields of Holland provide a sea of colour and a perfect setting, but not a perfect photograph.

UNSHARP MASK

I had never seen clouds from above until, with my camera in hand, I flew from London to the Channel Isles as a teenager. I found the cloud formations below me fascinating, and later discovered that of the 36 exposures on the one film I had with me, 28 were of clouds, all of which looked much the same. I learned my lesson so well that, even now, rarely will I take a second exposure of a subject when I think one will do.

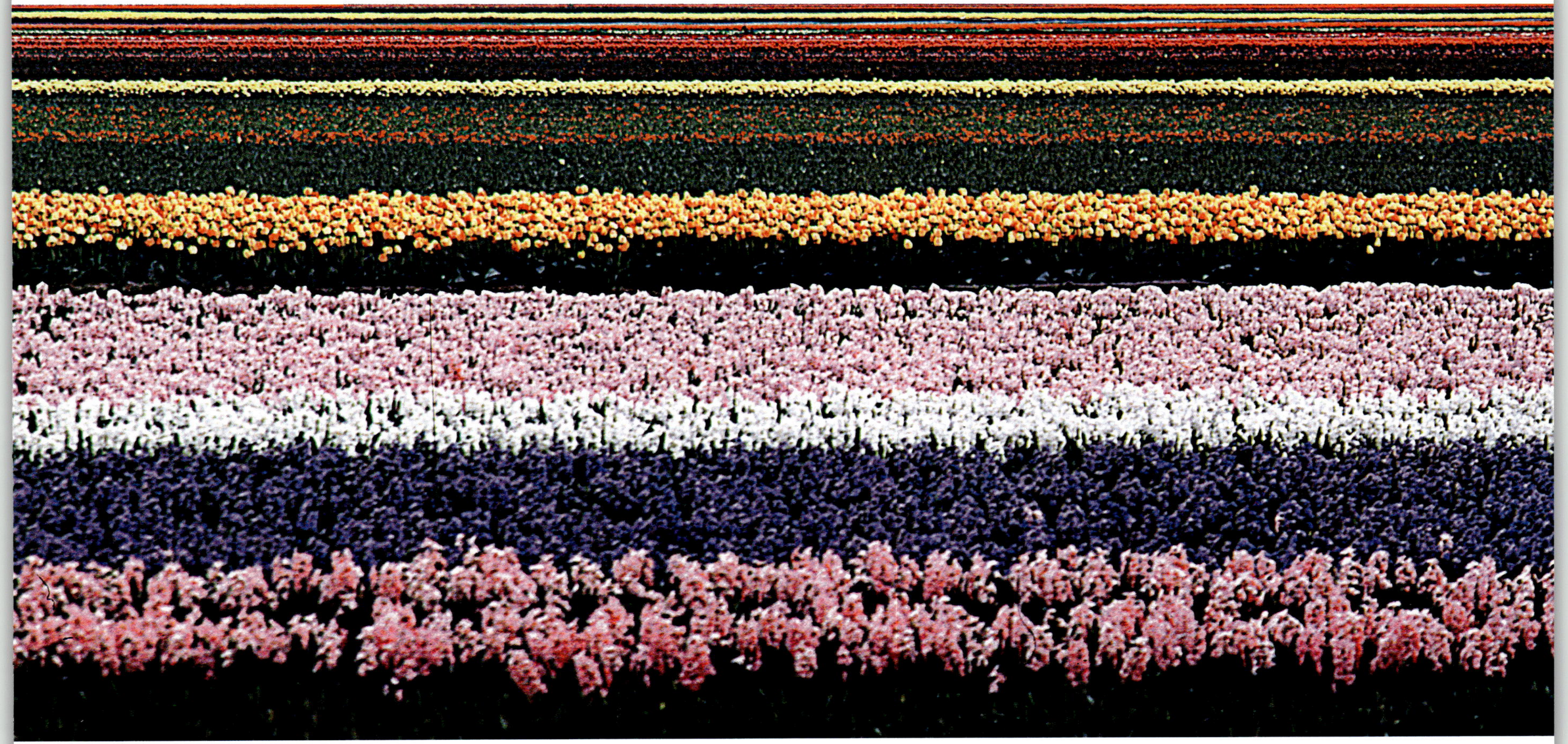

Fig 29.2 Why wait for the corresponding season next year to correct things when we can turn to the computer and perfect our photograph now?

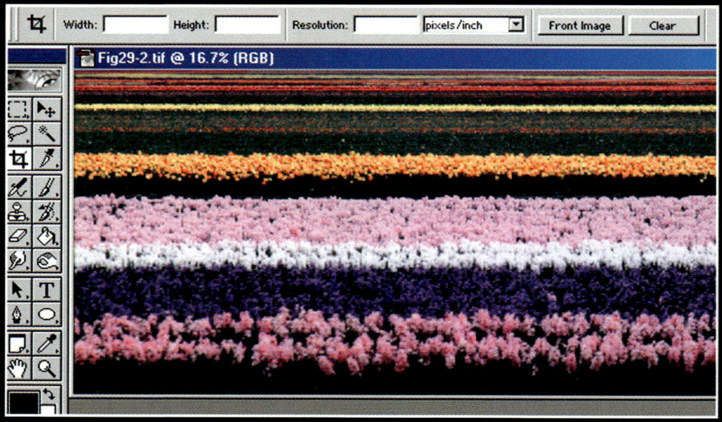

Fig 29.3

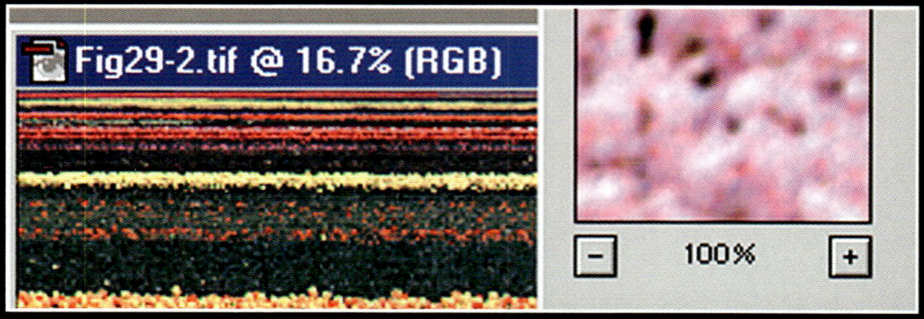

Fig 29.5

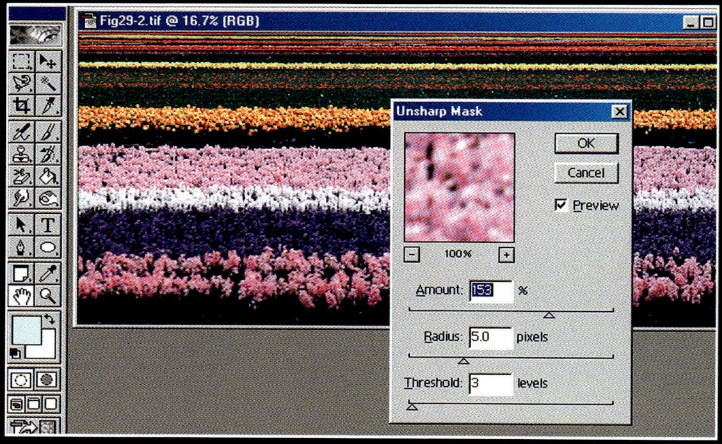

Fig 29.4

There have been a handful of occasions, however, when I have wanted to click on forever. Those exceptions included a fireworks display over Sydney Harbour, the Rocky Mountains near Banff in Canada, and Zimbabwe's Victoria Falls. Perhaps my expectation level rises amid such wonders, or maybe with so much to photograph I become over-excited and get a little careless with some of the basic techniques. Whatever the reason, I have noticed on such occasions that my overall standard of photography appears to drop. This goes to prove that a perfect setting does not automatically guarantee a perfect photograph.

I experienced another of these occasions one spring while travelling by train through Holland. At this time of year, it can seem as though the whole country is a flower garden filled with tulips and hyacinths. For mile after colourful mile, an amazing patchwork of beauty fills the view as far as the eye can see. To photograph this sea of colour, no matter how inadequately, is a challenge.

Was I to concentrate on design or colour, follow photographic clichés or try to be different, show the setting by using a wide-angle lens or zoom in close to focus on the flowers? *Bulb Fields* (fig. 29.1) typifies my dilemma. In this instance, by concentrating my attention on the distant horizon I let the foreground slip out of focus.

On reflection, I also feel that the horizon works against the rest of my photograph. The almost countless horizontal planes suggest a feeling of endless space, distance and depth. The avoidance of any hint of frame within the photograph suggests a further extension of the flowers to both right and left.

We load the picture, use the CROP tool to make the right selection (fig. 29.3), and then double click on the mouse (or press ENTER on our keyboard) to cut out our chosen selection. We can also use IMAGE/ADJUST/LEVELS to enhance the colours and increase the contrast of the image.

Our image-editing software allows us to apply a number of FILTERS, and the most important in photograph enhancing is the SHARPEN filter. Both images from digital cameras and scanners usually benefit significantly from its use. So we click on FILTERS/SHARPEN/UNSHARP MASK.

As with Project 22 (see page 102), the screen that appears shows three variables (fig. 29.4). The THRESHOLD value informs the computer to ignore image tone values that are similar. A value of 4, for example, ignores all the tones that are within 4 level values of each other. The RADIUS value determines the width of the edge contrast increase. A value that is too high or too low leads to an ugly dark or light halo around the edges. The AMOUNT determines the strength of the sharpening.

As before, whenever we want to sharpen a picture, we make sure the preview picture is the same percentage (i.e. scale) as the main picture, otherwise we can't judge the result accurately. We can see this figure on the main picture's top bar (fig. 29.5). Experience helps with this technique, so practising with it until you are satisfied with the result (fig. 29.2) is an advantage. For future reference when using this filter, it is helpful to note the different values arrived at on successful occasions.

project
30

reinforcing the focal point

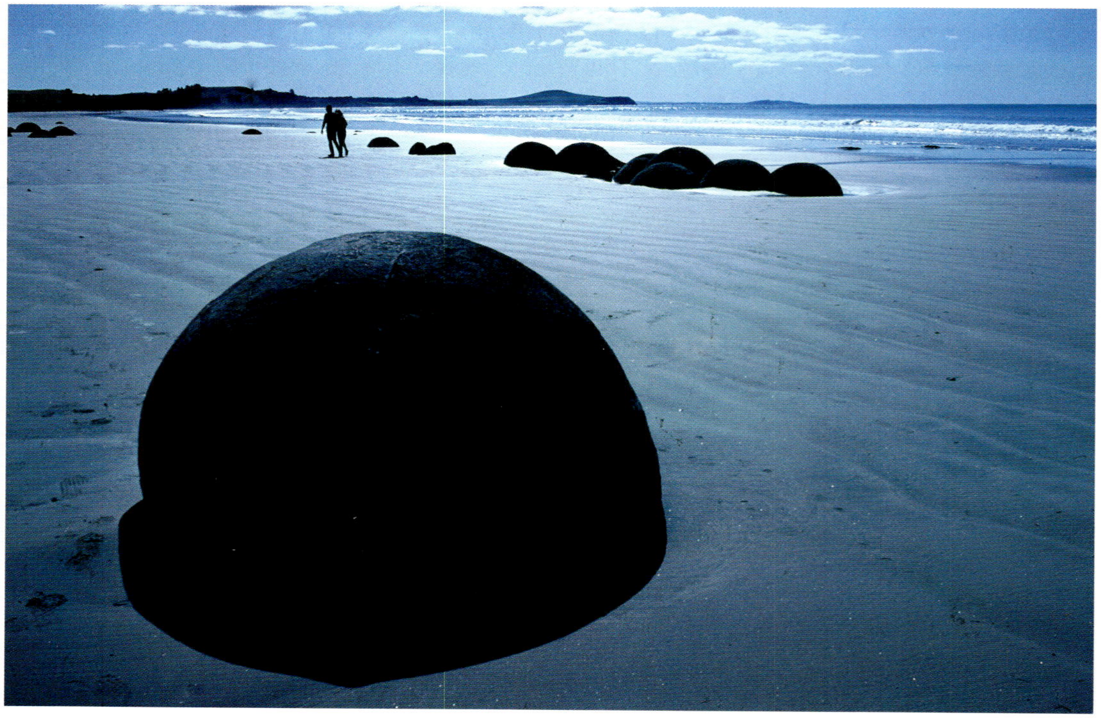

Fig 30.1 Including too much in this composition has meant that it fails to convey my mood of the moment.

CROP, ADJUST/COLOUR BALANCE

To many readers, the original photograph of *Beach Boulders* (fig. 30.1) may be more of a landscape photograph than its enhanced counterpart. Looking at it literally, the former satisfies the criteria of a landscape. Viewing it objectively, it is an honest record of the scene.

Fig 30.2 A more personal interpretation reflects my experience at the time with greater accuracy.

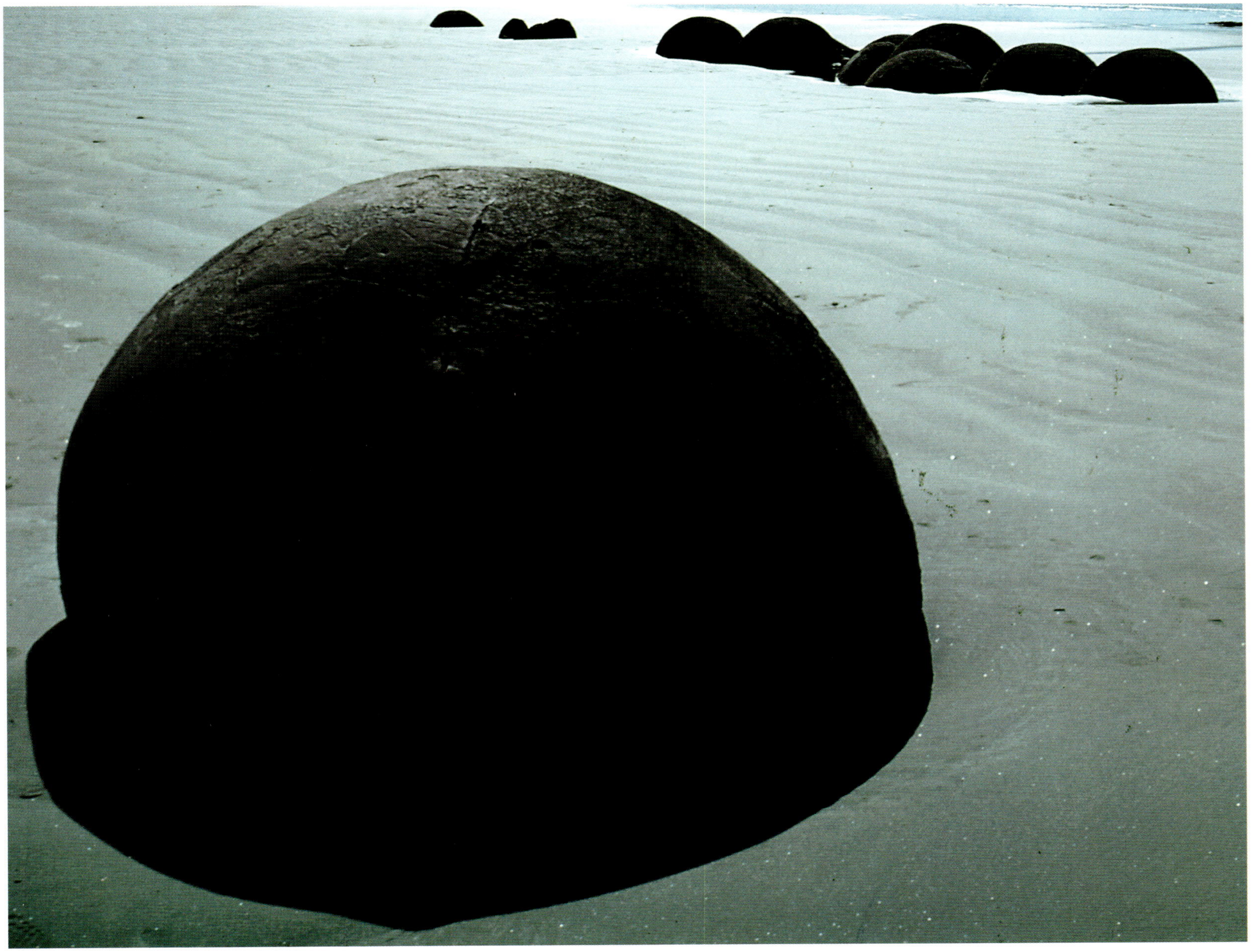

However, a photographer must also be honest with himself. One of the attractions I find in landscape photography is the subjective choice a photographer can enjoy. It is the satisfaction of a personal interpretation. A landscape photograph might only show the surface, but a landscape photographer may see much deeper. This may not be the case with every snap taken of the scenery, but the potential is there for it to happen. Further, the computer is available to enhance the photographic statement and to reinforce the photographer's personal point of view.

The original *Beach Boulders* shows what I saw: a beach, white-capped waves, blue skies, rocks and tourists. Described like that it is an average picture postcard and could have been taken at about half the holiday destinations on earth. What it does not do is describe how I felt at the time about what I photographed.

I had travelled to this beach specifically to photograph this rock formation. It is a public beach and the tourists had as much right to be here as I did, but at that moment I viewed them as an intrusion into my private world. Also, the cool blue of the scene that the final result reflects was not, to me, a true representation of the warmth I felt at the time.

You may recognize the techniques employed to enhance this image from some of the other projects in the book. This is deliberate. It is important to realize that each technique has infinite uses and can be applied in combinations limited only by our own thinking.

We load the photograph and use the CROP tool (fig. 30.3) to cut out the area we wish to keep. Having done so, we find that part of the two tourist figures, plus a couple of small distracting boulders on the water's edge, still remain. As usual there are a number of techniques we could employ to remove them. If we were to use the PAINTBRUSH in this instance, we would have to use the EYEDROPPER tool many times to ensure we included all the colour variations. A quicker way is to use the CLONE STAMP tool. So we activate it, sample a suitable area of the photograph with the ALT key pressed down, and 're-paint' the areas we wish to remove (fig. 30.4).

We use IMAGE/ADJUST/COLOUR BALANCE (fig. 30.5), when this has been completed, to change the colour to more closely match the original intention (fig. 30.2). (See Project 11, page 58, for details on using IMAGE/ADJUST/COLOUR BALANCE.)

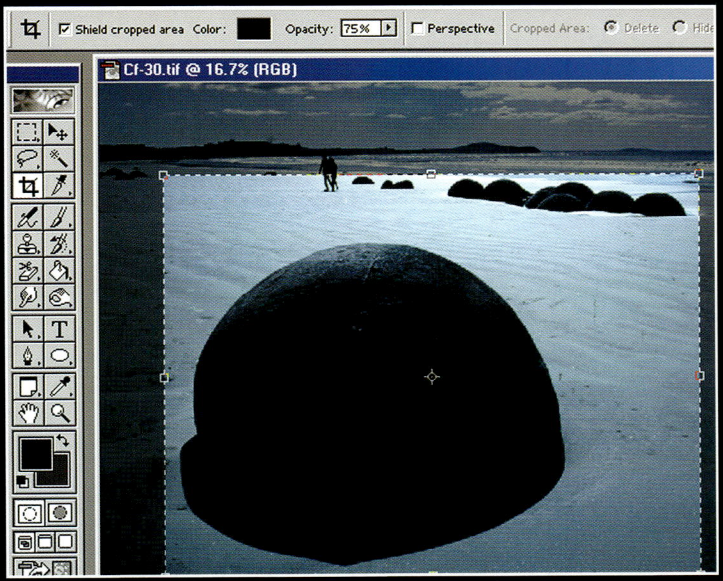

Fig 30.3

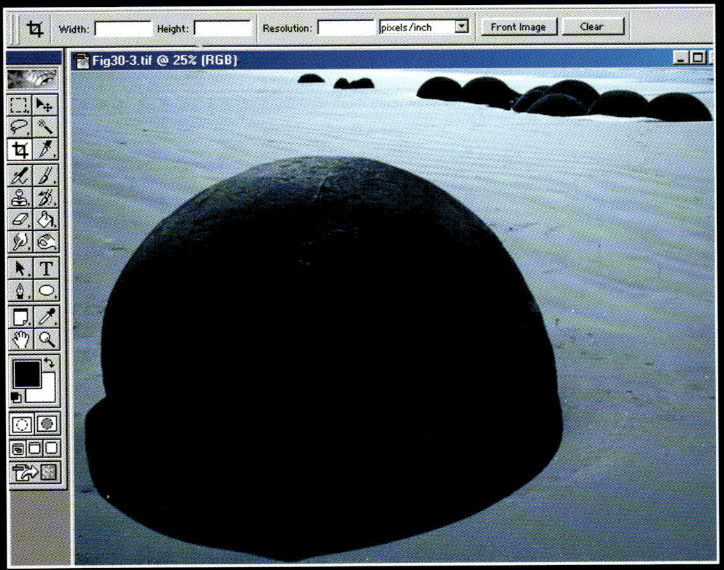

Fig 30.4

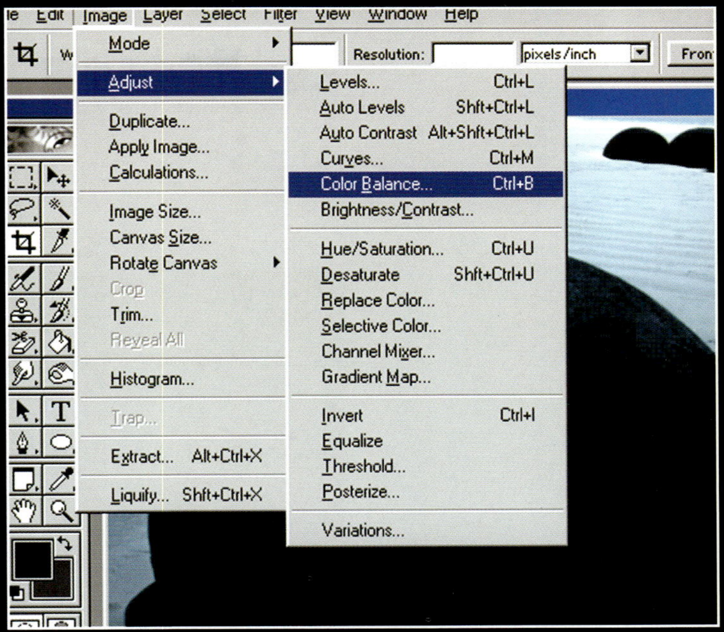

Fig 30.5

project 31

selecting colour variations

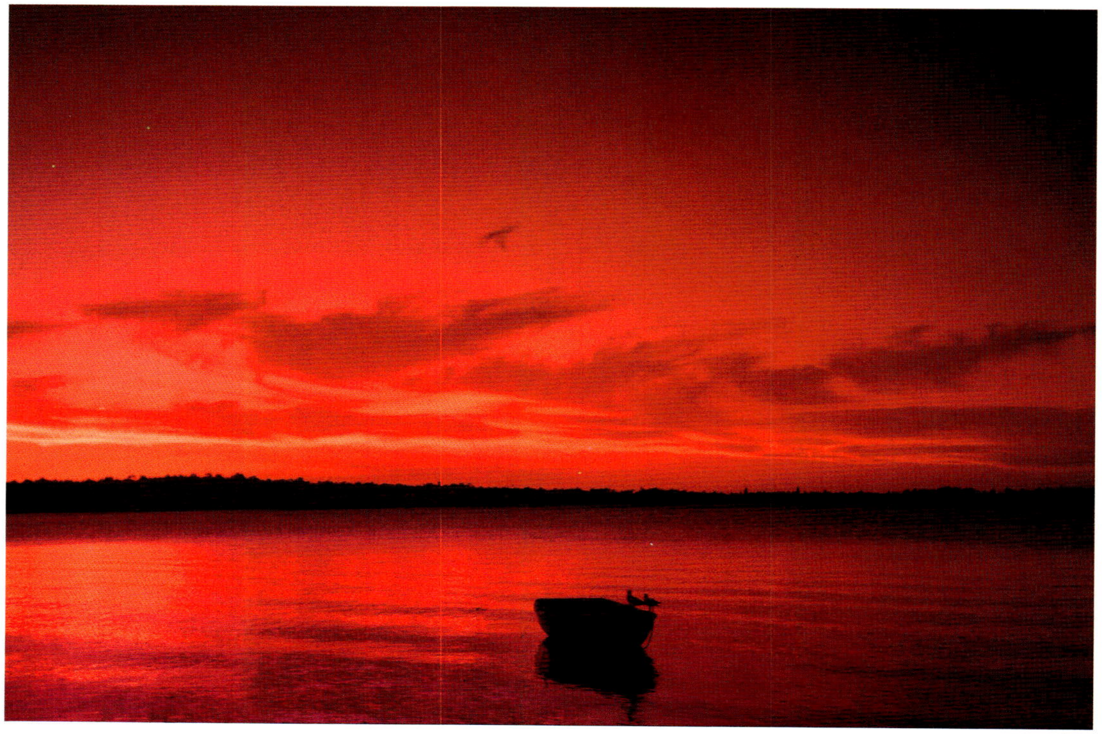

Fig 31.1 The intense colours of this image do not reflect how I felt at the time.

VARIATIONS

A subtle change in light resulting in the slightest change of colour can, due to the related experiences we have enjoyed or endured, effect us greatly. I can look back on two particularly prominent examples.

Fig 31.2 The computer allows us to make any number of subtle changes to colour in order to satisfy our interpretation.

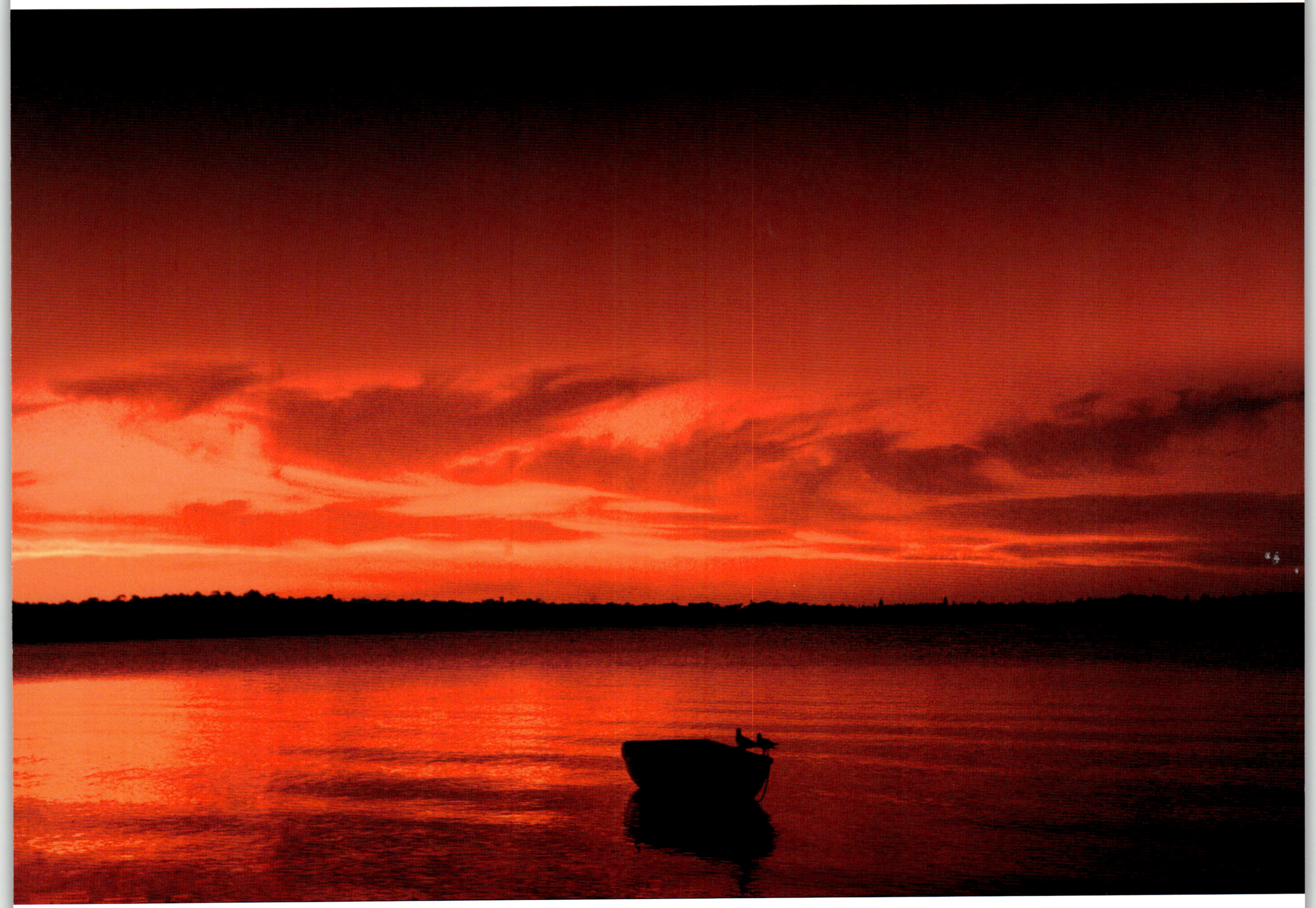

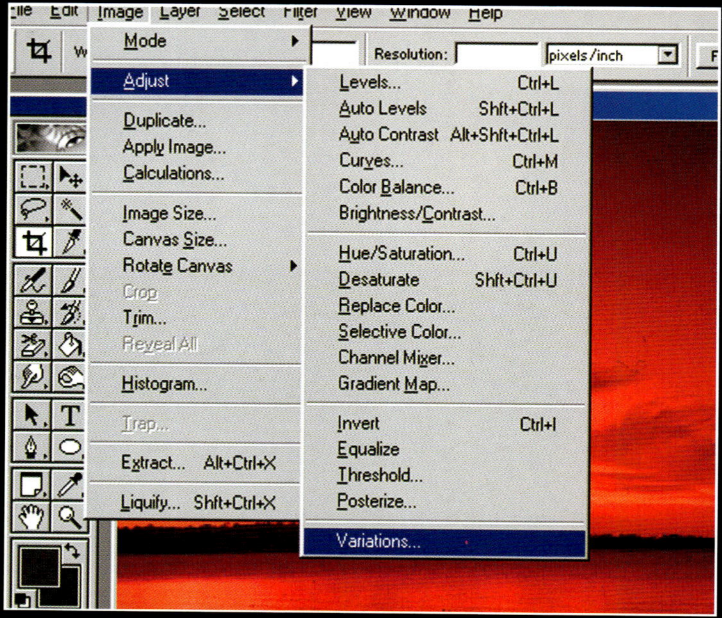

Fig 31.3

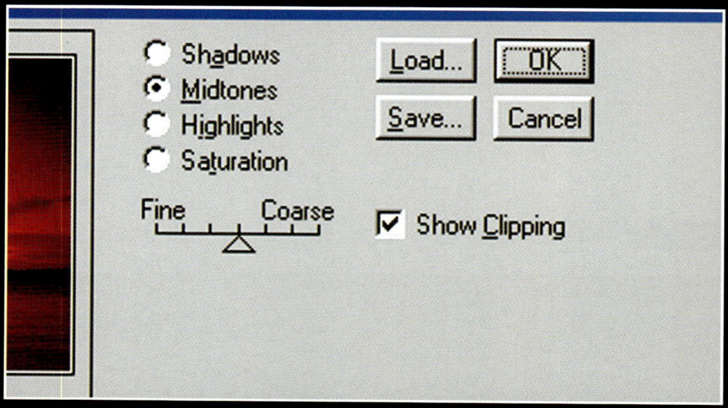

Fig 31.5

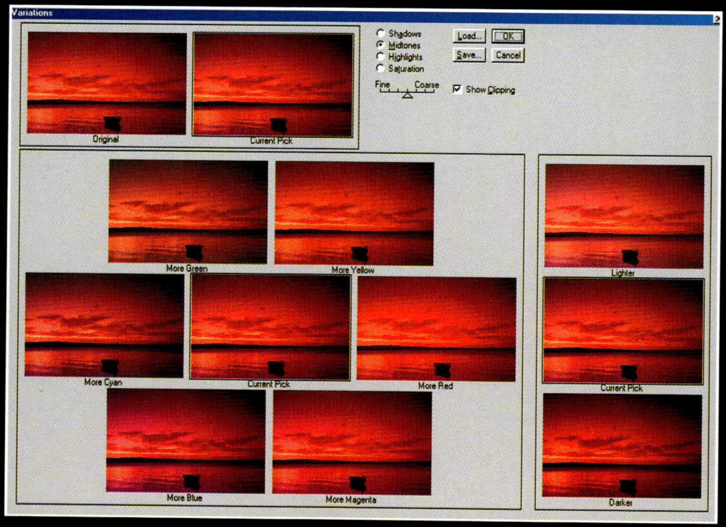

Fig 31.4

On one occasion, an erupting volcano, hundreds of miles away from where I lived, had created an enormous cloud of ash that had been blowing for days across the sky. It offered no threat, and had little impact other than to filter the sun gently and leave a surreal and pleasing lighting effect across the land. At the time I lived near a beautiful beach, enjoyed all the creature comforts imaginable, felt 'at one' with myself and happy with my world.

On a second occasion, bush fires had been raging out of control for days and man seemed powerless to stop the elements of nature. Lives had been lost, homes had been destroyed and the countryside had been devastated. A cloud of ash hung across the sun just as danger hung in the air, and a surreal light lay across the land. At the time I faced a crisis in my work, my health was suffering as a consequence and an unsure future lay ahead of me.

The atmosphere from both situations, though different, was similar. However, years later, whenever I see a photograph that reminds me of either of these two scenes my immediate reaction is a world apart from one to the other. Even now as I write, my mood alters as I think of the two.

I might never have shot *Red Sky* (fig. 31.1) if it had not been for the experience that had immediately preceded it. I had just completed directing two intense, three-hour photographic workshops and for a change of pace had headed down to this tranquil lakeside setting. A colourful sky was building towards sunset. In spite of how the scene may have looked through the lens when aided by a filter or two, it did not look so pleasing when I saw the result.

Of course, I knew the brighter the colour the less is needed to make a colourful impact. However, after the highs of the day I was not concentrating properly on the job in hand. As a result I was careless and failed to take what should have been a restful photograph.

The computer enables us to make, in a matter of moments, a wide range of subtle (or not so subtle) colour variations to an image. Given the complexity of the colours contained here, we choose IMAGE/ADJUST/VARIATIONS (fig. 31.3). This allows us to see and compare the widest range of colour variations possible (fig. 31.4). By moving the slider located at the top of the screen from FINE to COURSE (fig. 31.5) we can make all manner of changes. By clicking on the LIGHTER and DARKER options, and on the colour correction possibilities, we can produce the perfect picture every time (fig 31.2).

project
32

combining two images

Fig 32.1 This shot would benefit from a foreground silhouette to complement and complete it.

FLIP, MAGIC WAND, TRANSFORM/SCALE

Mountain Sunset (fig. 32.1), in spite of its colour, lacks a foreground platform from which to build a photograph to match the experience of taking it.

Being able to use the computer to edit your photographs will change the way you take them. When something is missing from a composition, you will still take the snap because you know that you can always find a remedy at a later date.

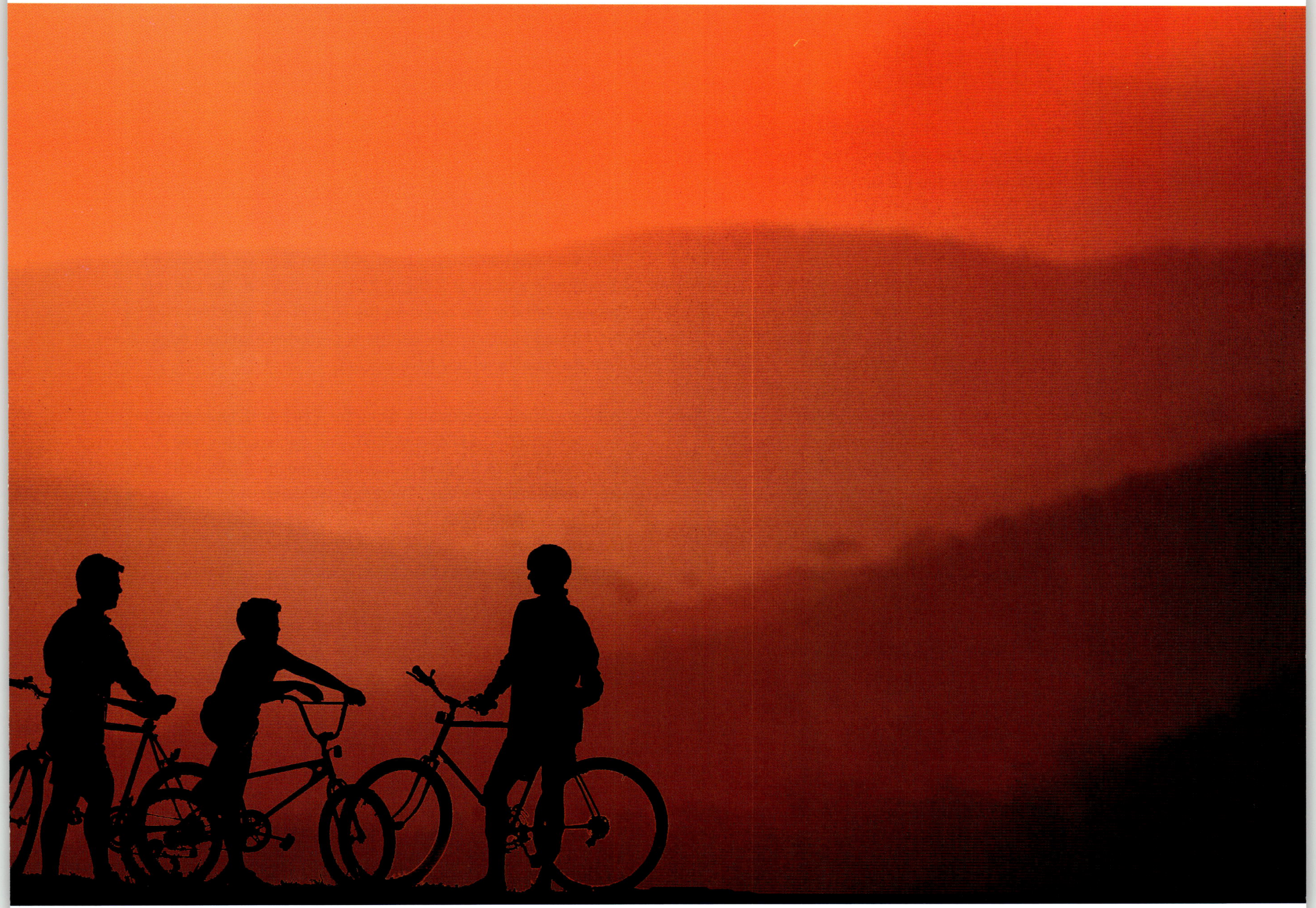

Fig 32.2 The simple combining of two photographs accomplishes our aim and illustrates, as with every other procedure in this book, the value of the computer in our photography.

Quickly looking through our slide database (another advantage of having a computer), we find a second sunset that has a foreground (fig. 32.3). If we can combine the two effectively we will have one very strong image. Imagine the cyclists fitting perfectly into the bottom-left corner of the original sunset. From this second image we need only the three figures with their bicycles, as we have the background sunset already from our first picture.

So, the task before us is to remove the three figures from the second photograph and place them appropriately in the first. As usual, there are different ways of doing this. Here, we will use the MAGIC WAND option, which is located under the MOVE tool in the toolbox. The MAGIC WAND enables us to remove everything in one colour, and slight gradations of that colour, from an image. This technique is easy to apply to our image of the cyclists, as they are largely one colour (i.e. black).

First, if we flip the sunset image, allowing the hills to rise from the left to the right, the composition will be stronger and the cyclists will fit even better. This is a very simple technique. With our image on-screen, we click with our left mouse button on the IMAGE pull-down menu and choose ROTATE CANVAS. Then we select FLIP HORIZONTAL (fig. 32.4). To save this reversed background we follow a similar procedure to loading an image but activate FILE/SAVE AS instead of FILE/OPEN, name it (e.g. *Reversed Sunset*) to identify it, and click OK.

Having established our background it is time to transfer the cyclists, using the MAGIC WAND. First, we load the picture of the cyclists onto the screen. If there is insufficient contrast between the black and the other colours we can use the LEVELS/ADJUST option to darken the black. You will see when you try something similar with one of your own images that the greater the contrast, the stronger the effect of this tool will be. We activate the MAGIC WAND and click the cursor on the black area we want to remove. The marching ants appear on the screen indicating our selection.

At this stage, we find that not everything we require has been selected. By holding down the SHIFT key and clicking on additional parts of our image, we can add to our selection. (We can also remove parts from the selection by clicking on them with the ALT key pressed down.) We continue doing this until our selection is complete. If we have trouble with details, such as the narrow lines of the spokes, we use the ZOOM tool to enlarge them.

With our selection complete we go to the SELECT FEATHER menu, type a value of 2 (fig. 32.5) and click OK. We use this because some of the pixels on the edge of our selection may be red instead of black; the feathering produces a smooth edge where a rough one may have existed.

We transfer our selection by using the EDIT pull-down menu. We click on EDIT and choose CUT. The cyclists have now disappeared from the screen leaving a smooth-edged white area that we no longer require. Therefore, we delete it by clicking on the X in the right-hand corner of the image bar. When asked if we wish to save the changes to this image we click NO. The selection has moved to the clipboard and is stored there.

To date we have flipped the main image and cut out the part we need from the second image. Now it is time to bring the two together into one new image. We load the saved *Reversed Sunset* onto the screen and add the cyclists by clicking on the EDIT menu and selecting the PASTE command.

By pasting the cyclists onto the image of the sunset we have added a new layer to our existing background layer. To carry out our next step, the layer containing the cyclists needs to be active. We use the mouse button to click on the MOVE tool in the toolbox. We bring the cursor over to the image, click the left mouse button and, keeping it pressed down, move the cyclists across the background. To reduce the cyclists to the correct scale, we click on the EDIT menu and select TRANSFORM and then SCALE (fig. 32.6).

A box appears around our image of the cyclists, with small squares located in the corners and at the centre of each side. We place our cursor on one of the corner squares. With our left mouse button and the SHIFT key held down, we move the cursor towards the centre of the image, making it smaller (holding the SHIFT key retains the proportions of the image while the size changes). Next, we click the mouse button on the MOVE tool and confirm whether or not we wish to apply the change. We click on APPLY and the image shrinks to its applied size.

Now, we have the background layer and a second layer containing the correctly sized cyclists. We use the MOVE tool again to place the cyclists in position. In their original setting the cyclists stood on a grassy knoll, which no longer exists in our new image.

Our image-editing software can also be used to paint in a foreground, but first we must make the two layers into one, or we end up painting only on the active layer. If we wish to make a print of our new image we must flatten it. Therefore, we go to the LAYER menu and click on FLATTEN IMAGE.

We use the EYEDROPPER tool to select the correct foreground colour and then choose a brush large enough to paint, in a single stroke, the necessary foreground for the cyclists to stand upon. Our sunset is now complete, or should we say 'perfect' (fig. 32.2)!

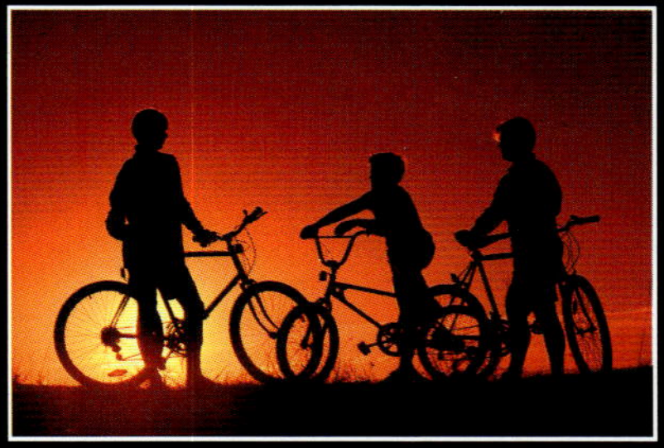

Fig 32.3

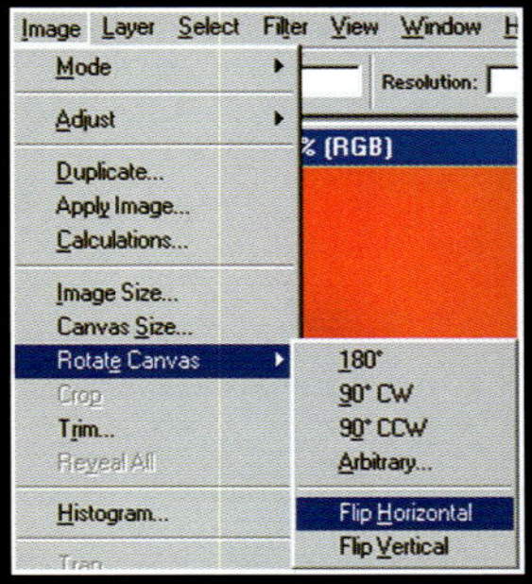

Fig 32.4

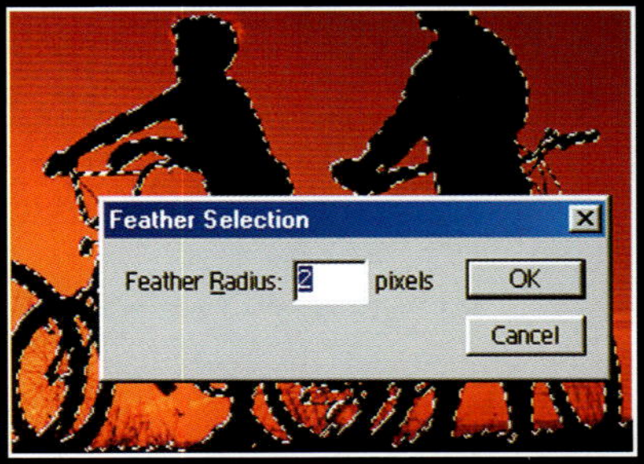

Fig 32.5

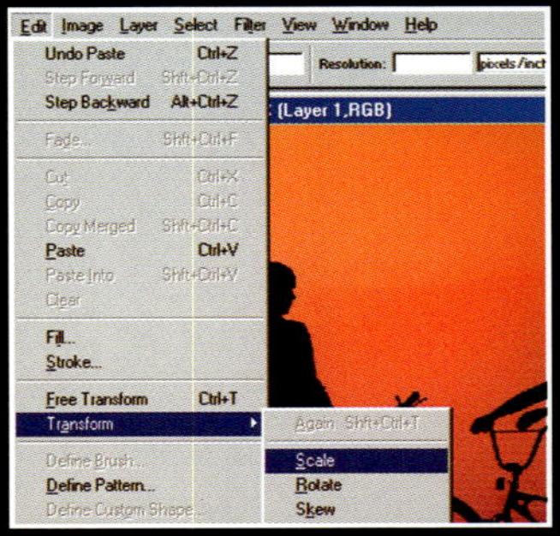

Fig 32.6

about the authors

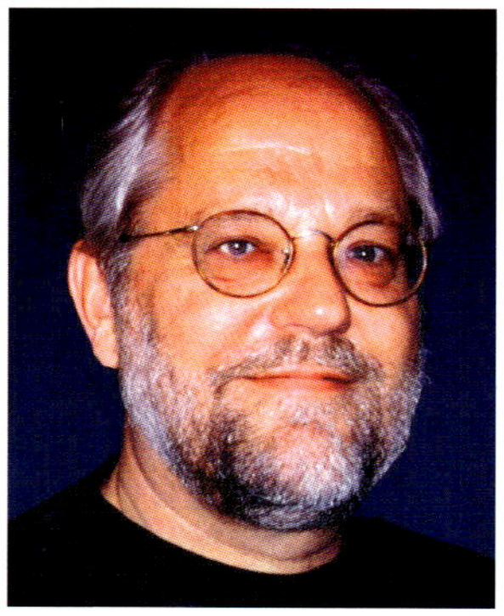

Dutch-born Arjan Hoogendam's interest in photography enabled him, through the sale of his photographs, to fund himself through university. Since then, he has combined his photographic talents with a long-standing interest in computers, much to the relief of the many friends and associates who have benefited from his expert guidance and tuition, including:

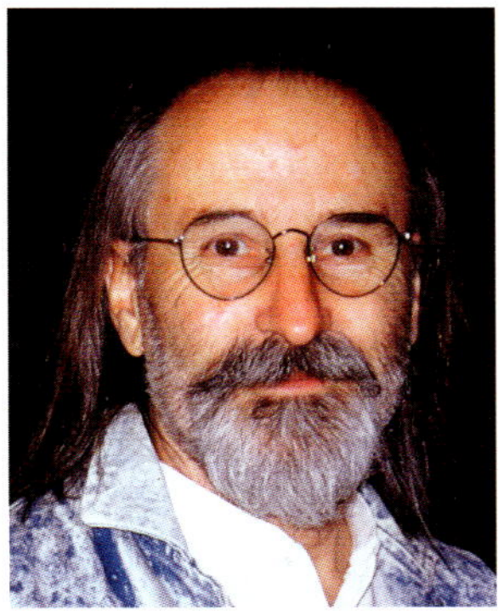

English-born Herb Parkin, whose work has appeared in *Photo World Magazine* (Australia), *Photography Yearbook* (UK), and the Nikon International calendar (Japan). His amateur photography has won numerous international honours, including a Gold Medal from the Photographic Society of America and a Fellowship from the Australian Photographic Society.

image index

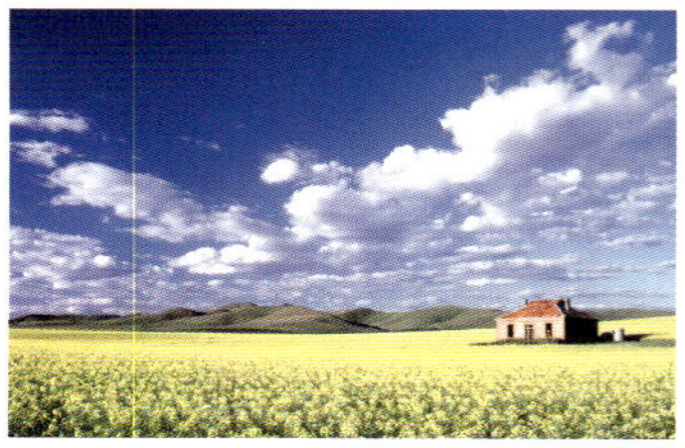
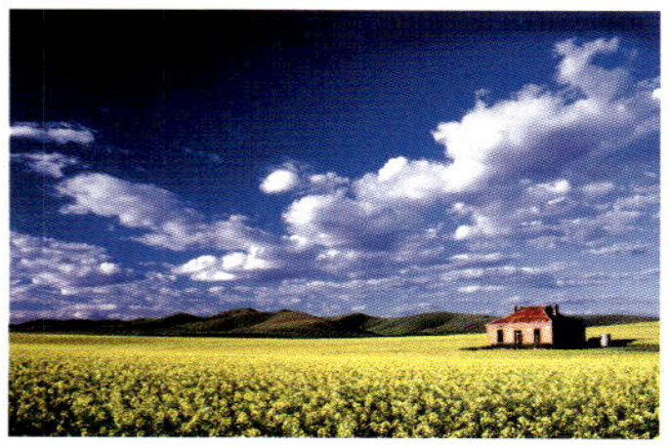

page 16 ADJUST/LEVELS

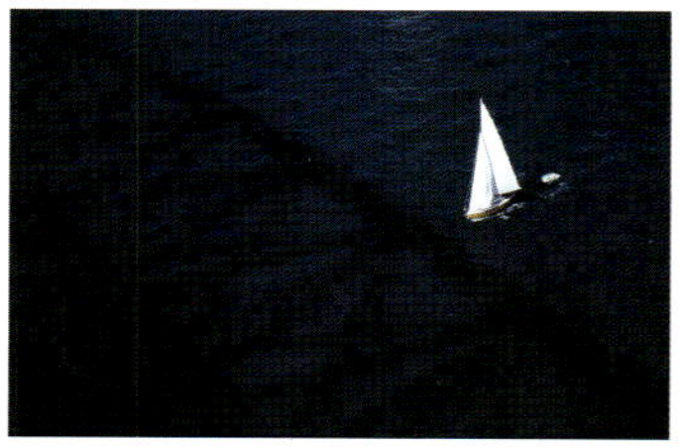
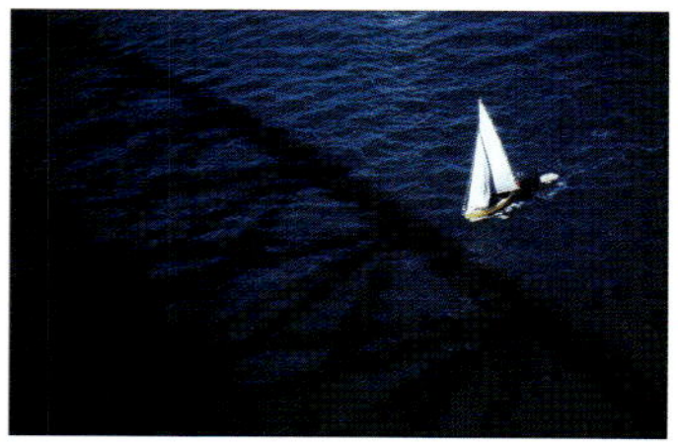

page 20 ADJUST/CURVES

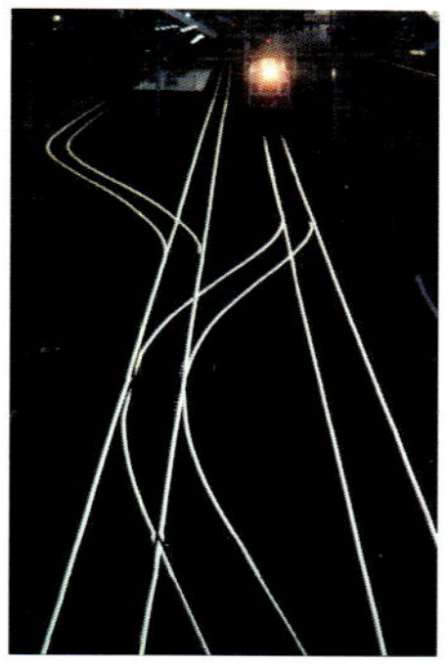
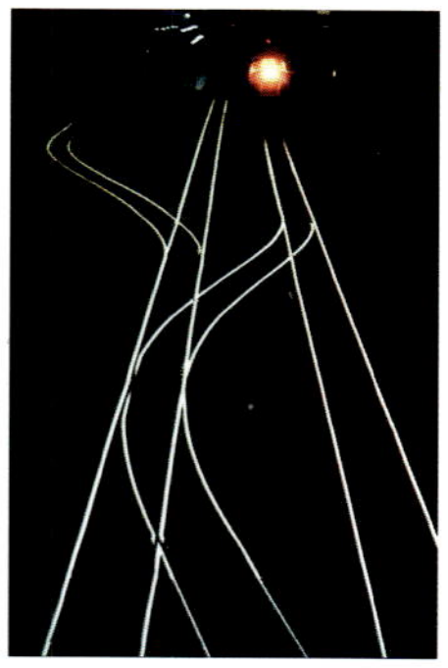

page 24 ADJUST/BRIGHTNESS-CONTRAST

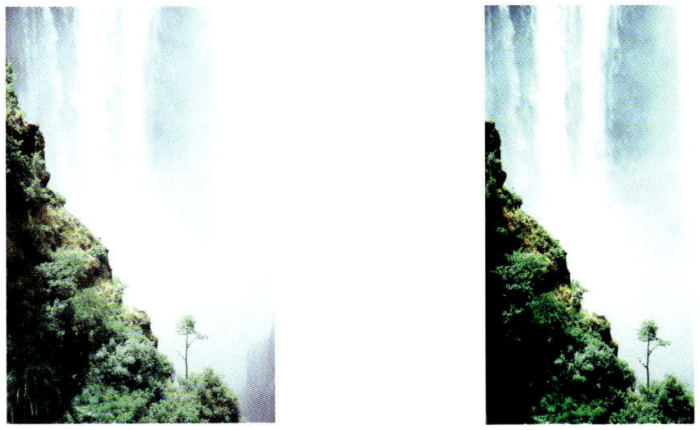

page 28 CROP, ADJUST/LEVELS

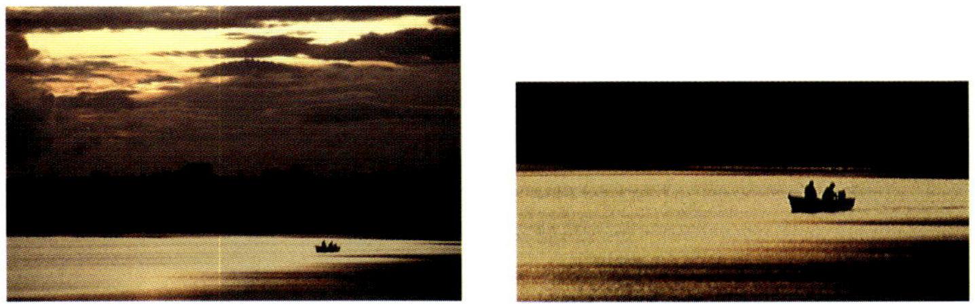

page 32 CROP, ADJUST/CURVES

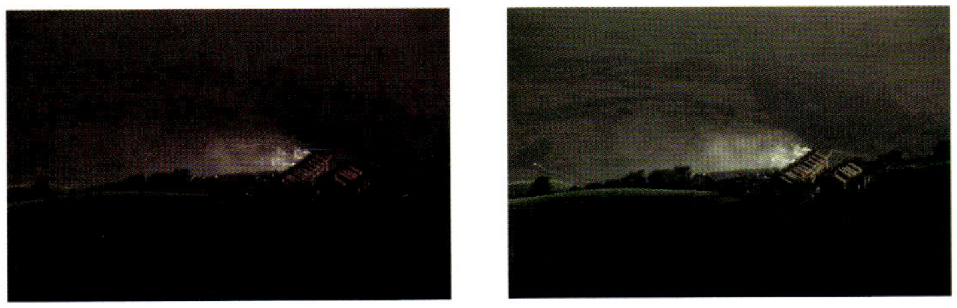

page 36 EYEDROPPER, PAINTBRUSH

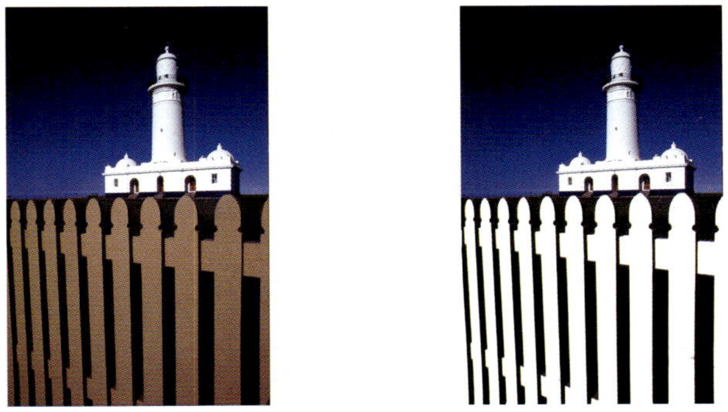

page 40 MAGIC WAND, PAINT BUCKET

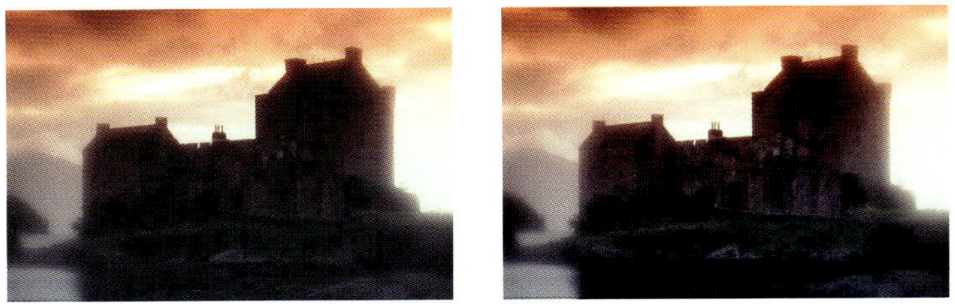

page 44 LASSO, BRIGHTNESS-CONTRAST

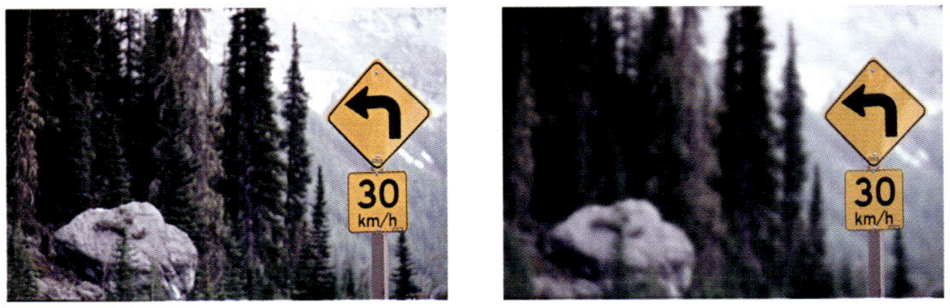

page 48 LASSO, GAUSSIAN BLUR

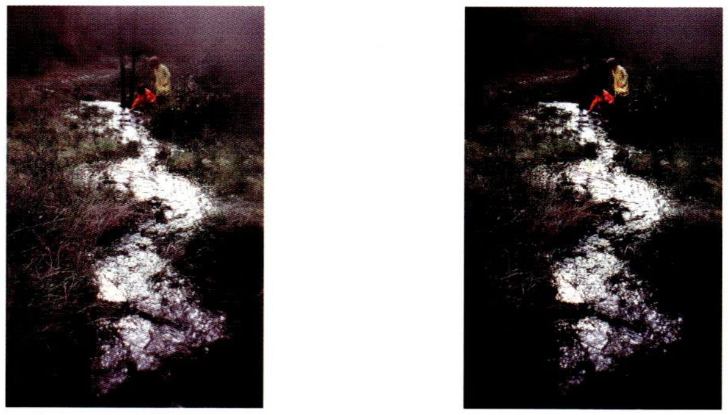

page 54 LASSO, ADJUST/LEVELS

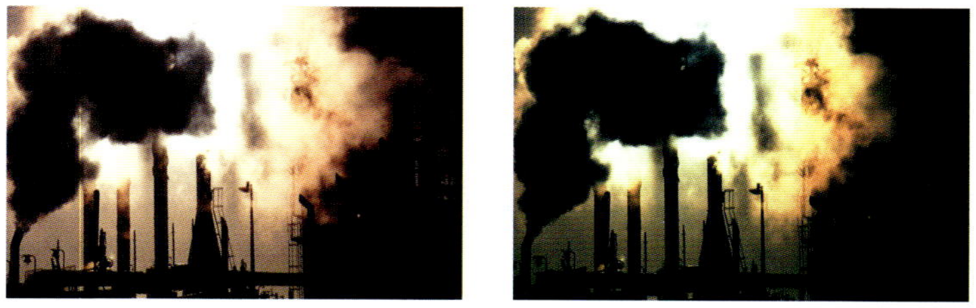

page 58 ADJUST/COLOUR BALANCE

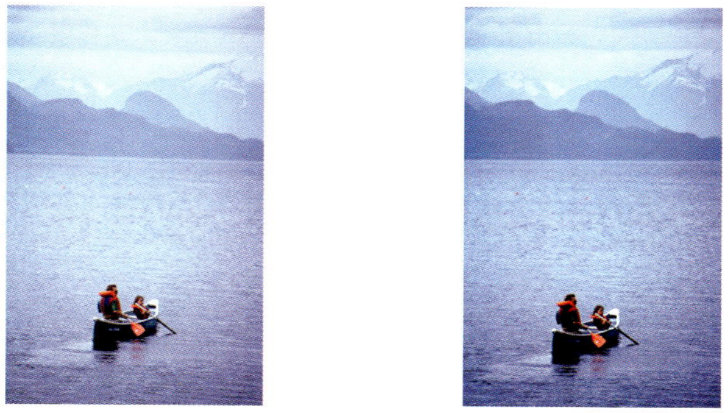

page 62 ROTATE CANVAS

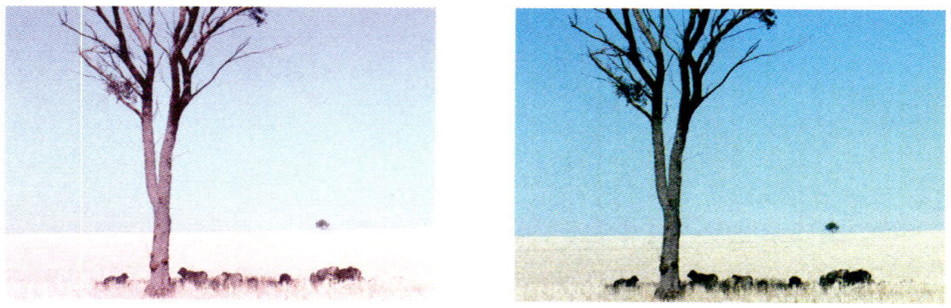

page 66 NEW LAYER/MODE/MULTIPLY

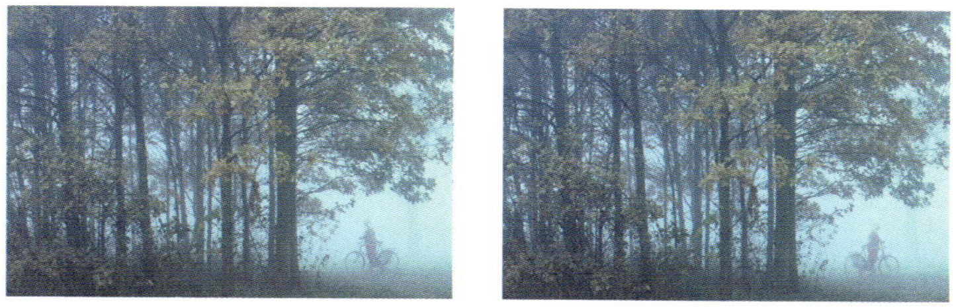

page 70 FLIP, CLONE STAMP

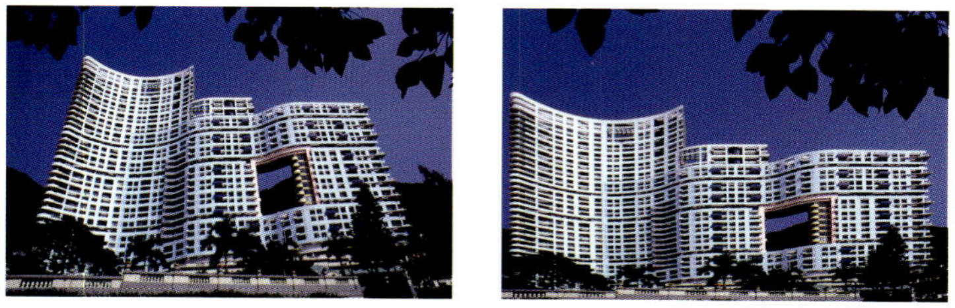

page 74 TRANSFORM/PERSPECTIVE

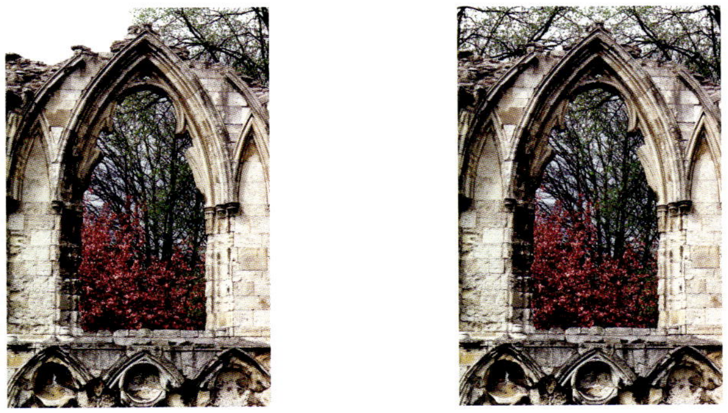

page 78 CUT, PASTE

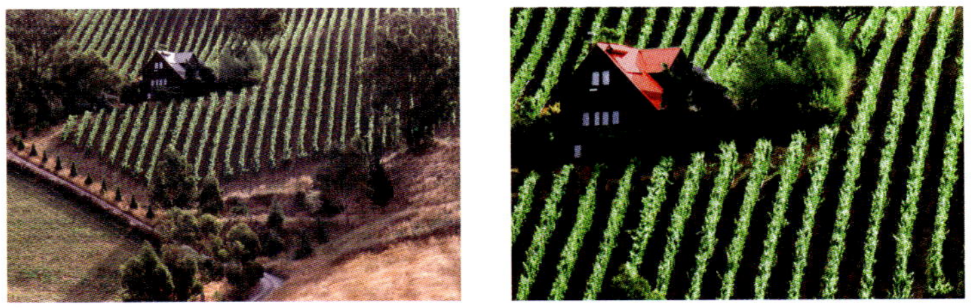

page 82 ADJUST/HUE/SATURATION

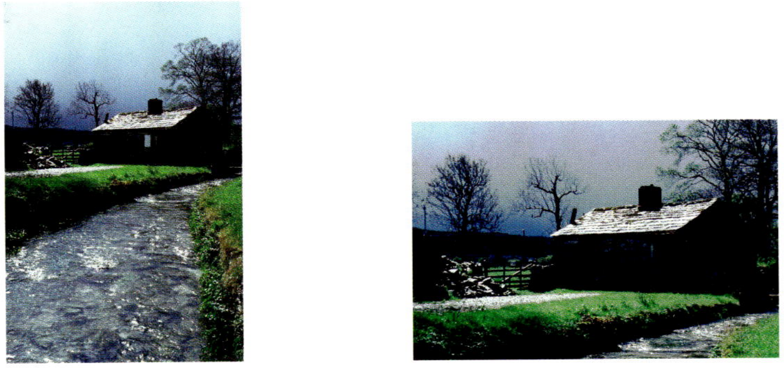

page 86 RECTANGULAR MARQUEE

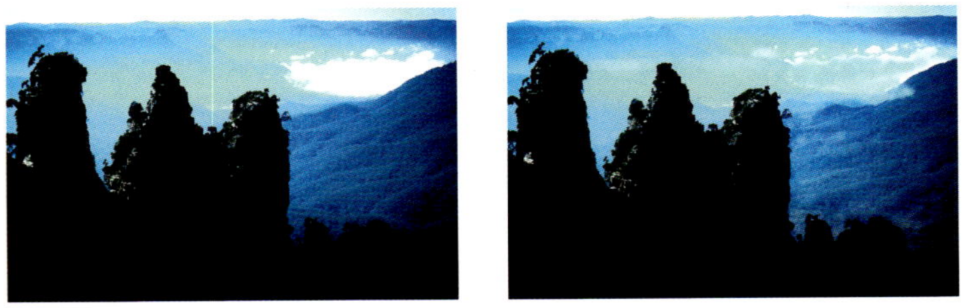

page 90 LAYERS, PAINTBRUSH

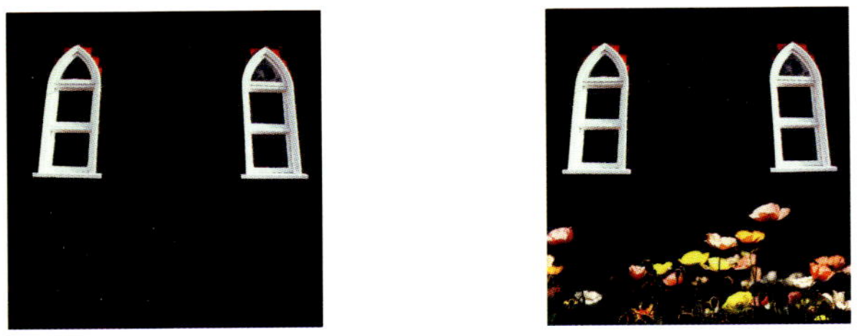

page 94 BACKGROUND ERASER, PASTE

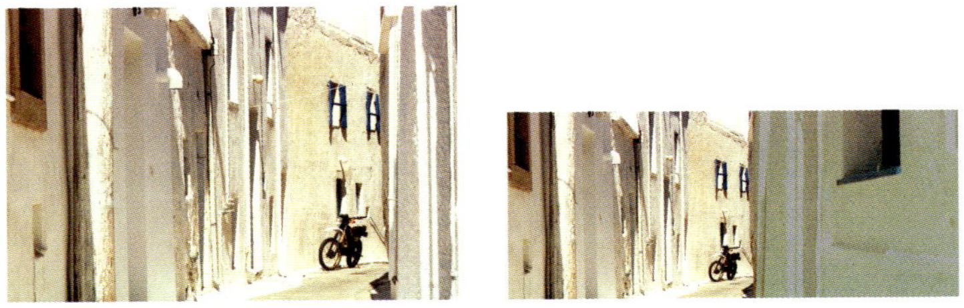

page 98 CANVAS SIZE, TRANSFORM/SCALE

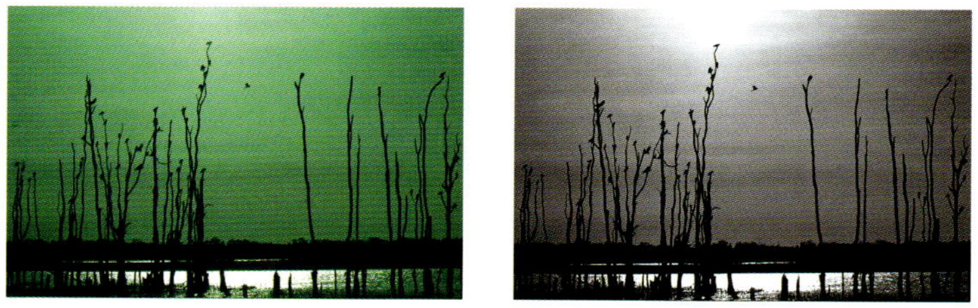

page 102 CHANNEL MIXER, UNSHARP MASK

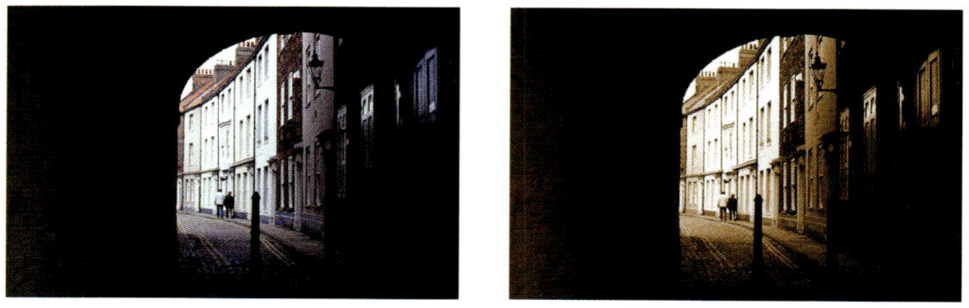

page 106 CHANNEL MIXER, MONOCHROME

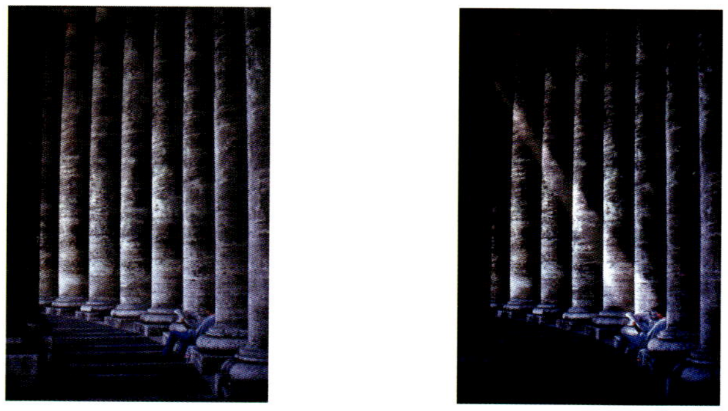

page 110 POLYGONAL LASSO

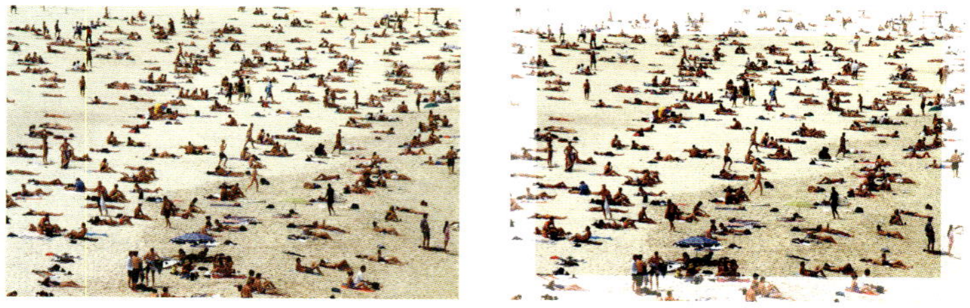

page 114 RECTANGULAR MARQUEE, RULERS

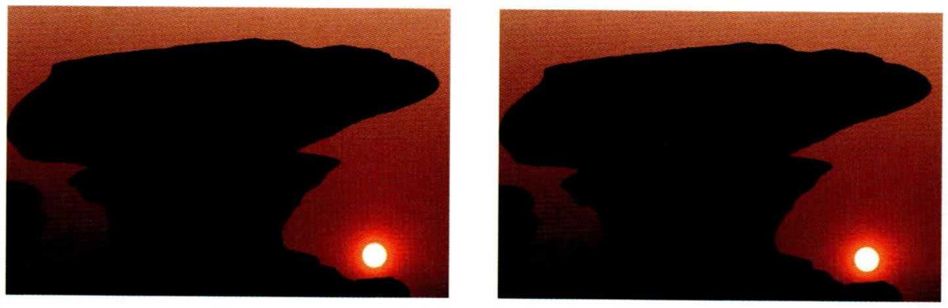

page 118 CLONE STAMP

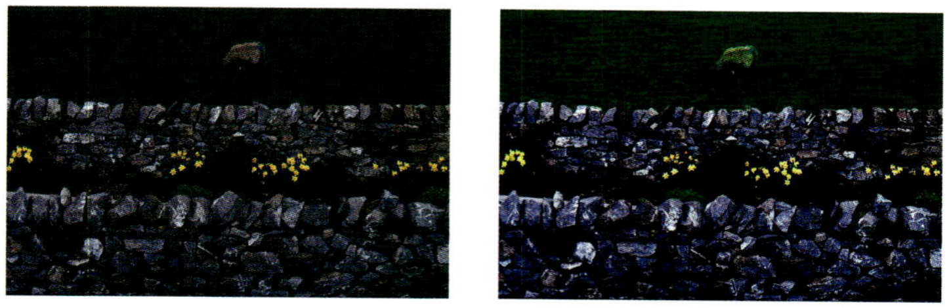

page 122 LASSO

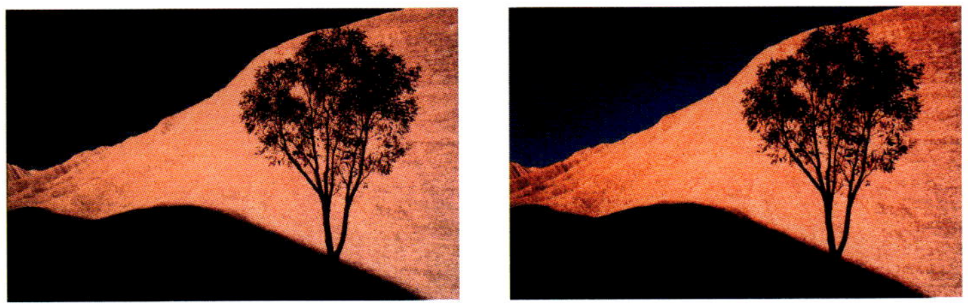

page 126 MAGNETIC LASSO, QUICK MASK

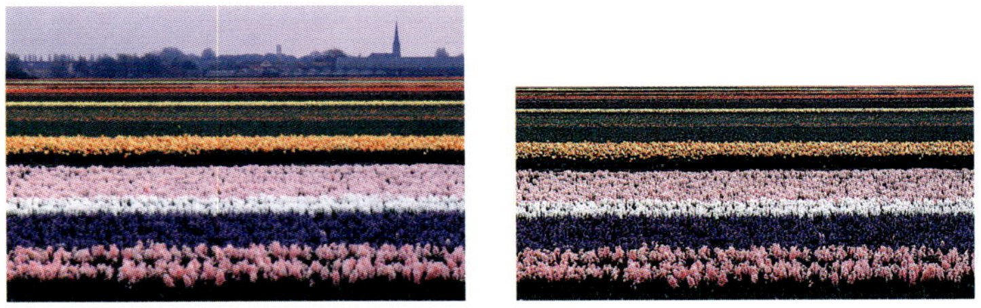

page 130 UNSHARP MASK

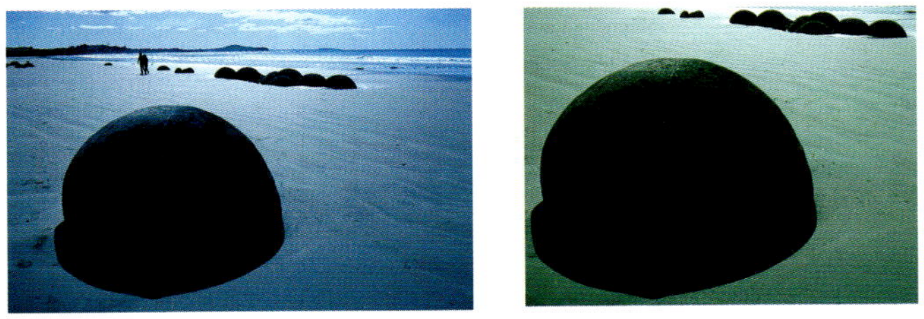

page 134 CROP, ADJUST/COLOUR BALANCE

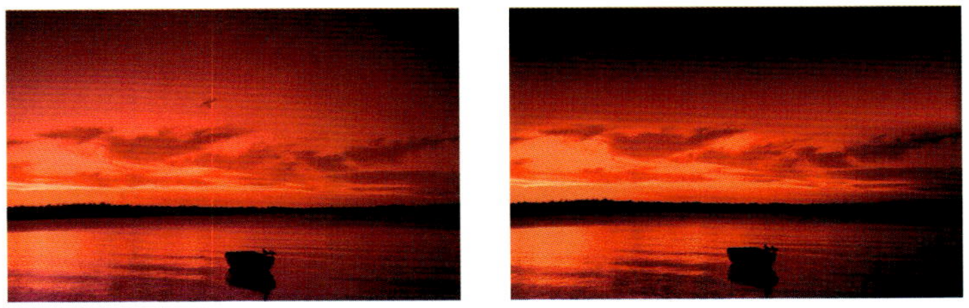

page 138 VARIATIONS

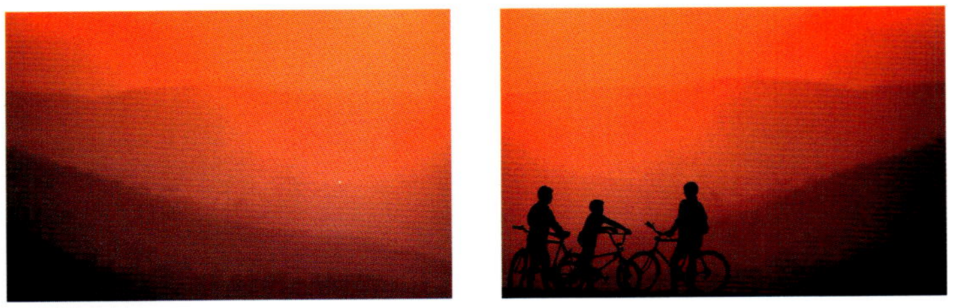

page 142 FLIP, MAGIC WAND, TRANSFORM/SCALE

index

D

E

F

G

H

I

L

M

S

T

U

V

Z

Dolls' Houses and Miniatures

1/12 Scale Character Figures for the Dolls' House — *James Carrington*
Americana in 1/12 Scale: 50 Authentic Projects — *Joanne Ogreenc & Mary Lou Santovec*
The Authentic Georgian Dolls' House — *Brian Long*
A Beginners' Guide to the Dolls' House Hobby — *Jean Nisbett*
Celtic, Medieval and Tudor Wall Hangings in 1/12 Scale Needlepoint — *Sandra Whitehead*
Creating Decorative Fabrics: Projects in 1/12 Scale — *Janet Storey*
Dolls' House Accessories, Fixtures and Fittings — *Andrea Barham*
Dolls' House Furniture: Easy-to-Make Projects in 1/12 Scale — *Freida Gray*
Dolls' House Makeovers — *Jean Nisbett*
Dolls' House Window Treatments — *Eve Harwood*
Edwardian-Style Hand-Knitted Fashion for 1/12 Scale Dolls — *Yvonne Wakefield*
How to Make Your Dolls' House Special: Fresh Ideas for Decorating — *Beryl Armstrong*
Making 1/12 Scale Wicker Furniture for the Dolls' House — *Sheila Smith*
Making Miniature Chinese Rugs and Carpets — *Carol Phillipson*
Making Miniature Food and Market Stalls — *Angie Scarr*
Making Miniature Gardens — *Freida Gray*
Making Miniature Oriental Rugs & Carpets — *Meik & Ian McNaughton*
Making Period Dolls' House Accessories — *Andrea Barham*
Making Tudor Dolls' Houses — *Derek Rowbottom*
Making Victorian Dolls' House Furniture — *Patricia King*
Medieval and Tudor Needlecraft: Knights and Ladies in 1/12 Scale — *Sandra Whitehead*
Miniature Bobbin Lace — *Roz Snowden*
Miniature Embroidery for the Georgian Dolls' House — *Pamela Warner*
Miniature Embroidery for the Tudor and Stuart Dolls' House — *Pamela Warner*
Miniature Embroidery for the Victorian Dolls' House — *Pamela Warner*
Miniature Needlepoint Carpets — *Janet Granger*
More Miniature Oriental Rugs & Carpets — *Meik & Ian McNaughton*
Needlepoint 1/12 Scale: Design Collections for the Dolls' House — *Felicity Price*
New Ideas for Miniature Bobbin Lace — *Roz Snowden*
Patchwork Quilts for the Dolls' House: 20 Projects in 1/12 Scale — *Sarah Williams*

Crafts

Bargello: A Fresh Approach to Florentine Embroidery — *Brenda Day*
Beginning Picture Marquetry — *Lawrence Threadgold*
Blackwork: A New Approach — *Brenda Day*
Celtic Cross Stitch Designs — *Carol Phillipson*
Celtic Knotwork Designs — *Sheila Sturrock*
Celtic Knotwork Handbook — *Sheila Sturrock*
Celtic Spirals and Other Designs — *Sheila Sturrock*
Complete Pyrography — *Stephen Poole*
Creating Made-to-Measure Knitwear: A Revolutionary Approach to Knitwear Design — *Sylvia Wynn*
Creative Backstitch — *Helen Hall*
The Creative Quilter: Techniques and Projects — *Pauline Brown*
Cross-Stitch Designs from China — *Carol Phillipson*
Cross-Stitch Floral Designs — *Joanne Sanderson*
Decoration on Fabric: A Sourcebook of Ideas — *Pauline Brown*
Decorative Beaded Purses — *Enid Taylor*
Designing and Making Cards — *Glennis Gilruth*
Glass Engraving Pattern Book — *John Everett*
Glass Painting — *Emma Sedman*
Handcrafted Rugs — *Sandra Hardy*
Hobby Ceramics: Techniques and Projects for Beginners — *Patricia A. Waller*
How to Arrange Flowers: A Japanese Approach to English Design — *Taeko Marvelly*
How to Make First-Class Cards — *Debbie Brown*
An Introduction to Crewel Embroidery — *Mave Glenny*
Making Decorative Screens — *Amanda Howes*
Making Fabergé-Style Eggs — *Denise Hopper*
Making Fairies and Fantastical Creatures — *Julie Sharp*
Making Hand-Sewn Boxes: Techniques and Projects — *Jackie Woolsey*
Making Mini Cards, Gift Tags & Invitations — *Glennis Gilruth*
Native American Bead Weaving — *Lynne Garner*
New Ideas for Crochet: Stylish Projects for the Home — *Darsha Capaldi*
Papercraft Projects for Special Occasions — *Sine Chesterman*
Patchwork for Beginners — *Pauline Brown*
Pyrography Designs — *Norma Gregory*
Rose Windows for Quilters — *Angela Besley*
Silk Painting for Beginners — *Jill Clay*
Sponge Painting — *Ann Rooney*
Stained Glass: Techniques and Projects — *Mary Shanahan*
Step-by-Step Pyrography Projects for the Solid Point Machine — *Norma Gregory*
Tassel Making for Beginners — *Enid Taylor*
Tatting Collage — *Lindsay Rogers*
Tatting Patterns — *Lyn Morton*
Temari: A Traditional Japanese Embroidery Technique — *Margaret Ludlow*
Trompe l'Oeil: Techniques and Projects — *Jan Lee Johnson*
Tudor Treasures to Embroider — *Pamela Warner*
Wax Art — *Hazel Marsh*

Gardening

Alpine Gardening — *Chris & Valerie Wheeler*
Auriculas for Everyone: How to Grow and Show Perfect Plants — *Mary Robinson*
Beginners' Guide to Herb Gardening — *Yvonne Cuthbertson*
Beginners' Guide to Water Gardening — *Graham Clarke*
The Birdwatcher's Garden — *Hazel & Pamela Johnson*
Companions to Clematis: Growing Clematis with Other Plants — *Marigold Badcock*
Creating Contrast with Dark Plants — *Freya Martin*
Creating Small Habitats for Wildlife in your Garden — *Josie Briggs*
Exotics are Easy — *GMC Publications*
Gardening with Hebes — *Chris & Valerie Wheeler*
Gardening with Wild Plants — *Julian Slatcher*
Growing Cacti and Other Succulents in the Conservatory and Indoors — *Shirley-Anne Bell*
Growing Cacti and Other Succulents in the Garden — *Shirley-Anne Bell*
Growing Successful Orchids in the Greenhouse and Conservatory — *Mark Isaac-Williams*
Hardy Palms and Palm-Like Plants — *Martyn Graham*
Hardy Perennials: A Beginner's Guide — *Eric Sawford*

Hedges: Creating Screens and Edges *Averil Bedrich*
Marginal Plants *Bernard Sleeman*
Orchids are Easy: A Beginner's Guide to their Care and Cultivation *Tom Gilland*
Plant Alert: A Garden Guide for Parents *Catherine Collins*
Planting Plans for Your Garden *Jenny Shukman*
Sink and Container Gardening Using Dwarf Hardy Plants *Chris & Valerie Wheeler*
The Successful Conservatory and Growing Exotic Plants *Joan Phelan*
Tropical Garden Style with Hardy Plants *Alan Hemsley*
Water Garden Projects: From Groundwork to Planting *Roger Sweetinburgh*

PHOTOGRAPHY

Close-Up on Insects *Robert Thompson*
Double Vision *Chris Weston & Nigel Hicks*
An Essential Guide to Bird Photography *Steve Young*
Field Guide to Bird Photography *Steve Young*
Field Guide to Landscape Photography *Peter Watson*
How to Photograph Pets *Nick Ridley*
In my Mind's Eye: Seeing in Black and White *Charlie Waite*
Life in the Wild: A Photographer's Year *Andy Rouse*
Light in the Landscape: A Photographer's Year *Peter Watson*
Outdoor Photography Portfolio *GMC Publications*
Photographing Fungi in the Field *George McCarthy*
Photography for the Naturalist *Mark Lucock*
Professional Landscape and Environmental Photography: From 35mm to Large Format *Mark Lucock*
Rangefinder *Roger Hicks & Frances Schultz*
Viewpoints from *Outdoor Photography* *GMC Publications*
Where and How to Photograph Wildlife *Peter Evans*

ART TECHNIQUES

Oil Paintings from your Garden: A Guide for Beginners *Rachel Shirley*

VIDEOS

Drop-in and Pinstuffed Seats *David James*
Stuffover Upholstery *David James*
Elliptical Turning *David Springett*
Woodturning Wizardry *David Springett*
Turning Between Centres: The Basics *Dennis White*
Turning Bowls *Dennis White*
Boxes, Goblets and Screw Threads *Dennis White*
Novelties and Projects *Dennis White*
Classic Profiles *Dennis White*
Twists and Advanced Turning *Dennis White*
Sharpening the Professional Way *Jim Kingshott*
Sharpening Turning & Carving Tools *Jim Kingshott*
Bowl Turning *John Jordan*
Hollow Turning *John Jordan*
Woodturning: A Foundation Course *Keith Rowley*
Carving a Figure: The Female Form *Ray Gonzalez*
The Router: A Beginner's Guide *Alan Goodsell*
The Scroll Saw: A Beginner's Guide *John Burke*

MAGAZINES

WOODTURNING ◆ WOODCARVING ◆ FURNITURE & CABINETMAKING
THE ROUTER ◆ NEW WOODWORKING ◆ THE DOLLS' HOUSE MAGAZINE
OUTDOOR PHOTOGRAPHY ◆ BLACK & WHITE PHOTOGRAPHY
TRAVEL PHOTOGRAPHY ◆ MACHINE KNITTING NEWS
GUILD OF MASTER CRAFTSMEN NEWS

The above represents a full list of all titles currently published or scheduled to be published.
All are available direct from the Publishers or through bookshops, newsagents and specialist retailers.
To place an order, or to obtain a complete catalogue, contact:

GMC Publications,
Castle Place, 166 High Street, Lewes, East Sussex BN7 1XU, United Kingdom
Tel: 01273 488005 Fax: 01273 402866
E-mail: pubs@thegmcgroup.com

Orders by credit card are accepted